DINNERS WITH RUTH

DINNERS WITH RUTH

A MEMOIR ON THE
POWER OF FRIENDSHIPS

NINA TOTENBERG

THORNDIKE PRESS
A part of Gale, a Cengage Company

Copyright © 2022 by Nina Totenberg.
Thorndike Press, a part of Gale, a Cengage Company.

ALL RIGHTS RESERVED
Thorndike Press® Large Print Biography and Memoir.
The text of this Large Print edition is unabridged.
Other aspects of the book may vary from the original edition.
Set in 16 pt. Plantin.

**LIBRARY OF CONGRESS CIP DATA ON FILE.
CATALOGUING IN PUBLICATION FOR THIS BOOK
IS AVAILABLE FROM THE LIBRARY OF CONGRESS.**

ISBN-13: 979-8-8857-8524-2 (hardcover alk. paper).

Published in 2022 by arrangement with Simon & Schuster, Inc.

Printed in Mexico
Print Number: 2   Print Year: 2023

To my husband, David, who put up with all the late nights of writing this book, and then apologized for talking me into it.

CONTENTS

7

PROLOGUE:
BOUILLABAISSE FOR RUTH

With Ruth, I always thought that there would be a next time.

For more than twenty years, she had defied not one but three bouts of cancer, not to mention other medical complications from bowel obstructions to shingles. And after each hospital stay, she had always come home. Her endurance, her will to live, even her plain old-fashioned grit, were unmatched. After one surgery, when most of us would be pushing the nursing station call button, she drafted a major speech. She even participated in Supreme Court oral arguments from her hospital bed.

But it was so much more than her repeated resurgence in the face of illness. For nearly fifty years, Ruth and I had knit ourselves ever more tightly into the fabric of each other's lives. Aside from my two sisters and my National Public Radio sisters, she was my longest-serving friend. She was loyal, clear-eyed, and deadpan funny. Although she enjoyed becoming an icon in her eighties, she enjoyed far more watching other people perform.

Still, she and I performed well together; I've lost count of all the times that I interviewed her onstage.

It helped that we were personal friends long before our professional lives propelled us into the spotlight. We first met over the phone in 1971. Ruth was a law professor in New Jersey; I was a print reporter. National Public Radio was in my future, but I would not be hired there for another four years, and nearly twenty-two years would pass before Ruth was appointed to serve on the U.S. Supreme Court.

Through everything, we could — and did — keep our boundaries. The irony is that while work introduced us, and work has defined each of us, in her own way, our friendship was never about work. I can recall only one time when Ruth pleaded with me not to ask her a question on a particular topic. In reply, I told her, "I'm sorry. I have to. It's my job." And, conversely, only one time when I said in frustration, "But, Ruth, why didn't you tell *me* that when I asked? It's news."

Instead, our friendship worked because

we held each other in the highest regard. From the start, we sensed just how hard the other had fought to climb the ladder to get to where she was. We shared a passion for music, opera, shopping (I more than she), and food, especially food prepared by far better cooks than we were. And a steady stream of good stories, jokes, and bits of gossip. We were both eager questioners, although with slightly different ends: I like asking questions to get information; Ruth liked asking questions to place an answer in a different light.

These traits were the easy parts. The bedrock of true, solid friendship is being there for the hard things. And there, our foundational rocks were sure and strong. Each of us saw the other through great personal joys and also deep personal sadness, through illness, loss, and widowhood.

During the long and devastating illness and eventual death of my first husband, Ruth was there to draw me out of my isolation and grief; twelve years later, I would, sadly, be able to reciprocate her kindness when her beloved husband, Marty, died.

When I remarried, she was the one who officiated at my second wedding to my husband, David, overseeing a joyous ceremony that she scripted down to the "spontaneous" jokes. She never let on until the end of dinner that she had been in the hospital the day before; she had "forbidden" Marty to tell me.

Throughout her final years, David and I were able to wine and dine her to keep her spirits up, particularly after Covid-19 struck. We shared so many small dinners together that Saturdays became "reserved for Ruth." Bouillabaisse, the light French fish stew, was her favorite, and David made it magnificently, adapting his version from Julia Child's recipe.

The last time I saw Ruth, it was for supper.

Ruth didn't teach me everything about friendship. I've had other wonderful teachers, expected and unexpected. All of them have taught me that friendship is precious, that it involves showing up, that it involves supporting and helping, that it is not always about the grand gesture, but rather about the small one. It is about extending the invitation, making space at the table, picking up the phone, and also remembering. Friendship is what cushions life's worst blows and what rejoices in life's hoped-for blessings. It can sometimes be as simple as a hug when the hug matters most.

Ruth's husband died at the very end of the Supreme Court term on June 27, 2010, and in the middle of Elena Kagan's Supreme Court confirmation hearings. Ruth was incredibly stoic through it all. She appeared on the bench with her colleagues the next day to announce an opinion she had written. When Chief Justice John Roberts opened the session by announcing Marty's passing, her eyes stayed dry. It was Justice Antonin Scalia, a close friend of both Ginsburgs, who wiped away tears.

Marty was buried at Arlington National Cemetery, and afterward there was a reception at the Supreme Court. The memorial events were, for me, scheduled at the worst possible time. I couldn't go to the funeral because I had to cover the Elena Kagan confirmation hearings. But then, almost miraculously, as the reception began, the Senate Judiciary Committee proceedings paused for a series of votes. I dashed across First Street to the Court building and raced into the conference room where everyone had gathered.

I can still see Ruth's face as I arrived, breathless. She looked up, saw me across the room, as I was searching for her, and her face lit up. "You made it! How did you make it?" she exclaimed. After we embraced,

I told her, "I had to come over and give you a hug."

You made it. Not exactly magisterial, Shakespearean prose, but words to live by, from beginning to end.

This book was written in large part as a tribute to friendship. Ruth and I never indulged in gossipy conversations about her colleagues on the Court. I never got a scoop from her, and she never volunteered any top-secret anything. Nor did we endlessly dissect cases or attorneys or debate what might become of *Roe v. Wade.* Mercifully, in fact, we did not have to talk shop when we were together in private. And Ruth, if you knew her, was perfectly willing to say in public what she was thinking, or as much as she would ever share with me. That same ethos applies to me.

We aren't from a particularly confessional generation. What we shared was the special warmth and closeness of longtime friendship. We were present in each other's lives, especially when it mattered most. We showed up.

What that meant and how it enriched and transformed our lives is perhaps even more meaningful in an age when people text rather than simply "pick up the phone." To me, video-gaming alone in a chair is a poor substitute for sitting in a darkened movie theater or concert hall among friends — no matter how many others may be playing in your alternative online world. And you just aren't going to convince me otherwise. My hope is that you might, after you read this book, open an actual door, make a phone call to hear someone's voice, write a paper note, set a table, or simply be there for a friend. Shakespeare did get it right when he wrote in *Richard II,* "I count myself in nothing else so happy, / As in a soul remembering my good friends."

ONE:
THE FIRST STIRRINGS
OF FRIENDSHIP

Friends play a unique role in our lives. We all, to varying degrees, have family, and for some, like me, it is a source of love, closeness, and wonderful support, but it is not that way for everyone. Beyond our biological, relational, or marital families, each of us is given the opportunity to establish a family of friends. Friends can sometimes do things for you that your own family cannot. They might even do some things better or see things more clearly. My appreciation of friendship has deepened over the years; life with its twists and turns has taught me much about the intensity of friendship and its value. I, who started out fiercely independent and doggedly focused, have found myself at various points humbled by events and challenges beyond my control. Repeatedly, the outstretched hand that has raised me up is friendship — and I am also deeply fortunate to count my sisters among my

17

closest of friends.

Friends are the ones who rush to you when trouble strikes, they are the ones who stand loyally by your side, they are the ones who find the helpful words and perform the acts of kindness that blunt the very rough spots in our world. Friendship is also reciprocal. Reach out to your own friends when they are in need, and you will be rewarded many times over.

In my career, I have been blessed to cover fascinating newsmakers and vital issues, and to break some big stories, but what resonates now are the extraordinary people I have come to know, and whom I have been able to call my friends. My life story is interwoven with them and has been infinitely richer for them. These pages are the stories of friends, my love letter to my friends, and ultimately the story of friendship with one very special woman. For nearly fifty years, Ruth Bader Ginsburg and I built our friendship. As with my other friendships, what we built made our lives immeasurably richer.

On the surface, Ruth and I were a classic example of "opposites attract." The superficial similarities of our backgrounds — we are both the children of immigrants and both of us came from Jewish homes — were outnumbered by the differences. She graduated tied for first in her law school class, I never completed college. She married and became a mother in her early twenties, I was single until my mid-thirties, and made the choice to forgo children, in part because I knew I could never be a superwoman like Ruth and others who somehow were able to do everything well. Ruth was my most famous friend, but as you will read in these pages, for women of my era who fought to get in the door, never mind break the glass ceiling, friendship was something special. In a very real sense, it became the Old Girl Network. Indeed, dig deeper and one will also find some very strong underlying themes in my friendship with Ruth. Our paths were not necessarily destined to cross — and how they ultimately did requires a bit of setup and explanation — but once we found each other, in the year 1971, we were destined to become friends.

When I was growing up, my parents were always surrounded by friends. My father, Roman Totenberg, was a virtuoso violinist who made his professional debut at age eleven as a soloist with the Warsaw Philharmonic. When he wasn't rehearsing or playing for fun, my father practiced for hours on end, preparing for long concert tours where he soloed with major orchestras around the world. And that practice frequently involved other musicians; our home swelled with the sounds of clusters of instrumental artists playing sonatas, quartets, trios, and quintets. The house didn't just come alive with music, it reverberated; the floorboards literally vibrated from the sounds of the violin. When I moved into my first apartment I was almost undone by the silence, the music so abruptly gone.

My parents seemed to know everyone from the literary lioness Dorothy Parker to great composers — Igor Stravinsky, Aaron Copland, Darius Milhaud — and they led an interesting and intellectual social life. My father arrived in the United States in 1935 at age twenty-four to make his American musical debut. He was such a sensation that he ended up playing for President Franklin Roosevelt at the White House.

Part of what made my father a master was hunger, not the metaphorical kind, the real kind. He was born in Poland, but his family moved to Moscow when he was five so that his father could take an engineering job, and it was in Russia that a neighbor volunteered to babysit him during the day. As it turned out, the neighbor was the concertmaster for the Moscow Opera Orchestra, and because he didn't know what else to do with this boy, he taught him the violin. Soon, my father began accompanying him to concerts, with his teacher playing the harder parts, and my father playing the simpler ones. During a terrible famine, young Roman Totenberg would play for huge halls of Bolsheviks, and after hearing the introduction "Comrade Totenberg," the whole place would burst into laughter when this little boy walked out with his violin. But the bread and butter he earned from those concerts fed his family. "Invariably, the people gave us white bread and butter and other things to eat, which we'd take home," he recalled years later. "And that was actually the first impression of the value of the art — what can it bring to you to survive, so to say."

Art helped him to survive again as Hitler rose to power. My father came to the United States on an artist's visa in 1938 and stayed. He was able to save his mother by getting her passage on the last ship to sail from Portugal for the United States before World War II began. Her passport was signed by Aristides De Sousa Mendes, the Portuguese diplomat who saved thousands of European Jews. But nearly everyone else in the Totenberg family perished in the Holocaust. One remarkable exception was my father's sister, Janina, nicknamed Janka. I was named for her, because at the time of my birth my father thought that she was dead. He didn't know that after her husband died she managed to escape from the Warsaw Ghetto with her daughter, Elzunia, and the two survived the rest of the war in hiding.

My mother, Melanie, had a very different life story. She was born in San Francisco, raised in New York, and met my father at a party in 1940. He was immediately besotted and would always recall how beautiful she was, the dress she wore that night, embroidered with birds, and her wonderful laugh as they danced the night away.

The year 1940 was a very dark time for him. He feared that many if not all of his friends and relatives were dead. He had failed to free his sister. But that night, when he met my mother, it was as if a light came into his life. She quickly captivated him and pulled him out of the darkness, even insisting at one point that he join her in skipping down the street.

For their first date, he took her to a very fancy party on Park Avenue, where he had been invited to play. She would remember the hostess descending a staircase, dripping with diamonds, and the guests, who ranged from the rich to the famous. It didn't matter to her one whit that he left her to fend for herself while he schmoozed with the partygoers and performed. She was dazzled by the interesting people she met and thrilled to hear him play. And he was equally thrilled by this independent-minded gorgeous woman, with a quick sense of adventure and a novelist's eye for the wonders of life. He always said that by the end of the evening, he knew she was the girl for him.

They were married in 1941. Their life together was a whirlwind; he performed with major orchestras, helped found music schools, was a fixture at summer music festivals, and taught legions of students. My mother supported him in everything he did, including taking dictation, writing business and thank-you letters, even sometimes acting as a "sound-meister" during recording sessions, while also managing three daughters and our overflowing home. There is no doubt that if she had been born forty years later, she would have had her own career separate and apart from his. As it was, she was his partner in music, always. Only later in life when we all had fled the nest did she take up a career of her own as a real estate broker. In typical fashion, she studied for the exam, realized she needed to learn more math, and called the local high school to find a tutor. She sold houses in the greater Boston area for years and in the process, mothered young couples through their first home purchase, made new friends for life, and became a genuinely beloved figure. She was a pip!

Ruth's early years were very different from mine. She grew up in quiet. Her older sister had died of meningitis at age six, when Ruth was fourteen months old; there were no other children. That loss was "devastating to both of my parents. I don't think they ever got over it," she told me during a conversation at the Museum of the City of New York in December 2018. Ruth did have music, but that came in the form of piano lessons in a building on the Upper West Side of New York, two subway train rides away. (She also learned the cello in high school to be able to play in the orchestra. That cello must have been bigger than she was.)

The Bader family lived in a lower-income, working-class section of Brooklyn, East Ninth Street between Avenue O and Avenue P. It was home to, as she remembered, "about an equal number of Irish, Italian, and Jews." Her father, Nathan Bader, was, like mine, an immigrant, but he came to the United States from what is now Ukraine at age twelve. He worked in the daytime and attended school at night to learn English, but he never finished high school. He eventually worked as a fur manufacturer, although few people were eager to purchase furs during the Great Depression. Her mother, Celia, the daughter of Polish immigrants, was a garment worker, who used her own wages to put her brother through college, and later helped her husband. She took Ruth to the library every week and, to introduce her to the arts, scraped together the money for tickets to a series of children's plays and book readings at the Brooklyn Academy of Music on Saturday afternoons — Ruth's favorite was *Mrs. Wiggs of the Cabbage Patch.*

"My mother never made me feel guilty," Ruth said. "But, she had very high standards for me." Once when Ruth came home with a grade of less than A, her mother "made clear that she never wanted to see that again." Her dream was for Ruth to finish college and become a high school history teacher, a job that Celia Bader thought would be both fulfilling and obtainable. As Ruth herself put it, her mother "never in her wildest dreams thought about the law.

That would be impractical because at that time women were less than three percent of the lawyers in the country." Ruth attended James Madison High School, named for the same Madison who advocated for the system of checks and balances that would give the United States its coequal, independent judiciary. If Ruth's life were a novel, the choice of James Madison High School might have seemed like some heavy-handed foreshadowing.

Celia was ill for most of Ruth's high school years and died of cervical cancer the day before Ruth, the class valedictorian, was to graduate from high school. Two of her closest school girlfriends would recall that they only intuited that her mother had died when they learned that Ruth wouldn't be at graduation. She had kept her mother's condition largely to herself.

Because Ruth spoke far more about her mother than about her father, years later, deeper into our friendship, I wondered aloud to her in private if her father might have been depressed. She told me that she thought he was. But when I gently broached the topic in a public interview, she demurred, quickly pivoted, and moved on. "He didn't talk much about his early years," as she put it. Much the same could be said of Ruth.

She did love to discuss her children and grandchildren, but otherwise, with Ruth, the past usually stayed past. She almost invariably deflected detailed conversations about her growing up, aside from her very fond memories of activities and places. She could reel off the list: Prospect Park, the zoo, the botanical garden, the Brooklyn Academy of Music, the Brooklyn Museum, and the Metropolitan Museum of Art, especially its Egyptian collection, and her first trip to the opera and watching the famous African American conductor Dean Dixon. For a bit of humor, she would also note that her stint as a high school baton twirler — "cold and little costumes, even then" — gave her a lifelong aversion to football games.

Her memories were also strongly shaped by World War II, "the overwhelming influence," she called it, adding, "Unlike our recent wars, there was a right side and a wrong side. There was nothing ambiguous about it. It was frightening because we came to know more and more what was happening to the Jews in Europe." Everywhere, she recalled, "there was rationing — gasoline, meat. In school, we peeled the tinfoil off our gum wrappers to make tinfoil balls. We had a victory garden in our public school. We knit squares. They were supposed to be combined into quilts. We used part of our allowance to buy savings stamps for savings bonds. When a book was filled, we'd have a savings bond." Patience, restraint, perseverance, and a true, abiding love for artistic diversions, especially music and opera, were what she took from her formative years.

Indeed, were she to have written the story of her own life, Ruth Bader would probably begin at Cornell University, where she studied literature with the Russian-American novelist Vladimir Nabokov and where she met Martin, a.k.a. Marty, Ginsburg. In many ways, Cornell is where she truly came alive.

Ruth famously joked that because Cornell's arts college had a ratio of four men to every woman, it was seen by many parents as "the ideal school for daughters. If you couldn't get your man at Cornell, you were hopeless." Her little zinger at the end was that, of course, this ratio also meant "that the women were ever so much smarter" than the men.

"Too many" of the women, she told me during that public conversation in 2018, "disguised their intelligence because they thought the highest degree that they could get was their 'M-r-s.' degree." Ruth, smart as she was — she attended Cornell on a scholarship — recognized the prevailing social landscape. She did not study in the open. Instead, "I found every woman's bathroom in Cornell. The one in the architecture school was by far the best. So, I would study in there. When I went back to the dorm, I could be just like one of the girls." When I suggested that she "had to" do her studying in restrooms, she corrected me, "I didn't have to. I wanted to." Translation: she wanted to fit in. But what she was learning would teach her to stand out, specifically in a class on Constitutional law taught by Robert Cushman, for whom she was also working as a research assistant.

"This was in the early fifties, and this great teacher wanted me to understand that our country was straying from its most important values. This was the heyday of Senator Joseph McCarthy from Wisconsin, who saw a Communist on every corner and was calling people to account, many of them in the entertainment industry." Various members of U.S. Senate and House committees were "quizzing" their targets about "some organization they had belonged to in their youth in the height of the Depression, some socialist organization."

"Cushman," Ruth explained, "wanted me to appreciate that there were lawyers standing up for these people and reminding our government that we have a First Amendment that guarantees us the right to think, speak, and write as we believe and not as Big Brother Government tells us is the right way to think, speak, and write. And reminding the government as well that there was a Fifth Amendment that protected us against self-incrimination. So, I got the idea that being a lawyer was a pretty nifty thing. I thought you could earn a living but also use your time and talent to do something that would make the world a little bit better. I must say that there was some reluctance on my family's part, being practical and knowing that women weren't really wanted by the law. But when I got married, that settled that problem. Because then the attitude was 'Well, Ruth wants to be a lawyer, that's okay. If she fails, she will have a husband to support her.' "

One person who did not have that attitude was Ruth's husband. As Ruth herself put it, "The remarkable thing about Marty is that he cared that I had a brain. No guy up until then was the least interested in how I thought. So, Marty was a revelation to me and throughout my life. I certainly wouldn't be here today if not for Marty, because he made me feel that I was better than I thought I was. When I went to law school, I was concerned in those first few weeks whether I would make it." Marty held the exact opposite view. He was a year ahead of Ruth at Harvard and told his buddies, "My wife will be on the law review."

Ruth, of course, did have very real reasons for being nervous. Before law school, Marty had been drafted into the U.S. Army, and as newlyweds, they moved to Fort Sill, Oklahoma, for two years. After taking the civil service exam, Ruth found work as a claims adjuster for the Social Security Administration, but she was promptly fired after she became pregnant, which was not only acceptable treatment but largely expected for a woman in the mid-1950s. Their daughter, Jane, was fourteen months old when Ruth entered law school. It was Ruth's father-in-law who started her down the path to becoming, in my view, a super-woman by giving her what Ruth viewed as simply very good advice. When she worried about how she would take care of a toddler, be a good wife, and do well in law school, her ever-supportive father-in-law told her, "Ruth, if you don't want to go to law school, you have the best reason in the world. And no one will think less of you. But if you really want to go to law school and become a lawyer, you will stop feeling sorry for yourself and you will find a way."

"That advice has stood me in good stead my entire life. The question is: Do I want this enough? If the answer is yes, I find a way," she said.

I was born nearly eleven years after Ruth. I have no memories of the Depression or World War II, although I clearly recall helping my mother pack suitcases filled with clothes and canned goods for my aunt Janka, her new husband, and my cousin Elzunia in Poland, and other memories of my father working tirelessly to free Elzunia from behind the Iron Curtain. My early years were not shaped by rationing or deprivations. Instead, the stories that my parents recounted — and that I remember — had overtones of American abundance. One of the early events in their married life was a party for a group of Poles and other Europeans after a concert that my father gave, I think at Carnegie Hall. My father was late returning to their apartment, and in his absence my mother had offered all the food that she had prepared for their guests, only to be told again and again, "I'm not hungry." So, she did what any Depression-era American would have done; she packed up the food and put it away. My father arrived, shocked to see an empty table. She quietly explained that "no one" was hungry. Oh my, he said, they are just being polite. You have to cajole them. Sure enough, after the food was returned to the table and my father had made his way around the room, every morsel was eaten. That may have been my mother's only entertaining faux pas; by the time I was old enough to remember, she had clearly mastered the art of being my father's entertainer-in-chief.

One of my mother's favorite tasks when we spent summers at the Aspen, Colorado, music festival, back when Aspen was a one-traffic-light town, was to host a big cocktail party. I say "favorite," but in truth, I think these big parties made her nervous. My sisters and I would spend two days helping her make the canapés. My mother had a party maxim: creative people drink bourbon, businesspeople drink scotch. Both flowed at these parties. But this was the 1950s, and when the adults gathered, our role was only to pass the food, and follow the rule "FHB," family holds back. For these kinds of events, children were to be seen and not heard.

Occasionally, my mother brought back funny stories from other cocktail and dinner parties, such as the time when she was introduced to Dean Rusk — who would later become secretary of state for Presidents Kennedy and Johnson. She assumed he was an academic dean, and proceeded to ask him, "So, Dean, what is your field?" To which he replied, "It's Mr. Rusk to you."

She always giggled when she told this story. It's probably from my mother that I learned the lesson never to be afraid to ask anyone anything. At the worst, it would be good for a funny story afterwards. At best, you never know what you might learn.

I was precocious, strong-willed, and for the first four years of my life, an only child. I was not all that happy to share my home with my two younger sisters when they arrived, and often was beastly to my middle sister, Jill.

I also was not an exceptional student. No one would have mistaken me for the valedictorian of anything. But I loved reading mysteries with girl sleuths. Like many girls of my era, I wanted nothing more than to be Nancy Drew, with her fast car, cute boyfriend, and independence. (A second choice was the Army flight nurse Cherry

Ames.) But I soon realized that I couldn't be a police detective, or a flight nurse for that matter. In the real world, women didn't appear in these occupations. So I turned my attention to politics. My introduction to the subject probably started in Aspen when, at age eight, I sat in the car with my mother as she listened to the 1952 political conventions. We listened in the car because that was the only place where we could get a radio signal, and she would explain who was who, and what was going on.

But it was the 1954 Army-McCarthy hearings in the U.S. Senate that formed the foundation of my political education. My mother followed them every day on TV, and when I got home from school, I would join her. I came to know every senator by name, what role he played, and a lot more; my mother would explain everything. About the only thing that puzzled me was a photo that kept flashing on TV of McCarthy's chief counsel, Roy Cohn, with his arm draped around another man, G. David Schine. Cohn had "hired" Schine, the heir to a hotel fortune, to be the unpaid chief consultant to McCarthy's Senate committee and had also pressured the military (unsuccessfully) to give Schine preferential treatment when he was drafted. What I did not understand

35

as a ten-year-old child was the subtext of that photo — and its thinly veiled suggestion that Cohn and Schine were lovers. Whenever I asked my mother about it, she would only say that they "were friends." A couple of decades later, in the early 1970s, I walked into Roy Cohn's apartment to interview him for an article and was dumbstruck as I looked at the artwork and realized that he was gay. My mind immediately traveled back to those afternoons watching the Army-McCarthy hearings with my mother and the photo of Cohn and Schine that kept flashing on the screen. As I tried to ask intelligent questions, I thought: "Finally, I get it!"

The intrigue and drama of those hearings helped cement my interest in politics. By 1960, as a high schooler, I was following the presidential election very closely and went door to door with campaign materials for John F. Kennedy. I also learned the congressional districts around the country and who the candidates were. I bought the leading weekly newsmagazines — *Time, Newsweek,* and *U.S. News & World Report* — and eagerly read *The New York Times.* When Theodore White's seminal book *The Making of the President 1960* was published,

I became overwhelmed with the idea that I could be a witness to history and was desperate to go to Washington, where the action was.

My mother could feel my restlessness. She knew Eleanor Roosevelt, having been a volunteer for Franklin Roosevelt during his presidency and because my father had played at the White House, and so she wrote to Mrs. Roosevelt, inquiring about an internship for me. At the time, I didn't appreciate what that meant. Almost fifty years later, during one of our public conversations, Ruth would reel off the books and writers that made a difference to her growing up — *A Tree Grows in Brooklyn,* and "that kind of risqué nasty boy's book, J. D. Salinger's *Catcher in the Rye,*" and, she added, "another person that I found inspiring was Eleanor Roosevelt, who wrote a column in the *Brooklyn Eagle,* 'My Day.' " Ruth read Eleanor from afar. My mother was able to write her, and even more amazingly, Eleanor Roosevelt replied.

With her intervention, in 1961 I — a mere seventeen-year-old — landed an internship with the Democratic Study Group, a research organization for liberal, as well as moderate, non–Dixiecrat Democrats. I lived with my aunt until my mother found me a spot in a group house. I paid my share of the rent and had a room with other girls. Each day, I rode the bus from the house to our offices near the Capitol. That was how I realized how segregated Washington, DC, was. Most days, I was among the relatively few white people on the bus. The job was fascinating. I did research and even once watched Attorney General Robert Kennedy testify before Congress.

Very quickly, I knew for sure that I wanted to be a reporter. I was much more interested in watching what went on and telling people about it than I was in fighting for any cause.

After my stint in Washington, I dutifully finished high school and enrolled at Boston University. My grades were what I'd call presentable, but I was bored to tears. After not quite three years, my Brown University–educated mother gave me permission to drop out.

I took the first newspaper job I could find, at the *Record-American,* which several mergers and years later would become today's *Boston Herald.* My spot was on the women's page, and there's no polite way to say it: it was a terrible job. The *Record-American*'s women's page bore no resemblance to a style or arts or food section in any newspaper today. The page was run by a woman named Ruth Mugglebee, a 1923 Boston University graduate who had covered many news stories and court trials — her reporting had even helped to solve a local murder — before she landed in fashion and food. By the time I worked for her, she was almost sixty-five and mostly doing small rewrites of fashion press releases and recipes. I knew nothing of her more daring past. I thought she was ancient, and I chafed. I wasn't allowed to do anything on my own until the society writer finally went on vacation, and for three weeks I was her designated substitute. I could write my own articles on weddings and the details of brides' wedding dresses, with their lace, satin, and seed pearls.

To escape a future professional life on the women's page, I volunteered for a second shift as the night reporters' "legman," helping to cover school committee meetings and the heated disputes around school busing in Boston. The main reporter would leave to file the story, and I would call in from a pay phone with new details to update the piece before it was filed. Through this unpaid assignment, I met the paper's night photographer, who had Boston police and fire, and Massachusetts state trooper scanner radios in his car. He would drive around all night searching for good photo material. He knew every "lowlife," as he dubbed them, in the city. We would hear a call and go careening to where the action was. I would phone in that information to the news desk too, for a long caption to accompany the photo.

I kept to that brutal double-shift schedule until one night when I ventured into an apartment where two women were engaged in a vicious fight, and one of them threw a knife that landed awfully close to where I was standing. I didn't say a word, but I also decided that maybe the night crime beat wasn't the best place for me.

Instead, I tried to prove my mettle in other ways, coming up with an investigative story to pitch to the newspaper's editor. At that time, contraception was illegal in Massachusetts. I called up the women's colleges around Boston — Radcliffe, Wellesley, Simmons, and a few others — and I made appointments at their health services for a contraception screening. Then I wrote a memo with my story idea and this information and gave it to the paper's executive editor. After reading my proposal, he appeared at my desk with an uncomfortable look on his face and an equally uncomfortable question: "Nina, are you a virgin?" My answer: Yes. Then he asked, "Have you ever had an internal examination?" My answer: No.

"I can't let you do this," he said with a pained expression. "I cannot let you do this." He wouldn't explain why. I argued that if I could get contraceptives at elite schools when they were illegal in the state, that would be a pretty good story, showing what a sham the law was. But my arguments were to no avail. He wouldn't change his mind.

Maybe he was concerned that I would have to have an invasive medical exam to write the story; maybe he believed that a pelvic exam would render me no longer a virgin — the same logic that used to be employed against women using tampons. Perhaps he thought it would be an ordeal for me or expose me to scurrilous criticism. Or maybe he just didn't want to expose the fact that wealthy young women attending prestigious schools around Boston were being allowed to break the law — and worse, a law about sex — while girls in Roxbury or South Boston had no such options.

My next reporting job was for *The Peabody Times,* north of the city. The paper was published twice a week, and for most of my time there, I was the principal reporter. I covered everything from the police to the local school committee to elections. My favorite journalistic moment occurred when we got a tip that there had been a robbery at the local bank. I immediately called the bank and I said, "Hi, this is Nina Totenberg from *The Peabody Times.* We understand there's been a robbery." And the guy on the other end replied, "Yeah, this is one of the robbers." They were so hapless that they fled the scene, dropping all the cash behind them. The cops followed the trail of bills and arrested them. I was able to write a hilarious front-page piece about it.

I covered the local courts too. One of the bigger trials was the murder trial of the Boston Strangler's prison roommate. The famous, or for some infamous, lawyer F. Lee Bailey was the defense counsel, and I was sent to report on the trial, held in Salem. It was summer, brutally hot, and the courtroom was not air-conditioned. One day I wore a sundress, not a very revealing dress, but a sundress. F. Lee Bailey called a bench conference and complained to the judge, tongue in cheek I think, that my attire was distracting to the jurors, and he unsuccessfully argued that I should be banned from the courtroom. That was how I met Mr. Bailey, with whom I stayed in contact for many years, sometimes receiving some good tips in return.

In 1968 a very big national story unfolded next door: the New Hampshire presidential primary. And I was determined to cover it. On the Republican side, the candidates were former Vice President Richard Nixon and Michigan Governor George Romney, a former CEO of American Motors and father of current U.S. Senator Mitt Romney. He seemed to me to be an incredibly decent man, but not a match for the far more crafty Nixon. On the Democratic side, President Lyndon Johnson was being challenged by U.S. Senator Eugene McCarthy, who was campaigning not just against Johnson but against the entire Vietnam War. Both were great stories. Every day after I finished my job in Peabody, I would make the hour-long drive to New Hampshire, lugging my little Olivetti portable typewriter, so I could watch the candidates campaign, interview people, and write about the races.

Women covering a presidential primary campaign were a rarity; the reporters' clique wasn't known as "the boys on the bus" for nothing. Some tolerated me, a few others were actually nice. But the majority had no interest in me whatsoever. Once I summoned the courage to ask a group of the men if I could join them for dinner. Their answer was "Sure, why don't you follow us?" They drove so fast that I had a hard time keeping up, and it was clear that they wanted to lose me. Lesson learned. Periodically one or another of the reporters would knock at my motel room door and try to come in, and I would have to figure out a way to say no, while at the same time preserving relationships with men whom I respected. I did that mostly by convincing them to go to the bar with me for a drink.

On the campaign bus, I nearly always sat alone. Then one day, a woman with short, pixie-styled gray hair appeared. The guys all knew her and waved. But she walked right over to me, and asked, "Is anyone sitting here?" I enthusiastically said, "No!" From then on, Nan Robertson of *The New York Times* was my seat companion. She had been all over the world and was fearless. Six years later, she would help launch a class action lawsuit against *The Times,* accusing the paper of discriminating against women in hiring and promotion. *The Times,* it turned out, was not much different from the *Record-American.* Women did not appear on the masthead; they were not featured as national correspondents or appointed to the editorial board. Even when they did advance, they were generally paid less than men. *The Times* eventually settled the lawsuit, offering some compensation to its female reporters and a more transparent path to promotion and advancement.

But those changes were more than a decade away. And I couldn't imagine them. In 1968 I was simply grateful to no longer be the only woman on the bus and to have a friend in Nan Robertson.

After the primaries, I gathered the clippings of my best stories into a scrapbook and headed to Washington. I interviewed anywhere I could and found a job working at *Roll Call,* a newspaper about Capitol Hill. Salary: seventy-five dollars a week. Then I got a call asking if I would be interested in becoming a reporter for *The National Observer,* the weekly publication put out by Dow Jones, which at that time also owned *The Wall Street Journal.* I got the job and was made a general assignment reporter covering Congress, the Justice Department, the U.S. Supreme Court, and anything else that the editors asked. Eventually, my main focus became legal affairs. And I started to win awards for my coverage.

For the first time in my professional life, a door had opened more than a crack.

"For women of my generation, getting the first job was the big hurdle," Ruth would say. "The woman who got the first job did it at least as well as the men, so the second job was not the same — it was not the same hurdle."

That was, in many ways, a characteristically Ruthian understatement. As one of nine women in her class at Harvard, she was invited to a dinner at the home of the law school dean, where he asked each of the female students to explain why they were taking a slot from a deserving man. At Harvard, Ruth would have two years of stellar academic performance and a position on the law review before Marty, a year ahead of her, got a job in New York. For her third year she transferred to Columbia Law School, where she was one of twelve women, once again made law review, and graduated in 1959 tied for first in her class.

Twelve law firms invited her for interviews, not one offered her a job. She was also recommended for a Supreme Court clerkship with Justice Felix Frankfurter, who wouldn't even grant her an interview. It took the intervention of one of her favorite professors, Gerald Gunther, to find her a job.

I loved asking her to tell the story during some of our public interviews. As she explained, Professor Gunther was in charge of locating clerkships for Columbia law students, "and he vowed he would find a place for me. I think he called every judge in the Southern District of New York and the Eastern District of New York, all of the Second Circuit judges, and there were no bidders. So, he called back one of them, who was a Columbia college and law school graduate, Judge Edmund L. Palmieri, and Palmieri said, 'Her record is fine, but she has a four-year-old daughter. Sometimes, we have to work on Saturday, even on a Sunday.' " The professor's response was "Give her a job, and if she doesn't work out there's a young man in her class who's going to a downtown firm, and he will jump in and take over." As Ruth put it, "That was the carrot. There was also a stick. And the stick was if you don't give her a chance, I will never recommend another Columbia law student to you."

When I suggested that it "worked out," she deadpanned, "It worked out very well." But the big firms still wouldn't hire her after she finished her clerkship.

Ultimately, she received a job offer from Rutgers Law School in New Jersey. It might not have been the path she envisioned, but it was a blessing in disguise. If she had been hired by a private firm, "I know what it would have been like," Ruth often reflected. "It's as Justice Sandra Day O'Connor said. She was a few years ahead of me in law school. She was very high in her class at Stanford. No one had offered her a job as a lawyer. So, she volunteered her services free to a county attorney and said, 'I'll work for you for four months. If at the end of that period, if you think I'm worth it, you can put me on the payroll.' That's how she got her first job in the law. But she said, 'Ruth, you know, if we had gone to a large law firm, do you know where we would be today? Today we would be retired partners. And because that opportunity wasn't open to us, look where we ended up.' "

Ruth wasn't working for free, but she wasn't treated equally either. She was hired by Rutgers University in 1963, the same year that the Equal Pay Act passed. "But the message hadn't gotten home," as she diplomatically put it. So, after a stellar academic record, a clerkship, and a subsequent research position at Columbia, the "kindly dean [at Rutgers] said, 'You will have to take a substantial cut in salary.' I said, 'I expected that.' Rutgers is a state university. But when he told me how much, I asked, 'How much do you pay so-and-so?' a man who had been out of law school about the same amount of time. He said, 'Ruth, he has a wife and two children to support, and your husband has a good-paying job in New York.' That's the way it was."

It *was* very much the way it was. Looking back, I think part of the reason that I got my reporting job at the *National Observer* was that they knew they could pay me much less than they would have to pay a man. I had been at the *Observer* for several years when the paper hired a guy right out of college. He sat next to me; our desks were side by side, our typewriters each clacked away. There were no dividers and no privacy. I was making $5,200 a year, $100 a week, and I soon learned that his salary was $7,500 a year, even though I had significantly more experience in journalism and more seniority at the paper! I requested a meeting with the editors, and I asked them flat out why he was making more money. Their answer was that "someday he would have to support a family." I listened and thought, "I guess that makes sense." It was only after I had walked out of the room that I realized I might also have to support a family someday. In my memory, I think I turned around and made that point. Still, the editors gave no indication that I would get a raise. Not long after, though, my salary jumped to $7,500, probably because it finally occurred to someone that such a gender disparity was illegal under the recently enacted civil rights laws. Though I, in essence, had to shame my bosses into a raise, the women at Rutgers-Newark brought an equal-pay claim. The university finally settled it in 1969. The smallest pay raise that any female faculty member received was $6,000 (or about $45,000 in today's dollars), which gives more than a little insight into the size of the disparity that existed at the time.

Of course, pay wasn't the only issue. When I worked at the *Observer,* one of my jobs was to supervise the printing of the paper. The *Observer* relied on old technology — hot type, where molten metal was injected into lines of type, and then the type was inked onto molds and the paper printed from them. Articles had to be cut to fit on the press, which meant if they were too long, a line of type had to be removed. It was my job to make the cuts, and I grew skilled at reading upside down and backwards to know exactly what words to cut. The typesetters and printers were all men, and they tended to be a little raunchy, but I put up with their comments because they were nice to me. When they weren't in the pressroom, four or five of them would often gather in the long corridor that led from the newsroom to a small lunchroom. Many days, I would walk past them, and I'd hear them say things like "Oh, boy, those boobs look pretty good today." I would just put my nose in the air and keep walking. But at least those men helped me do my job and were my partners in the pressroom.

In the House of Representatives, members would sit on the benches in the Speaker's lobby and catcall me as I passed, saying, "Come sit on my lap, honey." They didn't even know my name, they simply referred to me as "honey" and "girlie" and assumed I would answer to that. I probably didn't help myself, though; it was the age of the miniskirt, and I wore them, and in the mores of the era, that made me fair game in their eyes.

Still, just as I did with the typesetters, I stuck my nose in the air and kept walking. Or I made sure I sent a lot of very clear signals that they could read, once telling an overly interested U.S. senator, "Oh, Senator, you remind me so much of my father." Mostly they didn't have experience with women in the workplace, and they didn't have filters or brakes to dial back what they said or thought. It was perfectly acceptable for a cabinet secretary to walk up to me and say, "You have such lovely skin," as one did when I wore an off-the-shoulder dress to a White House Correspondents' Association Dinner.

Of course, their attitudes could work to my advantage too. I broke a lot of stories because I was sassy, I was good at what I did, and prominent men, often to their peril, did not take me seriously. With their guard down, because I was "just a girl," they answered my questions a bit more honestly, and my reporting often made news.

After Harry Blackmun was nominated to the Supreme Court, I wanted to do a story on how and why he was selected. Another possible candidate thought to have been under consideration was Robert C. Byrd, the U.S. senator from West Virginia, who had attended law school at night at George Washington and then American University while he was a sitting congressman. The degree was all the more remarkable because Byrd had dropped out of college to run for Congress. Like me, he never received his undergraduate degree.

For reporters, the practice was to sit in the room off the Senate floor and send messages to senators on the floor, asking if they might have time to talk. So when I was working on the Blackmun story, I asked for Senator Byrd, and he told me a very detailed story about being considered for the vacant Supreme Court seat, including his discussions with President Nixon regarding the job while flying on Air Force One to a strawberry festival in West Virginia. Later, Byrd was informed that the president had "decided to go with someone else." Our conversation was not for attribution — meaning I couldn't name him as my source — but everything he told me checked out, and after that, Senator Byrd was often a solid source for me.

I was also fortunate. *The National Observer* was a weekly. It wasn't a high-profile publication competing with the major daily newspapers. So most politicians weren't as wary when talking to me as they might have been for, say, a *New York Times* reporter.

At big events like the White House Correspondents' Dinner, I would be one of a handful of women in the room of five hundred or more people, and very likely in my early years, I was the youngest person there. In that era, most of the people at these dinners and the parties afterwards would become stumbling drunk by late in the evening. Except me. Instead, I would periodically excuse myself and head to the ladies' room, where I wrote down all the newsy things I'd just heard. I always kept a tiny notebook in my purse for this purpose, and I would leave every event with a story or at least leads for a story. It was nearly two decades later but not all that far removed from young Ruth Bader sneaking into the bathrooms at Cornell to study. The most successful way to get ahead was often to pretend otherwise.

The year 1971 was a watershed for Ruth Bader Ginsburg — and for me. I had two big journalistic coups; she wrote her first brief for a case before the Supreme Court, and suddenly, the divergent lines of our lives intersected.

My first headline-grabbing story was a profile of the legendary and by then very long-serving FBI director J. Edgar Hoover. The *Observer* gave me a month to work on the story, and by the time I was done, I think I had completed about fifty interviews — including Roy Cohn — many off the record or not for attribution, and some on the record. The resulting article, which I thought was reasonably balanced, so enraged Hoover that he demanded that *The*

National Observer fire me. Instead, the editors printed his long and vitriolic letter accompanied by a rebuttal to each of his complaints. As the paper's editor, Henry Gemmell, would later note to the entire staff, one of his great points of pride at the *Observer* was that he "had the guts to stand up for a member of our staff who was under attack from the head of the FBI. I'll recall with evil glee the joy of that combat — undertaken only after I had applied the microscope and found it was J. Edgar — not Nina — who was indulging in false and misleading writing."

Hoover, for instance, called it a "malicious lie" to state that his longtime deputy, Clyde Tolson, who lived with him and frequently traveled with him, "walked a respectful one step" behind the director. In response, the *Observer* printed three pictures of Tolson walking one step behind. Ironically, another of Hoover's allegations was that I used "faceless informers," an FBI specialty in its own investigations. By that, he meant that I used anonymous sources, which I did, including some of his friends and admirers who didn't want to be quoted by name. This was a common practice, and still is — I just had to ensure that the facts could be confirmed by multiple individuals. The people I interviewed didn't want to incur Hoover's legendary ire, and given how much power the FBI director had, speaking not for attribution was a reasonable precaution.

Hoover, I suppose, got his revenge by opening an FBI file on me. I knew there was a file, and it made me a bit paranoid. Even though this was the 1970s, I'd scurry from a party if people started smoking marijuana because I was afraid of being arrested.

After Hoover died, I repeatedly tried to get access to the file. In 1975 my neighbor and friend Marsha Cohen helped me file a lawsuit in federal court under the Freedom of Information Act. One thing I ultimately learned from that suit was that Hoover and his press rep had saved all my requests for interviews, and Hoover scrawled across one, "She certainly is a persistent bitch." (I wish I had that note. I'd frame it, but, alas, it was only shown to me by a Justice Department official, ironically in an attempt to coerce me to give up my FOIA lawsuit. Hoover's scrawl was not among the papers I finally received and was probably protected under the FOIA statute.) The Ford Justice Department fought me hard on getting the file; I only succeeded under President Jimmy Carter.

Not long after, I was having lunch with Harold "Ace" Tyler, who had been deputy attorney general in the Ford administration. He was a lawyer in private practice at that point, and I asked him why he had prevented me from getting my file. His response, with a smile, was "I was dealing with the FBI; I only had a certain number of chits, and you, my dear, were a chit I gave away." He was so charming that I couldn't be mad. In fact, even the Carter Justice Department wanted to be let off the hook. After we won in the trial court, the department threatened to appeal the verdict if we didn't waive the judgment, which included a requirement for the Justice Department to pay my legal fees. But Marsha and I refused. Eventually, they paid her five thousand dollars, which she planned to use to build a new deck on her house, to be named "the Nina Totenberg Memorial FOIA deck."

Truth be told, there wasn't anything terribly damning in the parts of the file that the Justice Department produced. The silliest was a document showing that the photographer hired by the American Bar Association to take photos of its Silver Gavel Award ceremony for outstanding journalism had lied; he told the ABA that a photo of Chief Justice Warren Burger presenting me with my award had "not come out." The photographer, however, was an FBI informant, and he wrote to Hoover that because of what I had written about the director, he was "not about to" make public any photo of me and the chief justice.

Some of these stories are funny in hindsight, but most of my journalistic life was hard work. That said, I loved the hunt for news, especially news that no one else knew about yet.

In the summer of 1971, the Supreme Court was aging. Two of the nine justices had been appointed by President Franklin Roosevelt, three by President Dwight Eisenhower. And two were seriously ill, including Justice Hugo Black, a politician and Supreme Court justice unlike anyone most of us could imagine today. Born in 1886, the Alabamian had served in World War I, joined the Ku Klux Klan in the early 1920s, resigned five years later, and was elected to the U.S. Senate, where he earned a reputation as a reformer, a powerhouse investigator, and an ardent New Dealer. President Roosevelt appointed him to the Court in 1937, and he resigned on September 17, 1971, eight days before his death.

Justice John Marshall Harlan II was thirteen years younger than Black. Born in 1899, he was the grandson and namesake of Justice John Marshall Harlan, who became famous as the "great dissenter" in a series of cases when the Supreme Court upheld the legality of racial segregation and struck down or eviscerated key civil rights laws enacted after the Civil War. Harlan II was a well-known trial and corporate lawyer, appointed to the Court by President Eisenhower in 1955. A conservative justice, he nonetheless had no respect for President Nixon, and hoped not to retire on his watch. But in terrible pain from spinal cancer, he resigned six days after Black, and died three months later.

That meant Richard Nixon had not one but two simultaneous vacancies to fill. Two previous Nixon nominations to the court had failed to win confirmation by the Senate, something that had not happened since Herbert Hoover was in office.

It's hard to believe now that senators would cross party lines over judicial nominations when they thought those nominees were in some way unqualified to serve on the Supreme Court, but they did back then.

Nixon's first Supreme Court nominee, Judge Clement F. Haynsworth, of South Carolina, was rejected by a vote of fifty-five to forty-five, with seventeen Republicans joining the majority of Democrats in opposition. Nixon, who was determined to name a southerner, then nominated Judge G. Harrold Carswell of Florida, only to see him defeated as well, with significant numbers of Republicans in opposition. Haynsworth would continue to serve as a distinguished federal judge until his death. Carswell would leave the federal bench after his defeat to run for the U.S. Senate, but he lost and later was arrested for making sexual advances in a public bathroom to an undercover police officer.

On his third try Nixon succeeded, picking Federal Appeals Court Judge Harry Blackmun of Minnesota.

With that arduous nomination process completed, in September 1971, everyone knew that the White House was putting together a new list of potential nominees; I also knew that there were unlikely to be any high-profile judges on that list. The president's advisers had sent a list of six names to the American Bar Association's Committee on the Federal Judiciary. I didn't know how many names were on the list, but I did know that Nixon's people had asked the bar association to take a look, following a tradition started by President Eisenhower. So, I thought, why not aim for the stars? If I could figure out who was on that list, it would be a helluva scoop.

I called a ton of law school professors and big-time lawyers, asking who they thought would be on Nixon's list and asking them if they had been contacted by the ABA or the FBI. The responses to those calls gave me a start. But I needed to confirm which of the names on my list had been sent to the ABA. The best way to do that was through the bar association's committee. Although I was only twenty-seven, I knew the committee chairman: Lawrence "Ed" Walsh, the senior partner at Davis Polk in New York. He was a high-powered litigator. I had visited him at his firm, and in my young life, I had never been in an office like that, with three secretaries sitting outside his door to handle his workflow, a huge arrangement of fresh flowers at the main desk, and a massive, largely empty reception area. I had never seen so much space that was apparently only for show.

Ed Walsh was of an entirely different generation. He had been a federal judge and had served as deputy attorney general in the Eisenhower administration. Yet I remember him greeting me like a colleague, not some girl reporter, which is what I was far more used to. He addressed me as someone who deserved his respect and never treated me otherwise. He was a genuinely distinguished gentleman.

So, to create my final list, I called Walsh. He was on Cape Cod, but this was the Nixon era, Hoover still ran the FBI, and Walsh certainly knew enough to be paranoid about his phone. I thought it was silly, but in hindsight I realize he was probably right. He told me he'd call me back, and he did, from a pay phone. The first thing he said was "You know I can't tell you who's on the list. That would not be appropriate." But I wasn't giving up that easily (Hoover wasn't entirely wrong). I asked, "Is Judge Gignoux on the list?" (Edward Gignoux was a revered federal district court judge in Maine appointed by President Eisenhower). Walsh laughed a bit ruefully and said, "We should be so lucky. I wish it were somebody like Eddie Gignoux, but it's not. I won't tell you who is on it, but I'll tell you that he's not on it."

I had my first clue. It wasn't going to be a traditional, Republican jurist. So, I added other names to my list, including Mildred Lillie, a midlevel appeals court judge in California, Nixon's home state. One of my White House sources told me Mrs. Nixon very much wanted a female judge, and I knew that her husband thought appointing a woman would be a political plus.

Another source told me that Nixon thought picking a conservative woman would "really sock it to them." So I went to work researching Judge Lillie's record. This is a reminder that in good journalism, there is no substitute for the sometimes tedious work of tracking down crumbs of information. Those crumbs can lead to a major scoop.

Through my friend Marsha Cohen, I found a clerk on the California Supreme Court who had easy access to the state's unpublished opinions — which contained a treasure trove of information about many California state court judges. I confess I still don't completely know the rules for published and unpublished opinions in California, but when I told the clerk that Mildred Lillie was on the Supreme Court short list, she was horrified. Soon I had a thick stack of Judge Lillie's unpublished opinions, including one in a redistricting case where she had cited a California Supreme Court opinion that even I knew had been overturned. Amazingly, as I combed through the file, I discovered that it wasn't the only time she had cited an opinion that was no longer good law.

Only recently did I learn that the White House apparently didn't know about those unpublished opinions when they put Lillie's name on the list. According to *The Washington Post,* John Dean, Nixon's White House counsel, "was dispatched to California to vet the candidate. In a recording of an Oval Office meeting on October 15, 1971, Bob Haldeman, Nixon's chief of staff, relayed Dean's assessment of Lillie to the president, 'He says she's a goddamn jewel.' " I, however, knew otherwise.

I got my list together, but because the *Observer* was a weekly and we didn't want to be scooped, my editors released my list of names on the Dow Jones wire, without any of the supporting information. My *Observer* editor later described it as my "exclusive on the horrid six under consideration for Supreme Court appointment, which could find outlet only on the DJ ticker." Ed Walsh had already asked me in one of our conservations what I had learned about Lillie, and from his probing tone, I knew that if she were nominated, I was sitting on a couple of bombshells. But instead, in the back room maneuvering of the era, the ABA quietly nixed her as "unqualified," which apparently came as a relief to Nixon, who, I later learned, really didn't want to name a woman.

Lillie wasn't the only problematic name on that ill-fated list. Another top potential choice, Arkansas lawyer Herschel Friday, had represented the Little Rock school district when it tried to fight desegregation. The bar association balked at his name too, apparently because he wasn't exactly what they considered to be Supreme Court material. When Nixon eventually did announce his two nominees, neither had been on the advance list he had sent to the ABA. Instead, he chose Assistant Attorney General William H. Rehnquist, forty-seven, and the distinguished Richmond lawyer Lewis F. Powell, Jr., sixty-five, who as president of the Richmond Public School Board had presided over the desegregation of the city's public schools. I knew Rehnquist from covering the Justice Department, and I would come to know Powell very well. But I still had a lot to learn.

In 1971, despite the recurring moments of drama, covering the Supreme Court wasn't considered important enough to be my full-time job. But I realized fairly quickly that covering the Court was something I could do that other people weren't as interested in at the time. So I could carve out a small piece of territory for myself.

I can say this now, decades later: I was also completely in over my head. I knew nothing. I wasn't a lawyer, and most of the people covering the beat were. The press corps at the Court was a small, tight-knit group, with occasional interlopers, like me.

But I loved it, and soon I moved from interloper to someone who showed up with increasing regularity. Not knowing "shit from Shinola" in some ways made me a better reporter. I had to write things so that regular people, people who weren't lawyers but who might be interested if I wrote a story well, could understand them. But first, I had to learn as much as I could. I wanted to know all about the Court, from how the justices did their jobs to the cases themselves.

In those days, the Supreme Court docket was twice as big as it is now; the Court took on between 140 and 160 cases each term. Usually the justices heard two cases in the morning and two in the afternoon. I couldn't follow all of them, but for the cases I was reporting on, I immersed myself. I would spend hours reading the briefs and, just to get my bearings, other material that my sources referred me to. I even read some law review articles, which, God help me, I try to avoid today. While a Supreme Court brief isn't a literary work akin to Shakespeare, it does have a few similarities to the Elizabethan-era bard's work, namely that the language can at first be very peculiar to our modern ear. In the beginning, I struggled to understand that opaque legal jargon. Then slowly, the rhythm and the wording became clearer. Once I could decipher the structure and the cadence, I could see that the arguments were powerful, captivating, and often involved some of the greatest and most controversial issues of the times.

One of those cases that at first mystified me was *Reed v. Reed,* a challenge to an Idaho law that automatically preferred men over women as executors of estates. The combatants were Cecil and Sally Reed, the divorced parents of a son who had committed suicide. Each parent applied to administer their deceased son's estate. Sally Reed didn't even receive a hearing. The probate judge automatically appointed Cecil because Idaho law decreed that "males must be preferred to females" when more than one person was qualified. If Sally had at least been granted a hearing, she likely would have argued that her son had died using a gun owned and kept in the house by his father, and she was thus more qualified to administer the estate. Sally's lawyer refused to appeal the decision, saying that she would certainly lose. Sixteen additional lawyers refused to take her case, until finally attorney Allen Derr agreed. He also thought that she would lose, but he believed it was an important case, with a constitutional issue at stake.

As Derr had predicted, Sally Reed lost in every lower court. Her last appeal was to the U.S. Supreme Court. But on this appeal, Sally Reed and Allen Derr were joined by the American Civil Liberties Union. The ACLU asked Ruth Bader Ginsburg to be the principal author of the brief, even though Derr would argue the case before the Court. The brief asked the Court to do something revolutionary: to declare a law unconstitutional because it discriminated "on the basis of sex."

I still remember reading that brief and being flummoxed. It argued that the Fourteenth Amendment's guarantee "of equal protection under the law" applied to women. I knew that the Fourteenth Amendment was enacted after the Civil War to protect newly freed African Americans and to guarantee them equal protection under the law. But that was on the basis of race, not sex. Indeed, when it came to rights like voting, no woman living in the United States had the right to vote when the Fourteenth Amendment was ratified. I flipped to the front of the brief and saw that it was written by a law professor at Rutgers named Ruth Bader Ginsburg. Her telephone number was listed under her name.

In those days, only the big news organizations with full-time reporters at the Court had assigned desks, with phones, in the pressroom. Since I didn't work for one of these organizations, I didn't have an assigned desk, but if I was working on a story, I would camp out at one of the open desks. If I wanted to make a call, I had to use one of the tiny phone booths in the pressroom. I would scrunch up inside and either feed nickels, dimes, and quarters into the phone or use my phone card from the *Observer,* which required calling the operator and asking to place a long-distance call. These were the phone booths where I had spent hours compiling my list of possible Court nominees a few weeks earlier. I thought at the time that those were the most significant calls I would make that year. But the one I placed in October to Newark, New Jersey, would prove to be more enduring.

Fortunately, when I called Ruth, I used

my phone card, rather than pocket change. She was in her office. I introduced myself and asked my very simple question: I thought the Fourteenth Amendment applied to African Americans after the Civil War. How does it apply to women? Ruth spent an hour walking me through her argument, that the Fourteenth Amendment guarantees equal protection of the law to *all* persons, and "women are persons," as she put it. I emerged from that phone booth like a goose that had been stuffed in preparation for foie gras. Or as Ruth later put it, "That was our first conversation, and we have been close friends ever since."

The argument may seem obvious today, to the point where it is hard to conceive of how revolutionary it was in 1971. At that time, women had very few rights beyond the right to vote. They could be fired for being pregnant. They often could not apply for credit cards in their own names — only in their husbands' names; a woman generally could not get a mortgage by herself. Even if she was married, banks routinely refused to count her income. In fact, when one of my male reporter colleagues at the Court and his wife were trying to buy a house, the bank refused to consider her income on their joint mortgage application

— even though at the time she was a partner at a large law firm and earning substantially more than her husband. She was indignant, but the loan officer explained that the bank didn't consider her salary "real income" because it was earned by a woman. In the United States, banking and credit rules for women were not that different from the rules of conservatorship or guardianship that had prevailed in Victorian England; women almost universally needed the participation or the guarantee of a man.

Not only that, but almost every time a woman brought a legal challenge — asking to be admitted to the bar in the state of Illinois, or to work as a bartender, or to be paid minimum wage, or to prevent her work hours from being restricted — the courts ruled against her, declaring that a woman's primary job is to take care of the children and make hearth and home happy and safe. So, for a case to directly ask the questions why and on what grounds? was truly revolutionary.

In 1971, the Supreme Court applied two tests for evaluating whether a law violated the equal protection clause: "rational basis" and "strict scrutiny." Rational basis was a much lower threshold, and most laws easily survived a challenge because the only justification required was that the law represented a rational state interest. Applying that test was how the laws that treated men and women differently had survived.

But "strict scrutiny" was a much higher standard, used only for racial minorities, and it required, among other things, that the state prove that it had a compelling interest for treating people differently. The brief that Ruth wrote in support of Sally Reed's claim argued that laws that discriminated on the basis of sex should also be subject to strict judicial scrutiny, because, like race, sex is an inborn characteristic, and women, like racial minorities, had been historically discriminated against. They had been restricted in their ability to own property, serve on juries, hold certain jobs, and vote. Voting was especially important, because the limits on voting meant that for generations women had also lacked political representation. They did not have equal power or the ability to change discriminatory laws through the legislative process, and they needed the courts to intervene.

Reed v. Reed was argued on October 19, and slightly over a month later, the Court delivered a 7–0 decision, a unanimous ruling because there were two vacancies at the time. The decision didn't address what the standard should be for evaluating gender discrimination claims. It simply said that "to give a mandatory preference to members of either sex over members of the other, merely to accomplish the elimination of hearings on the merits, is to make the very kind of arbitrary legislative choice forbidden by the Equal Protection Clause of the Fourteenth Amendment . . . The choice in this context may not lawfully be mandated solely on the basis of sex." It was a complete victory, and Ruth's first win in the Supreme Court. But it was also the most minimal step; while the Court ruled that the treatment was unequal, it declined to say what the standard for equal treatment was when it came to women. It also said nothing about what level of scrutiny the courts should apply in the future.★

There would be many battles ahead, both legal *and* legislative, and it would take years. But ultimately, in the simplest terms, the law, whether handed down by the Supreme Court or enacted by Congress, would mean

★ The court did not adopt an "intermediate scrutiny" test until five years later, in another case that Ruth argued and won. The test would be strengthened further in a 1982 opinion written by Justice Sandra Day O'Connor.

that many of the most blatant but tolerated forms of discrimination against women had to end. A woman like Ruth couldn't be demoted or removed from her job because she was pregnant. She had felt the burden of this type of discrimination when she and Marty had lived in Oklahoma and again ten years later when Ruth became pregnant with their son, James. She hid her pregnancy from her law colleagues at Rutgers. She was teeny, so she simply borrowed her mother-in-law's clothes. By the time her fellow professors discovered that she was pregnant, the school year was over, and she had already signed her contract for the following year.

Changes in the law also meant that someone like me could not be told, "We pay him more because someday he will have to support a family," or "We don't hire women for the night desk" or just flat out, "We don't hire women." Women no longer had to accept that.

My first remarkable conversation with Ruth about her argument in the *Reed* case stayed in my mind long after the case was decided, and I started calling her regularly. She was almost always there, and she always answered her phone or would return my calls.

She took the time to answer my questions and became one of my first translators of the finer points of law. Her explanations were very clear, her answers were always concise and to the point, also a rarity, although I did find that lawyers and even judges were more willing to explain things to me than people in the political world were. And their explanations were often better.

We finally met in person at a legal conference in New York. As with many momentous events that are momentous only in retrospect, many of the individual details of that day are lost; my mind didn't think to preserve them. I don't know if we had planned to meet or if it was an accident. For years, we could not agree on the topic of the conference — I'm pretty sure it was about alternative dispute resolution, although I don't remember if it was held at Columbia University or NYU. She always maintained the topic was something else. Normally, I would have trusted her memory, but I was not yet thirty, and everything was so fresh and new to me, and imprinted on my brain, that I think I'm probably right. What matters most is the fact that the conference was unbelievably boring, even to her. And so, we hopped in a taxi and went shopping.

Frankly, I can't remember anything about the shopping. What I remember is the cab ride. We must have been stuck in traffic for some time. Indeed, as we rode down Fifth Avenue, she was still simmering about the way she had been treated by a screening committee appointed by New York's two senators to recommend potential judicial nominees for the lower federal courts. Ruth had applied for a job as a trial court judge; the committee — all male and all very Wall Street — informed her that they would not recommend her because she didn't have enough experience in securities law. I still remember her muttering quietly to me in the back of that cab, "And how much experience did *they* have in dealing with sex discrimination law?"

Mostly though, we just talked. And what I realized was that even though she was very accomplished, while I was younger and still had a lot to learn, we were similar in a very significant way. We were outsiders to the world in which we operated. We both had our noses pressed up against the windowpane, looking inside, and saying, "Hey, men in there, let me in!"

TWO:
MAKING FRIENDS AND
A FEW ENEMIES

Is that all it takes for a friendship to take root? Professional phone calls, a volley of questions and answers, and then skipping out on an incredibly boring conference, where we were likely the only women in attendance, to roam the aisles and ride the escalators at Saks Fifth Avenue or Bloomingdale's or Lord & Taylor — I'm guessing here, I don't even remember where we shopped (nor did Ruth) or whether it was for more than a few minutes. The conversation drowned out everything else, at least for me. We were both chronically busy women and taking time for shopping was a rarity, but also a necessity. Some women hate shopping or don't want to think about their appearance, while other women think their appearance is part of their persona. It's always been part of my persona, and it was part of Ruth's.

Clothes are also a language. It's hard to

appreciate now how rarely in the professional world, particularly the legal world, we saw other women. In a photograph of Ruth amid her second-year law class, she is one of two women — the photographer put them on either end of the grouping, saying, that it was "nice to see two roses amid the thorns." The other female student wore a white blouse, but Ruth blended in with her male classmates. They were dressed in dark jackets and white shirts; she wore a dark top with what would become, many years later, on the nation's highest court, her signature white collar. But in many ways, blending in was impossible. To be a woman was to stick out.

And Ruth was a beautiful young woman. Once at a dinner party, I sat next to a man who had been in her law school class. "She was not just beautiful, but exotic looking," he said, adding that on the first day of their torts class, when the professor addressed her as "Mrs. Ginsburg," there was an audible groan from her male classmates. That response may have been one of the reasons Ruth wore her hair pulled back in a scrunchie for most of her life. She had glorious, luxuriant hair, but she pulled it back to keep it out of her face and so that people would take her seriously. Only occasionally when she dressed up would she wear it down.

Being taken seriously was a major struggle for women, particularly when we were young. And, like it or not, that impression started with clothing and hair. When I was in my twenties, I dressed to the nines. I wore tailored suits and my hair up, with a hairpiece to add volume and structure, as was popular in the 1960s. I wanted to wear clothes that were tailored, but distinctive. If I was going to stand out by being female, I wanted to stand out well.

Ruth recognized this too, and by the time I knew her, she had developed a very distinctive style and a love of presentation. The woman who adored opera also understood that life is in its own way a performance, and she was prepared to command the stage. That said, shopping with Ruth was a humbling experience. She was petite and beautiful and could wear almost anything, and everything she put on fit; her sizes were two and occasionally four. Mine hovered around ten or twelve, the first sizes to sell out. I also could never have worn what she did; on me, most of her clothes would have looked ridiculous. The one item of clothing I remember her complimenting me on was a scarf that I mistakenly spent a huge amount of money on. I bought it in a rush, wore it, and then a bill for six hundred dollars arrived, and I was shocked. I thought, "Nina, are you crazy? You don't buy a scarf for six hundred dollars!" But I couldn't take it back, and it is beautiful, and Ruth loved it every time I wore it.

Ruth's personal style wasn't like anything in a fashion magazine, it was completely different. When she went to the opera or a dinner party, she wore mandarin silk jackets and flowing designer pants; she also preferred oversize necklaces and intricate pins. It was the exact opposite of what professional women were advised to do — namely not to call attention to themselves. For that era, it was quite rebellious to dress as she did, or at least it was highly unconventional. Most things she did were unconventional — except for her work, although she did keep an unusual schedule, working until the early hours of the morning.

Ruth loved to shop at judicial conferences because being completely away from the office, she had time, and these conferences were often held at nice hotels where there was at least one place inside the hotel or nearby that carried fancy clothes. On one occasion, when she was giving a speech at a conference for the Tenth Circuit, she bought a black and white jacket — the material was cut to look like black and white feathers, very textured and delicate. It was among her favorites; she wore it with black pants until the white parts of the jacket started to develop a yellow tinge. I was on the verge of telling her that the beloved jacket needed to be retired when she said to me, sadly, "I had to give up my black and white jacket. It was really falling apart."

Marty shopped for her only once that I know of — for her Supreme Court confirmation hearings. While she was madly preparing, he went to Saks Jandel, a very high-end women's clothing store that used to be located near their apartment at DC's Watergate, and picked out four or five suits in jewel colors. It wasn't exactly her usual style, but the suits fit her perfectly, and she added her own jewelry and commanded the hearing room from the moment she entered. Other than that, however, she rarely wore suits.

She also rarely wore more than a touch of makeup. Indeed, while she was stylish, she was not vain. Her only noticeable bit of vanity came in the last years of her life when she donned thin crocheted gloves to hide the dark marks on the backs of her hands caused by her many chemotherapy treatments. By the end of her life, those thin black, gray, and cream gloves had become another signature of her iconic status.

Otherwise, there was no artifice. The first time I interviewed her, at the Ninety-second Street Y in New York City, I remember that she wore a dress, but no makeup, aside from maybe a light dusting of powder and some lipstick. I wondered later if she had decided to be so minimalist because she was appearing before an intellectual crowd in New York. But the truth is she didn't need any enhancements from jars or tubes.

She held on to her style throughout her life. I can still picture her paying her respects to her fellow justice and dear friend Antonin "Nino" Scalia in the Great Hall of the Supreme Court after his death. She wore high heels and a beautiful gray tweed button jacket with a solid skirt.

Even when she was undergoing radiation treatment for cancer in the year before she died, she decided that she would treat what to anyone else would have been an ordeal as a "vacation" in New York. This was classic Ruth. She was determined to go shopping, attend events, and enjoy herself, so she wasn't consumed by the radiation treatments. She would gaze at the windows of the small shops on Madison Avenue near the Lotos Club, where she stayed, and go into stores with her hair hidden under a babushka-style scarf, so people didn't recognize her. At one point, she walked into a Stuart Weitzman shoe store somewhere in Manhattan and asked to try on a pair of the same shoes that she was wearing, but in red. The shop assistant said, "We don't make that style anymore." And Ruth replied, in classic Ruth style, "Well, why not?" After the store associates finally figured out who she was, I think Stuart Weitzman had the shoes custom-made for her in the exact color she wanted.

But many years had to pass before that moment. Decades of friendship had to unfurl. And first, Ruth and Marty had to move to Washington.

After *Reed v. Reed,* Ruth's life and mine initially moved in rather different directions. In 1972, she was offered a tenured professorship at her alma mater, Columbia University Law School, becoming the first woman to receive such a position. She also became the director of the ACLU's Women's Rights Project, would eventually argue six cases before the Supreme Court, write briefs and argue cases in dozens of other gender discrimination cases in the lower courts. I started down a rockier path; I got fired.

I had a great editor at *The National Observer.* Lionel Linder taught me how to write ideas in paragraphs, and he taught me the value of the "nut graph" near the top of a story, in which the author synthesizes the story's essence. It took me forever to learn, but I did learn it. And the paper sent me all kinds of places — from Northern Ireland to cover "the Troubles" to Arkansas to cover the gubernatorial race. The incumbent in Arkansas was Winthrop Rockefeller and the challenger was a young upstart named Dale Bumpers. I covered both, joining Bumpers for a day or so and then traveling with Rockefeller. Everywhere I traveled, I had to learn the local customs. One morning in Arkansas, I accompanied one candidate to a breakfast and when I got to the person spooning grits, I said, "No grits, please." And along the entire line, I could hear people repeating, "No grits? No grits? No grits!"

I was reasonably sure Rockefeller would win, but I was wrong. The story I wrote was good, or so I thought. But one of the editors, Wes Pruden, who would go on to work for *The Washington Times* and was a wonderful writer, put it through what I privately called "the Pruden machine," and it came out a million times better. I learned from that. I learned a lot at the *Observer* in the roughly six years I worked there, enough to help earn me two Silver Gavel Awards from the American Bar Association.

Then the new executive editor started hitting on me. He wasn't the executive editor who had hired me, and in all other ways, he treated me very well. He lived a block and a half from where I shared a house with several other young women. He was in his fifties and married. But he was all over me, literally pawing me, and it was incredibly embarrassing and awkward. At first, I just tried to ignore it. I had given him a ride home and found myself fighting him off the whole time, to the point of pulling over to the side of the road to try to get him to stop. But he persisted, and it was, let's just say, pretty bad. There was no place to go, no one to report it to. It was just what was accepted and tolerated by women in the workplace at that time, in the early 1970s.

In 2018, at the height of the MeToo movement, I was asked to interview Ruth at the Sundance Film Festival before the debut of the documentary *RBG.* I told her in advance that I was going to ask her if she had ever been harassed. It turned out to be a gonzo interview. "The attitude to sexual harassment was simply 'Get past it. Boys will be boys,' " she told me, adding, "Well, I'll give you one example." She proceeded to recount how, during a chemistry course at Cornell, "because I was uncertain about my ability in that field," she asked her professor if there were particular materials that she should review. He then volunteered to give her a practice exam. The day after she took the practice test, she took the real one. And to her horror, it was the same as the practice exam. "And I knew exactly what he wanted in return," she said, mincing no words. "And that's just one of many examples. This was not considered anything you could do something about, that the law could help you do something about."

I followed up. "So, just to close the loop here, what did you do about the professor? Did you just stay clear of him? What did you do?" I was thinking that I likely would have hidden from him. Not Ruth. Her eyes narrowing, she said, "I went to his office, and I said, 'How dare you! How dare you!' And that was the end of that." I remarked that she likely aced the exam, and Ruth replied, "Well, I deliberately made two mistakes."

But, back to my firing, which coincidentally or not occurred after I had rejected my boss's overtures. I had been assigned to write a short profile of House Speaker Tip O'Neill. It was a small article, but my sister, who was visiting, became quite ill, and instead of telling my bosses that I needed a couple of days off, I rushed to complete the job, lifting quotes from lots of people about O'Neill that had appeared in other publications, most prominently *The Washington Post.* And I didn't credit any of them, even though I knew I was supposed to. I lost my job over it. But, unlike today, when that mistake might have ended my journalism career, I got a second chance. My *Observer* editor, the one who had been harassing me, gave me a wonderful recommendation.

The memo to the paper's staff announcing my "resignation" stated that during my "service" I had worked "when necessary to the point of exhaustion." It also noted that while "women have a role in journalism, and deserve equal treatment," upper management "wasn't entirely sure they are really equal, in capacities for our craft." But in my time at the paper, I had helped demonstrate that in fact "women can be," in what was a "pleasant surprise." That was how compliments to female employees were handed out in 1973.

I moved to *New Times,* a start-up magazine that lasted only a few years. I was the Washington bureau "chief" because there was no bureau, just me. I covered anything in Washington that I wanted to, but I also continued covering the Court, with more of an edge. I would talk to anyone about anything. And I was particularly interested in how the Court worked — or didn't work. In July 1974, I wrote an article titled "The Supreme Court: The Last Plantation" detailing a range of appalling and discriminatory employment practices, nearly all of which were directed at African Americans who worked at the Court. The article called attention to the fact that the Court was exempt from federal employment laws, and it showed. I filled the piece with statistics and examples of how Black Court personnel, especially messengers, who were personal assistants for the justices, responsible for everything from delivering documents to serving lunch, were subject to particularly egregious treatment. Messenger Cyril Mitchell, for instance, worked sixty to seventy hours a week for Justice William O. Douglas. He was fired shortly after he refused to serve at a private party in Justice Douglas's home. Douglas officially blamed Mitchell for not giving him correct directions to an event but gave his ultimate reason as wanting a messenger who would provide "more personal" service. Another African American messenger, Philip Brooks, was required to drive Justice Stanley Reed to his farm in Kentucky and stay at a nearby hotel in case he was needed. Brooks's lodging was paid for, but not his meals. When the Supreme Court neglected to forward his paycheck, he ran out of money. Justice Reed refused to provide a temporary loan, instead telling Brooks that he needed to work on his farm if he wanted money. Instead, he returned to Washington on a long-distance bus and was demoted.

A Black janitorial employee who was dating a white law clerk was forbidden to speak to her or acknowledge her in the hallway. He was eventually fired and escorted from the building by police. He and the former clerk later married. Black police officers, some of whom had worked at the Court for decades, were summarily fired and denied retirement benefits after they developed health conditions. A Black officer who attempted to organize a union was falsely accused of producing a fraudulent letter, a charge which the Court's press office later had to retract.

One of my favorite quotes in the article

came from a Court employee who said, "Now that they've made the rest of the country comply with the Constitution, it would be the right and moral thing if they did it here." The justices could get away with this because they were not covered by the nation's civil rights laws and the justices led lives much more remote from the public than they do today. They didn't write books or give many speeches. Confirmation hearings were not televised. The members of the Court existed in their own world.

But if I were to write that same piece today, I would skip the indignant tone. Rather than be judgmental, I would have given the readers just the facts. Because I had the facts. I had the statistics showing Black employees were largely confined to the janitorial force, and I had the facts on the mistreatment of the Black messengers and police officers, many of whom wept when I interviewed them.

The article did cause a minor stir, but, as I would learn many years later from papers sent anonymously to me, Chief Justice Warren Burger assigned his top aide the task of minimizing the fallout. The aide's name was Mark Cannon and to this day I have a file labeled, "Cannon Fodder."

At about the same time the article was

published, Ruth had concluded her second argument before the Court, which she lost, by a vote of 6 to 3. The case involved a Florida property tax exemption for widows but not widowers. Ruth argued that it violated the equal protection clause. Justice Douglas, the son of a widow left destitute at a young age, wrote the majority opinion, observing that single women face more hardship in the job market than single men, and that, he noted, was especially true for widows as opposed to widowers. It sounded rational and certainly reflected his own experience, but the opinion, instead of requiring a level playing field, used employment discrimination against women as a justification for upholding the Florida law.

I don't know if Ruth ever read my piece about the Court's discriminatory practices, but we talked on the phone episodically, and when in the mid-1970s she and I were at an American Bar Association meeting in Atlanta, we arranged to have dinner, joined by my sister Amy (today a federal judge), who was a young lawyer living there. The three of us spent the night laughing and gossiping, although neither Amy nor I can remember now about what. We may even have talked about a *New Times* cover story I wrote called "The Ten Dumbest Members of Congress." After the article appeared, the senator I had dubbed "The King of Dumb," Virginia's William Scott, held a press conference. As *The Washington Post* headline put it the next day, "Scott Denies He's 'Dumbest.'" It was the first real breakthrough for the magazine, and I liked to joke that until Scott's press conference we probably had a circulation of about fourteen readers in all of Washington, DC.

Ruth continued her pursuit of cases that would expand women's rights — really, everyone's rights. Then on August 8, 1974, an event occurred that would shape both of our lives in ways we couldn't have predicted. Richard Nixon resigned the presidency. The unprecedented resignation and its aftermath paved the way for Jimmy Carter to become president. Carter is one of four presidents who did not have the opportunity to appoint a Supreme Court justice. But he was the president who brought Ruth to Washington as a federal judge. And Carter's presidency and politics would have a direct effect on my personal life, although I didn't know it then either.

THREE:
UNEXPECTED FRIENDS

The first Supreme Court Justice who became my lasting friend was Lewis F. Powell, Jr. I had gotten to know other members of the Court. Justice Potter Stewart was enormously helpful in explaining to me how the Court worked when I first started covering it. And he remained incredibly kind to me over the years. I would eventually become friends with other justices too. But my friendship with Powell and Justice William Brennan, Jr., would last until their deaths, as would my friendship with Justice Scalia and with Ruth.

My first interaction with Powell was, well, pushy. On the day he was sworn in, Powell held a reception at the Court. He invited some of the high-profile reporters who covered the Court. I, however, wasn't invited. I wasn't anyone notable, but I was gutsy and, looking back now, probably more than a tad inappropriate. I wrote to Powell and said in essence that he had put me at a terrible professional disadvantage by not extending an invitation, but I was sure he had not realized that. I ended by politely asking him to have lunch with me. Powell was a genuine Southern gentleman and replied that he would be delighted to do so. My response was "When?"

We had lunch in his chambers served by his messenger — nothing very elaborate. He couldn't have been more gracious.

A few years later, in the mid-1970s, I invited Powell; his wife, Jo; and another couple to dinner in my tiny, thirteen-foot-wide house in the Capitol Hill neighborhood. I didn't even have a real dining room; instead, I had a dining room table tucked into an alcove, and I cooked and served the meal myself.

It was an unseasonably warm February day, above seventy degrees, and while I don't remember what I cooked, I do remember what I wore — a brand-new, green-and-white Diane von Furstenberg wrap dress. I was terribly nervous, but they couldn't have been sweeter. They came and ate dinner as if they were dining in a palace.

Powell was expected to be a reliable conservative, but he turned out to be a staunch advocate of reproductive rights for women, starting with *Roe v. Wade.* Long after he retired in 1987, we met regularly for lunch. I would ask him why he voted certain ways, nothing that I could ever ask a sitting justice, but part of the historical record for a retired one.

The interesting thing about retired justices is that while their law clerks love them, very few other people pay much attention to them. But I really liked Powell; in some ways, he was one of my best educators in the law.

One thing I asked him in those post-retirement conversations was why he was such a strong supporter of abortion rights when abortion had been illegal for so long. In his very soft Southern drawl, he told me the story that had formed his views. It dated back to his days as a young partner at the law firm of Hunton & Williams when he got a call from one of the firm's messengers, a young Black man, only eighteen or nineteen years old. The messenger was in tears, and he asked, "Mr. Powell, would you come, please. I am in trouble." He gave Powell the address, and Powell drove over to a house in what was then known as "the Black part of town." There he found his messenger and the woman he lived with, who was in her early twenties. She had bled to death after either enduring a back-alley abortion or trying to perform the abortion herself. Powell persuaded the local district attorney not to prosecute the young man because, as he explained it to me, this was a decision by a woman, "an older woman," and no good could come of prosecuting him.

Then Powell said to me, "After that, I thought to myself, This is not the business of the government. This is a choice that people ought to be able to make." It was as basic as that, and why he was a very firm supporter of abortion rights.

Another case we discussed involved an engaged couple who worked in the Harris County, Texas, constable's office. When President Ronald Reagan was shot, the woman, Ardith McPherson, looked over the divider and said to her fiancé, "If they go for him again, I hope they get him." Someone overheard the remark, and McPherson was fired. She sued, arguing that the comment had been intended as private and that the firing violated her First Amendment free speech rights. Powell sided with McPherson, providing the decisive fifth vote. I was surprised by his vote and told him so. And in his gracious way, he said, "Oh, Nina, you can't fire people for the stupid things they say to a friend in private. You just can't do that." It wasn't even a hard decision for him.

He was someone who, in the late 1930s, had gone around the country as a lawyer trying to convince people to support the United States getting into World War II. When the nation finally did enter the war, Powell, by then in his thirties, volunteered, and toward the end of the war he was assigned to the Ultra project, monitoring Axis communications in Europe. That work made him quite sympathetic to government secrecy claims, but it also may have made him wary of government wiretaps without court permission. Justices, I was discovering, were complex individuals, shaped by many factors.

Indeed, it's worth remembering that for many decades key figures on the Court were not necessarily steeped in the law; many had been powerful senators or governors and played significant roles in the nation's political life. Chief Justice Earl Warren, who was serving his last term when I started covering the Court, had been a hugely popular Republican governor of California, elected three times, once with the endorsement of both the Republican and Democratic parties. Even Warren Burger, who would succeed him after spending a life in the law, began as a Republican political activist and played a significant role in securing the presidential nomination for Dwight Eisenhower. Harry Blackmun, who would write the majority opinion in *Roe v. Wade,* had been the general counsel for the Mayo Clinic. Understanding the justices, their backgrounds and experiences, helped me to understand the Court. But these were interesting relationships that evolved over time. I didn't go into reporting expecting to become friends with any of these men, and I never got any sort of a scoop from any justice, but I thought it was always worth getting to know the people I covered. In my brash youth, it never occurred to me that some might view my approach as unseemly.

Even today, the Supreme Court is enough of a monastery that it pays to know the justices even a little bit to pierce the veil of secrecy that pervades the place. As I am writing this, the Court, because of the pandemic, is closed to the general public, and the justices have abandoned their long-standing practice of summarizing their opinions from the bench so that the lay public — who were always in attendance prepandemic — and the press can hear a quick summary of the law that is being established. Also gone is the practice of justices summarizing their dissenting views when they feel strongly that the Court has taken the wrong path. One can only hope those practices — linking the Court to the outside world — will resume.

When I first started covering the Supreme Court, I had no idea how it worked, how opinions were assigned, written, agreed upon, and much more. So I set out to learn as much as I could about the Court, its history, and how it ran. Justice Powell, for instance, once described the justices as operating "like nine different law firms." In his chambers, he told me, any opinion he wrote would go back and forth between him and his law clerks "like a shuttlecock" until he thought it was good enough to circulate to the other justices. Another justice ruefully admitted that sometimes an opinion ends up "fudging" on a point when a majority can't agree on language. I would not be the reporter I am today without those kinds of insights.

It was also a very different time. These men had come of age in an era when Supreme Court justices regularly played poker at the White House with Harry Truman; indeed, the poker game tradition continued well into the Reagan years. Chief Justice Rehnquist, who appreciated a good wager, played in a White House poker game while he was on the Court. There were lawyers who argued cases before the Court who also played poker with the justices — Leonard Garment, a well-known attorney, was one. As late as the 1980s, he played in a long-standing monthly poker game with Justices Rehnquist, Scalia, and Stewart, as well as Judge Robert Bork and the Reagan drug czar and education secretary William Bennett. When Garment had a case before the Court, he reluctantly sat out of the game for a couple months. And in addition to those bonds, Garment's wife, Suzanne, wrote a column entitled "Potomac Watch" about Washington for *The Wall Street Journal.*

In retrospect, it's possible to make multiple arguments: that Washington was too chummy or that it was simply friendlier and more collegial. Neither I nor other reporters who covered the Court were ever aware of an opinion that changed because of a poker game. I have to assume that the men in the game never discussed business because any such conversation would surely have leaked; Harry Truman once tried to sway some of his justice friends in the steel seizure cases — not only did it fail, but word got out. However any of this may appear now, the rules were different then.

But there's another facet of these relationships, on all sides, that no one should confuse: objectivity and fairness are not the same thing. Nobody is purely objective. It is not possible. Justice Powell was shaped by what he had seen in World War II and by the personal devastation of his young messenger in Richmond. To pretend otherwise would be simply to pretend. What all of us are capable of is fairness. Many times I read Supreme Court briefs, and when I'm done, I've changed my mind from what I thought at the beginning. Of course, what I think the *outcome* of a case should be is irrelevant. But the whole idea of reporting as an enterprise is to make people think. And when you think, really think, you should be a little torn. Most cases are not slam dunks. If I'm doing my job in the best possible way, I want people to think about what the repercussions are if you do X as opposed to Y, and what the background on this issue has been for one hundred years, and what will change if the Court changes its course.

The other crucial aspect of friendships in that period, from the 1960s to the 1980s, is that they were different. For women of my generation, it was not natural to find an immediate group of friends at work. Indeed,

101

for more than a decade, in every job I had, except for my brief foray working on the "women's page," I was the only woman, or if there was one other woman (emphasis on *one*) she worked in a different area, and our paths rarely crossed.

Then too, there was the fact that I almost exclusively reported on men. It was lonely at work. That's the only way to describe it. If you were a woman, you were always fighting to get a chance. The workplace was not a haven. It could, as the end of my time at *The National Observer* had taught me, be very much the opposite.

So when I walked through the doors of National Public Radio in 1975 and saw other women working there, not just as assistants but holding important jobs, it was a complete reversal of everything I had come to expect. The women at NPR treated each other differently. The organization was so small, there were so few of us and so many things that needed to be done on a shoe-string budget that there was no time, energy, or inclination for competition. We were just trying to get out a radio show and fill a big news hole, ninety minutes for *All Things Considered,* every day. And we were all women who had been told, even by our mothers, that you shouldn't really expect much in terms of a profession because the doors are closed. My mother had said, "Well, you'll be somebody's administrative assistant like I was, and you'll go further doing that." I said I wanted to be a reporter. But while she refrained from outright rolling her eyes, she didn't think that was possible.

I knew nothing about radio, but I was thrilled with what I saw at NPR. I was eager and willing to learn, and there was a lot to learn. The first time I did a two-way conversation live on the air with Susan Stamberg, I thought I had done pretty well, but after we finished, she said, "Nina, while you were speaking you were covering your mouth. Don't do that on the radio." It was such basic advice, and yet it was so important. She was helping me succeed. Linda Wertheimer and I immediately hit it off. She was very generous always.

Linda didn't make fun of me when I didn't know how to do things. She taught me tricks for using a tape recorder and how to physically cut tape with a razor blade so that I could splice the beginning of a long sentence to the end, cutting out the entire middle, and making it sound seamless — the radio version of hot type. Entire sentences and paragraphs ended up on the cutting room floor that way, although the technique took me a while to master — I have scars on my hands from many old wounds to prove it. After Cokie Roberts arrived, the three of us immediately sat together and quickly became close friends. Everything at work, we did together. We covered many of the same stories and we helped each other out. Linda and Cokie covered the Hill, while I covered legal stories, but I ended up covering the Hill a lot because I was also covering congressional hearings about scandals, from the investigation of the Kennedy assassination to corruption in the intelligence agencies and CIA plots to kill foreign leaders. And of course, there were Supreme Court confirmation hearings.

We were three women who were the same age, at the same stage in our careers and trying to figure out how to do it all, how to be married, how to have children — or not have children in my case and Linda's too — and how to navigate our professional worlds and our private worlds. The confluence of what we did, where we were, and the stage of life we were in — as well as the stage of life America was in for women in the workforce — made us natural allies as well as friends.

We were also friends who attracted other women. When NPR moved to larger office space, we claimed a ratty old couch and put it in our corner. Women on staff would come and sit on that couch if something was wrong. I don't know that I was a terribly generous person then, or would have had the foresight to play that role on my own, but I do know that Cokie and Linda were. They taught me. Certainly some of the guys resented the fact that we were a pack — they famously dubbed our corner "the fallopian jungle" — but from our perspective, it was great to be a pack and not a solo act. There was safety — and power — in numbers.

As hard as it was to be a working woman, it was harder to be a working mother, and in that category among the three of us, Cokie was a supermother. I remember several times when her daughter, Becca, was in elementary school and the school dismissed early for snow. Back then, there were no texts or emails, not even a telephone tree. The school simply put the kids on the buses, because of course their mothers or someone would be home. Cokie, however, was at work. She was incensed that they would send her child home without calling her. And she was right to be incensed.

Ruth told a similar story about her son, James, when he was young. In a slightly wry way, she explained, "This child was what his teachers called hyperactive, and I called lively," adding, "I would get called by the head of the school or the school psychologist or the room teacher to come down 'immediately' to hear about my son's latest escapade. Well, one day I think I'd been up all night writing a brief. I was at my office at Columbia Law School. I got the call, and I responded, 'This child has two parents. Please alternate calls. It's his father's turn.' " Chastened, they called Marty, who went to the school, only to be told, "Your son stole the elevator." Marty's response was "Okay, he stole the elevator, but how far could he take it?"

After that, the calls came barely once a semester. As Ruth speculated, "I don't know if it was Marty's sense of humor. I suspect it was that the school was reluctant to take a man away from his work but wouldn't hesitate to call a mother away from hers. Anyway, there was no quick change in my son's behavior. But," she continued, the administrators "had to think long and hard before asking a man to take time out of his workday to come to the school."

I knew about these challenges, but they

were abstract for me. When I started at NPR, I was very much single. The popular CBS comedy *The Mary Tyler Moore Show*, featuring the character Mary Richards, a single television producer (one of the early reviews of the show labeled her a "spinster"), could practically have been about me, except Mary Tyler Moore was a gorgeous actress with a live studio audience to laugh at her jokes.

FOUR:
FRIENDS AND LOVE

Two of my most wonderful friends have been my husbands. Each man is/was very different, in part representing the different person that I was at the time we met. Marriages, or romantic relationships in general, are friendships that need a particular kind of care and nurturing. And of course, each one is unique. When you fall in love, you feel as if you are walking on air. Even if no one else seems to have noticed, you feel special. After you have weathered the hard times of marriage, you are committed in ways you were not in the beginning, when life together has a rosy, champagne toast glow. And then, of course, there is lust. Young people may think it wanes later in life. They are wrong!!

I met Floyd, my first husband, on the patio at Dick and Ann Schmidt's house. Ann was a reporter for *The Denver Post* and Dick was a lawyer who represented a lot of big news organizations, like the American Newspaper Association. I'm not even entirely sure how I first met the Schmidts all those years ago, but they invited me to their house for cocktails, and Floyd Haskell, the junior U.S. senator from Colorado, was sitting on their patio. He was twenty-six years older than I was, and one of the most handsome men I had ever seen.

He looked like a rugged Westerner, although he grew up in New Jersey. And he was exactly not the person anyone, including me, ever thought I should be married to. In addition to the age difference, he was definitely not Jewish, hilariously not Jewish. He once wondered how I knew that several campaign contributions were from Jewish members of his Harvard class and was astonished to learn that names like Goldfarb and Steinberg are traditional Jewish names. And he was a U.S. senator, which was a problem for a reporter who often covered the Hill. But that night, I just thought of him as very handsome and quite charming, which he certainly was, especially in a small group.

To this day, I cannot imagine how he got elected to anything, let alone the U.S. Senate. His idea of how to campaign or how to connect to his constituents was to walk into a bar, sit down with a bunch of people, never tell them who he was, and instead ask them how they were doing and what they thought about things. Then he would walk out. They never knew who that "masked man" was, my Lone Ranger.* Sometimes people would ask him what he did and he simply said, "I work for the government." He may have been the only U.S. senator who sounded like a spy. But with that independent streak came an equally deep vein of inherent decency. He was principled almost to a fault. He didn't have patience for lobbyists who came asking for favors for undeserving corporate clients, and he was willing to take an unpopular position if he thought it was right.

Floyd had been a lifelong Republican, but he had changed his registration to Democrat over President Nixon's decision to bomb Cambodia. He had fought in World War II and was among the first troops to enter Japan after the United States dropped the

* The Lone Ranger was a 1950s TV western, featuring a perpetual "good guy," a mask-wearing, crime-fighting cowboy, known only as "the Lone Ranger." Each episode ended with someone asking, "Who was the masked man?" to which the answer was, "Why, that's the Lone Ranger!"

two atomic bombs. For him, as for many veterans, war was not to be taken lightly, and when he served in the Colorado state legislature as a Republican, he managed to win passage of the first anti–Vietnam War resolution in the country. He was out of politics in 1972, when the Democrats asked him to run against the sitting Republican U.S. senator, Gordon Allott. It was considered a safe Republican seat, and Floyd was to be a sacrificial lamb. Allott must have thought that too. He would show up for their debates in a fancy chauffeur-driven car, while Floyd arrived by himself in an American clunker. Amazingly, with a budget of about $180,000, Floyd won.

People knew Floyd was the real deal. When one of the longtime doorkeepers in the Senate heard that I was dating a senator, he told me flat out, "There's almost nobody I would be okay with you dating in this lot." When I said that it was Floyd, the doorkeeper made an exception, adding, "He's about the only one of them."

We, however, did not start dating after that night on the patio. The next time I saw Floyd was a complete accident. I was flying to an American Bar Association convention in Montreal, and he was flying to Maine. We were on a small plane, and he was seated

111

diagonally across from me. He reached over, tugged on my skirt, and said, "We met at Dick and Ann Schmidt's house." And we talked for the rest of the trip.

Weeks and months passed until he called and asked me out on a date. It was a terrible date. Just awful. All that I remember was that I talked incessantly while he sat in silence, puffing on his pipe, with reams of smoke circling his head. He was not a big talker, and I was nervous, determined to fill every gap by yammering away. When it was over, I figured that was never going to happen again. Months later, he called and asked me out again. Normally, I would have said no, but I think it was a long holiday weekend and nobody was in town (I have no idea why he was). I was bored and lonely, and it was a free dinner, so I said okay. That evening, we had the best time. We laughed and swapped stories, and discussed the news of the day. After he escorted me back to my little house on Eighth Street NE, I invited him in and we made out on the couch. This was a much better date.

I started seeing him, but there were some bumps along the road. He had been dating another woman, and I think when he asked me out it was after they had a fight. When he started seeing her again, my response was "Just go away." I wasn't always that tough in my personal relationships, but I had reached my early thirties, and I thought, "I'm just not doing this." So, I flew to Saint Martin for a vacation with a girlfriend. She went out almost every night while I would sit on the porch of our tiny bungalow and read. When I returned to Washington, there was a message on my answering machine. I played the tape and heard, "This is Floyd. I'm an idiot. Can we talk?"

As we got to know each other more, my respect and admiration for him deepened. Time after time, I saw him make decisions that most politicians would not. Time after time, I saw how kind he was to others, and time after time, I saw what a gentle soul he was. And most of all, I think I loved him because he loved me — unreservedly. As a woman who for many years had put on a tough exterior because I had to, I finally had a protector in my life.

After we had dated for a while, Floyd matter-of-factly said we should live together. I had never lived with anyone before, and I was petrified. I would only agree to live with him in my small house, not in his cookie-cutter bachelor apartment in Southwest DC. We set up housekeeping, and one day, almost out of the blue, he turned to me and said, "I think we should get married."

I was scared; I did not want to be left a widow. I went to visit my sister Amy, who had finished law school and was applying for jobs, and told her, "I don't know whether I should do this. What if he dies?" Amy very thoughtfully replied, "Nina, you could marry someone your age, and he could walk out on the street and be hit by a truck." She went on, "You love him, he loves you, and if you have fifteen really good years out of your life, you'll have done better than most people do in their marriages." Everything Amy said, including, sadly, the timing, was exactly right.

Two of the enduring, loving relationships I saw up close, Cokie and Steve Roberts and Ruth and Marty Ginsburg, were partnerships that had been forged when both were in college. Floyd was already a grown man when I was born, and that created some very different worldviews. Not long before our wedding, we had a conversation about two life choices. We were sitting on the couch in my living room and I said, "You know, Floyd, I'm not going to change my name for you." Floyd's eyebrows were the type that furrowed, and they furrowed then. "Why is that?" he asked. And I said, "Well,

I have worked very hard to have a profession and a recognizable name, and I don't want to change that." I paused and added, "How would you feel if somebody said to you that when you married me, you would have to become Floyd Totenberg?" He looked over and said two words, "Got it." That was the end of the conversation and the topic. He truly did get it.

Our next conversation was about children. I told him that I always thought I would have children, and he told me, in that terse, laconic way he had of speaking, "If you really want to have children, I will do that, but I've done that. I don't have to do it again." He was sixty years old, had three daughters from his first marriage, and I thought about it for a long time. I could not honestly say that I could be like Ruth or Cokie. I'm not a superwoman — and I couldn't see how I could do it all. Another part of the calculation was that I lacked true financial security and so did Floyd.

When we got married, all I had was a savings account of about ten thousand dollars. Floyd had more money, but he had also just lost his reelection bid, in part because of voter dissatisfaction with Jimmy Carter's presidency, and depending on what he did next, we were going to need to use some of those funds for our life together. I had to consider whether I could pay for childcare, and there was the fact that I was turning thirty-five. It was now or never, and it was a decision I had to make myself. Floyd had left it up to me. Bringing a child into the world at that moment implied a significant chance that I would have to give up working or working in the manner I was accustomed to. To put it bluntly, I wasn't prepared to make that sacrifice. So, I had my answer.

We held our rehearsal dinner at the Tabard Inn, and my father had to give a toast. It was always a bit of a surprise when he spoke because he was a genius violinist, not a genius public speaker. That night, though, he was magnificent. His eyes twinkling, his Polish r's rolling, he said, "When I first met Senator Haskell, he came with Nina to visit us in Maine in the summer. I didn't know what we should talk about, so I took him to the golf course. And I said to him, 'Senator, you have three daughters; I have three daughters.' " (pause) "What to do?"

On our wedding day, in February 1978, I was a basket case. Right up through my walk down the aisle, I thought, "What have I gotten myself into?" I'd been independent all my life and now I had to accommodate somebody else. Arranging the wedding had already been a challenge: I needed neutral ground and a neutral officiant, without any religious affiliation. Cokie told me that the National Presbyterian Church allowed interfaith marriages without clergy, and that's where we wed. To officiate, I asked Federal Appeals Court Judge John Minor Wisdom, revered for some of his civil rights decisions. Like Ruth, he had been one of my calls as a young reporter, asking him to explain some point of law to me, and from our phone conversations, we had become good friends.

Cokie and Linda were my ushers, in charge of seating people; I had only one bridesmaid, my longtime friend from Boston, Valerie Bradley. Ushering was quite a challenge because we had a very eclectic guest list. Linda almost seated Judge Wisdom's wife, Bonnie, next to Jimmy Carter's attorney general Griffin Bell. These were not people who much liked each other, dating back to Bell's time on the appeals court with Wisdom. Cokie, a politician's daughter twice over — her father had been the Democratic House whip, and when he died in a plane crash, her mother took over the seat — swooped in and practically yanked

Bonnie from her seat, saying, "Oh, no, we want you to sit here." When I walked out of the church after the ceremony, someone handed me a glass of champagne. To this day, I still think, "Thank God for that person."

I loved Floyd dearly and he really loved me. But being married to somebody twenty-six years older had its challenges; we were so different in our experiences and expectations. He was always very proud of what I did and never for a moment suggested that I not work, but he really wanted me home at seven o'clock, which I couldn't manage most of the time. Seven-thirty was the best I could do, and many nights, I would work a lot later. He didn't like that.

We didn't fight. Rather, he would shut down and stay silent. He came from a home where nothing was discussed but everything had to be done exactly right, and I came from essentially the opposite. If I had a beef, my philosophy was to say what I was thinking and then move on. We both realized that if this marriage was to work, we needed to do things differently. We began meeting with a female therapist, who was a perfect fit for two such different people. She was quite a bit older than I was and more in tune with Floyd's generation, but she was also a working woman and could understand me. We met once a week for about six months and in that time worked out most of our disagreements, which ranged from the inconsequential to the large — from which pictures should be hung where to why do I have to come on a vacation with your family at Christmastime? We both learned that neither of us could have our way all the time.

One funny point of contention, when I consider that Floyd had been a U.S. senator, was that he really didn't like big parties. He would ask me, "Is this going to be a mob scene?" And then follow up with "I don't want to go." Of course, I liked big parties with lots of interesting people and lots of possibilities for finding stories. Our compromise was that we would go, but I would leave when he wanted to leave. He pithily summed up our party life by joking, "I leave without saying goodbye. Nina says goodbye without leaving."

Another thing I didn't fully appreciate was that I had married Floyd right after he lost his reelection bid by a wide margin. He claimed it didn't bother him, that he had always expected to be a one-term senator, but it was a terrible rejection. I believed what he said without digging deeper. I didn't see it and wasn't understanding enough. It was my friend Val, my maid of honor, who finally said to me, "Nina, I think he's actually really depressed." I brushed it off, saying, "No, he's not." But this is why women friends are important. She was right and made me think. I became a more sympathetic partner. During that first year of marriage, Floyd and I both became better partners.

We, most of us, may be born with an innate desire for friendship, companionship, and love, but being good at any of those things takes work. There is no quick method for learning how to do it right. Floyd ultimately became a very wonderful and supportive husband. No marriage is perfect; it's a question of whether the marriage matters to you enough to be able to make adjustments and repairs — and we did that.

The one friend I had not invited to our wedding, and instantly regretted not doing so, was Ruth. But she was living in New York, and I didn't want her to feel pressure to make the trip. She was still teaching at Columbia and litigating for the ACLU, but what she was hoping for was a federal judgeship. In 1978, Congress expanded the size of the federal judiciary by 33 percent or 152 positions. President Jimmy Carter was also making a concerted effort to appoint more women and people of color. When he took office, only eight out of five hundred federal judges were women, and there were only thirty-one judges of color. In his one presidential term, Carter appointed forty women to the federal bench, many of them minorities, and another fifty-seven men of color. The challenge was even greater because the legal profession was overwhelmingly white and male. In 1980, women made up just 8.1 percent of the profession; people of color were only 5 percent. Carter declared that he wanted to change the complexion of the federal courts — he even issued an executive order in May 1978 calling for "special efforts . . . to seek out and identify well qualified women and members of minority groups as potential nominees." Ruth always credited Carter with making her a federal judge, years after her aspirations had been shot down on her first try.

With Carter now president, her first choice was a position on the United States Court of Appeals for the Second Circuit in New York City, but that opening went to Amalya Lyle Kearse, a distinguished African American attorney who had practiced on Wall Street. Another obstacle for Ruth was that her academic expertise carried less weight with the American Bar Association evaluators than working at a large firm or serving as a prosecutor. Next Ruth applied for a position on the U.S. Court of Appeals for the District of Columbia Circuit, commonly known as the DC Circuit. (There are thirteen U.S. courts of appeal in all). That process dragged on for months, and her nomination was not announced until April 1980, which was a problem because 1980 was a presidential election year. In those days, both parties had a tacit agreement not to put through any federal judgeships after June. The clock was ticking.

As the deadline approached, I did something I had never done before. I stepped outside my reporter zone and wrote an op-ed for a legal publication. I called for Ruth's nomination to be moved and voted on in the Senate, arguing that she was an extraordinary person who had done so much for women's rights. I'm sure my op-ed had no impact, but I felt better writing it, even if in hindsight it was not a professional choice I should have made or would ever make again.

What did make a difference was that Marty Ginsburg had a friend who was the counsel to the Business Roundtable, an influential lobbying organization whose members include top executives of U.S. corporations. The friend made a call to Senator Orrin Hatch, a Republican and leading member on the Senate Judiciary Committee. The result was that Hatch invited Ruth to lunch.

Ruth was shy in most social circumstances, but she also was a woman who had argued before the Supreme Court. She understood how to perform. If she hadn't been a person of the mind, she could have been a great actor. And she wowed Hatch. She was confirmed by the U.S. Senate on June 18, 1980, and sworn in the same day. Ruth was moving to Washington, and neither of our lives would be the same.

Today, perhaps because of our ever more electronic lives, proximity is less important in the care and nurturing of friendship. But perhaps not. Perhaps familiarity, that simple act of showing up in each other's lives, is essential to friendship. When Ruth moved to Washington, I saw her much more. She loved concerts, the theater, and the opera, although opera in Washington wasn't all that good in those days. Whatever the venue, we would chat at intermission or while waiting for the performance to start. Ruth and Marty lived at the Watergate, which was only a short walk from the Kennedy Center. They attended performances frequently — Ruth a bit conspiratorially smuggling a bag of grapes inside her pocketbook for a snack. We saw each other at legal events too, but it was the cultural ones where we could talk and laugh.

And of course, there was dinner.

I regularly invited Ruth and Marty for dinner, although it was a bit of a production on my end. Floyd did not cook, and we did not cater anything — the preferred refuge for many busy people in Washington. I was a pretty good cook but had a limited repertoire. One of my go-tos was leg of lamb, which I carved myself in the kitchen. Both Floyd and Ruth were reserved by nature, so the conversational underpinnings often fell to me and Marty. It could be hard work, and Marty, whom I had not known as well before, was quite simply a godsend. He was not just funny, he was hilarious. He was also a great cook, and he would always insist on bringing something. Once he brought a chocolate cake. I think it was a white cake with chocolate icing, and I could never get him to make it again because he couldn't remember what he had done to the cake and how he had made the frosting, but it was the best icing I've ever had.

Neither of the Ginsburgs knew much about cooking when they married, but one of their wedding gifts was *The Escoffier Cookbook,* the bible of French cooking. And so Marty, a chemistry major, began at page one and worked his way through the entire volume while he was stationed at Fort Sill, Oklahoma, when they were newlyweds. As Marty himself put it once in a speech, "I learned very early on in our marriage that Ruth was a fairly terrible cook and, for lack of interest, unlikely to improve. This seemed to me comprehensible; my mother was a fairly terrible cook also. Out of self-preservation, I decided I had better learn to cook because Ruth, to quote her precisely, was expelled from the kitchen by her food-loving children nearly a quarter-century ago." Ruth had her own reply, namely that, she thought his storytelling was "most unfair to his mother. I considered her a very good cook. In fact, one of the seven recipes I made was her pot roast." (For the record, two of the others were tuna casserole and hamburger.) This is only a small inkling of why it was indeed great fun to have Ruth and Marty over. Floyd was always happy when they came to dinner.

All those small moments, sitting in a darkened theater or concert hall, having a catch-up chat, or sharing a meal, evolved — without me even recognizing it — into a very close friendship. For Ruth's fiftieth birthday in 1983, Marty asked each of her closest friends to write a letter to Ruth, which he carefully placed in an album. I have always been certain I did not write a particularly good letter. But I was pleasantly surprised when Ruth's daughter, Jane, recently sent me a copy.

In the letter, I recalled our first meeting and the cab ride, including her fury at how she had been dismissed by the judicial screening committee. "I remember that on that day we both wondered if women would be forever cut out of the judging business," I wrote. I closed by asking her if she remembered a "riddle" that used to puzzle almost everyone: A father and son are injured in car crash, and when the boy is wheeled into the operating room, the surgeon says, "Oh my God, it's my son." Question: How could this be? Answer: The surgeon is his mother. "It's in no small part because of your work as a lawyer that this isn't a riddle anymore," I wrote. "Happy 50th! Love, Nina Totenberg."

Note that I signed my whole name. I think that was because I had not realized what Marty had — that Ruth and I were real friends. A few years later, Ruth returned the favor, writing a far more beautiful and eloquent letter to my parents to say how much she enjoyed meeting them at my fortieth birthday celebration. "I have great affection for your daughter and much admiration for her intelligence and courage," she wrote. "Talking to Melanie Saturday evening, I gained some sense of why Nina grew up brave, strong, and wonderfully human. Roman's incredibly beautiful playing was one of life's extraordinary treats. I alternated between smiles and tears as I listened and cannot imagine a finer birthday greeting from parent to child. With very best wishes, Ruth." I do not think I was worthy of those words, then or now. My mother carefully saved the letter, along with folders of my article clippings going back to when I started at *The Peabody Times.*

Gradually, year by year, my friendship with Ruth grew and deepened, until a day came when I needed it most.

FIVE:
FRIENDS IN NEED

It was the last week of June 1976, early in my NPR career and well before my first marriage. The end of June is when the Supreme Court usually releases its remaining opinions, and it is always a very busy week for me. Sitting in the office, reading one of those opinions, I suddenly realized I was having trouble seeing. I thought the problem must be dirty contact lenses, so I rushed to an eyeglass store to have the lenses professionally cleaned. As I waited, I tried to read the eye chart on the wall. That's when I noticed there was a black curtain over half of my dominant eye — I've had a "lazy" eye since I was a child. I returned to NPR and called my doctor, telling him that I either had a "brain tumor or a minor infection." By then it was 5:00 p.m., so he told me to come in at 7:30 the next morning.

By 8:30, I was headed to the hospital for

surgery to repair a detached retina. Laser technology was in its relative infancy. It was very possible to go blind from a detached retina; in fact, I knew someone who had become blind in both eyes from retinal detachments. I called my mother, and she immediately got on a plane from Boston. (When I woke up after the operation, I told her that I had had the most wonderful dream, that all the passengers on the Air France plane that had been hijacked and flown to Entebbe, Uganda, had been saved and only one commando had died in the raid. My mother told me it wasn't a dream. The TV had been on, and reporter that I am, I must have been glued to the news in my subconscious.)

To recover from the surgery, I was to remain lying down, with my eyes patched and the window shades drawn, and I was not supposed to move my head. My mother had to feed me because I couldn't see. My recovery was not promising; the head nurse would periodically drop by and try to prepare me for the fact that I might be blind. But I refused to believe it.

I was also taken aback by other people's kindness; it was one of my first lessons in the pure giving of friendship in a time of need. The most thoughtful gesture came from Richard Perle, who at the time worked for Senator Henry "Scoop" Jackson and later became a major figure in Ronald Reagan's Defense Department. A mutual friend had once tried unsuccessfully to fix us up on a date; instead, we became casual friends. Richard also loved classical music, and he arrived at the hospital bearing a stack of records, so I would have something to listen to in my darkened room. All these decades later, though I have not seen him in years, Richard still holds a special place in my heart because of that moment of thoughtfulness. After seeing the records, one of the nurses brought me recordings of books, what they used to play for the blind, the distant precursor of audiobooks today. I spent three weeks listening and attempting to tough it out. No matter how many times a medical person tried to gently or not so gently suggest that I might not see again, I resolved to be gritty. I would not cry, until the morning when the surgeon came in to check my eyes again, picked up the phone, and canceled another surgery that, unbeknownst to me, had been scheduled for the next day.

Now, however, there were signs of recovery. After I heard those words, I finally burst into tears.

■ ■ ■ ■

Intellectually and emotionally, I had learned how a single moment could change everything when it came to health and life. Ruth knew it too. Long before we met, when Marty was in his third year of law school and she was in her second, he was diagnosed with testicular cancer. There was no treatment, other than surgery and massive radiation. Marty's friends rallied to take notes in his classes, but Ruth took care of Marty; their toddler, Jane; and the responsibilities of law school for both of them. She made sure she was home by four in the afternoon to play with Jane. She gave carbon paper to the best note takers in his classes, and they would give her the carbon copies, which she typed up at night. Because the radiation treatments left Marty so depleted, he was only able to rouse himself around midnight. From midnight to 2:00 a.m., Ruth took dictation from him for his third-year paper. When he drifted off to sleep, she would continue her own work, often staying awake until three or four in the morning. She learned to survive on a couple of hours of sleep a night and slept extra on the weekends. For months, she did everything, enabling Marty to graduate with top grades and on time. I don't think I could have done what she did.

I interviewed Marty once after Ruth had been nominated to the Supreme Court. It was just Marty, me, and my little tape recorder. He agreed because he trusted me, but Marty, who was so entertaining and so funny, was quite nervous with the microphone in his face. When we were done, I asked him a very personal question. I told him I'd always wondered why there was such a large age gap between their two children, because their son, James, is ten years younger than Jane. His answer was candid; he said, "Well, after I got testicular cancer, we all assumed that I was infertile because I'd been bombarded with radiation. Ten years later, we were at a conference in Puerto Rico, and Ruth started throwing up. And she kept throwing up. So finally, when we got back to New York she went to see her doctor. He examined her, did some tests, and he said, 'Ruth you're pregnant.' And then sitting down next to her, he asked, 'May I know who the father is?' "

Of course, as Marty told it, it was a very funny story — and James looks just like his dad. But it also underscored how serious his diagnosis and recovery had been. It was impossible to imagine that a man who had been bombarded by that much radiation could have fathered a child — and it was unthinkable to the Ginsburgs too. Most couples face the challenges of illness and caregiving after many years together; for Ruth and Marty, the weight and intimacy of illness and caregiving were rooted in their marriage early on. The thing that I had feared most at age thirty-four — being left a widow — Ruth had faced a decade earlier in life, at age twenty-four.

Now I was a few days away from turning fifty. My seventy-six-year-old husband was a very young older man. He was a gifted athlete, and a beautiful tennis player, and was writing a novel while working on various human rights issues. But that was about to change.

My birthday is in January, and Floyd had been busily planning a party for me. That winter was a terrible one in DC. We had bouts of freezing rain and snow, followed by ice. Everything was coated in ice. I can remember trying to walk up our street and having to grab the metal pickets on the wrought-iron fences and having trouble holding on because even those were completely iced.

For years, I have replayed the moments of that morning in my mind: I was getting dressed for work. Floyd had already left to make last-minute arrangements for the party. The next thing I heard was my once-a-week housekeeper, Jenny, running inside, yelling, "Nina, Floyd down." I raced out in my robe to find that he had slipped on the ice, and he couldn't get up. I called 911, and the ambulance took us to Howard University Hospital. Floyd was alert and joking with me, telling me that he was going to be fine. But he couldn't sit up. His brain was filling with blood from a large subdural hematoma. I hadn't absorbed how serious this was. I even dashed out to tape a quick report for ABC News's *Nightline*, where I was a regular contributor, and then returned. One of my NPR colleagues, Julie McCarthy, came to wait with me. Gradually, by the end of the day, I realized that Floyd could die.

The reporter in me took over and I started hunting down information. At one point, Julie and I followed a long hallway and may have even opened a door to an operating room. Floyd had multiple surgeries to try to remove the blood and free up space for his swelling brain. After that, there was nothing left to do but monitor him in the ICU —

and wait. He was in and out of conscious-
ness, and the moments when he was aware,
he was very disoriented. His chief legislative
assistant from the Senate and by now
longtime friend, Rob Liberatore, came to
see him. Floyd grabbed him by the arm and
said, "Rob, you've got to spring me out of
this joint. I need to go home."

But our home was dark, quiet, and empty;
except for the nights when I went back to
sleep, I was practically living at the hospital.
Three weeks passed, but the fog in his brain
had not lifted. Floyd was not getting any
better, and I said that to the doctor, Sylva-
nus Ayeni, the senior neurosurgical attending physician.

He agreed and told me that there is a
condition called ICU psychosis, in which
patients become very disoriented. At the
time, Howard's ICU was in the basement,
so there was no natural light, no way to
know what time of day it was. So Dr. Ayeni,
known as "Tokes," had Floyd moved up to
a big suite at the top of the hospital, which
also had a pullout couch, and that's where I
assumed I would stay.

I heard from many friends, but one piece
of advice in particular stood out. Ruth's.

She was on the Supreme Court by then,
but somewhere, somehow, she took me

aside and in that gentle, blunt way she had of speaking, with a small pause after each phrase, she said, "You know, Nina, you can't be there all the time. It's not good for you and it's not good for him. You need to go there, to the hospital. You need to make sure that he's being properly cared for. You need to make your presence known to him. But you should only go for an hour. If you spend your whole day there, every day, you will lose who you are."

She paused and added, "He has to be able to come home, and you have to be able to really take care of him when he comes home, and you won't be able to do that if you let yourself get sucked into this. You need to go back to work. It may not be your best work, but it will be good enough." Of course, she was speaking from experience, from Marty and probably even from her mother's long illness. She knew. She could read the exhaustion on my face in a way that other friends, whose hardest days still lay ahead of them, could not. And it was exactly the right advice, the best advice, and the words that I needed to hear.

There is a terrible practicality that settles over every life-changing accident or illness: the economic cost of full-time care-giving is often not sustainable. I had to go back to earning a living, and I had to return to work for Floyd's sake as well.

I went to see him at Howard every day, but I stopped all but living in his room. I told the hospital that we didn't have a lot of money, but I could hire nursing help around the clock for a short time, because it was clear to me that he needed the extra care. One night when I got home from work, one of the nurses called, and my heart dropped. But her voice was happy, and so was her news. Floyd had moved his left thumb; until then he hadn't moved anything on his left side. I began to cry with relief. It was a beginning.

Very slowly, he started to come out of this netherworld. He still couldn't always place his visitors — once, he thought his internist was Supreme Court Justice Byron White, a friend from his Colorado days. But soon he was reading the newspaper, and I knew things were looking up when he read a story about White House Counsel Bernard Nussbaum refusing to give Justice Department lawyers access to First Lady Hillary Clinton's papers. Floyd put down the paper and said out loud, "Bernie, you're going to have to do it." For the first time I thought that maybe he would be all right, even though he now weighed only about 130 pounds.

What I didn't fully appreciate was that I had been in a different kind of fog myself. I look back, and I don't know how I would have survived had it not been for my friends and my family. In the beginning, I was so scared and spooked and half crazed with what lay before me that my sister Jill came down from New York almost every weekend, even after she had knee surgery, just to sleep in the bed with me and keep me company. My sister Amy was in Atlanta, but she called a friend in Washington and said, "You need to go get Nina a decent TV. Her TV is ancient, it can only get a few channels, and she needs to be able to get more channels so she can divert her attention." My parents came from Boston as much as they could. And Cokie and Linda made sure that I was never alone. On the weekends, they would include me in movie and dinner plans, and they told me, "Look, if you're feeling lonesome and like you're losing your grip, and you really need somebody that night, one of us will be free. We will either go to you or take you with us somewhere. But one of us will always be free."

And Ruth, incredibly thoughtful Ruth, called regularly. Where once the phone had been a professional bond between us, now it was a personal lifeline. It seemed she always had an extra ticket to take me to a performance or an extra seat at the table for a dinner out, and please would I come. It wasn't asked as a question; it was asked in a way that I couldn't say no. I could sit with her in a darkened performance hall, lost in the sounds of an orchestra or opera, no conversation required, just the sense of companionship and the knowledge that I was not facing this personal trial alone.

Sometimes, the invitation came at the last minute, like the time she called to ask, "Would you like to come to dinner, it's my birthday. It's just a few people at Beth and Steve's house." (Her cousin Beth is married to Stephen Hess, who has worked for or advised four presidents and is a scholar at the Brookings Institution.) It was a true family party to celebrate Ruth's sixty-second birthday. We even wore party hats — I was handed a silver crown. Ruth's granddaughter, Clara, then five, tried to talk me into a crown trade, because she liked mine more, but I was not one to easily give up my shiny paper crown.

The day after the party Ruth, as she always did, wrote a note to the Hesses, thanking them for "a sparkling party," and noting that "for Nina T it was a much needed spirit restorer." I have noticed in recent years the transformation of the word "intentional" into something personal, something that an individual does with clear purpose or intent. Ruth was intentional long before it was fashionable. Just about everything she did was intentional.

This compassionate care from friends and family — Ruth, my sisters, Cokie, Linda, my father, and before her death, my mother, as well as many others — lasted for nearly five very long years.

After about six weeks at Howard, Floyd was transferred to the National Rehabilitation Hospital to relearn the basics of how to function in the world. There, his will to survive really kicked in. But it was a long haul. At first, Floyd complained that the nurses would not come when he hit the buzzer, and I got annoyed on his behalf, until finally a nurse explained to me that they didn't come on purpose. "He has to learn to do some things for himself." One of those things was to walk, something he might not have mastered without his own friends. Everyone came to visit Floyd, especially his tennis pals. He organized their visits so they could join him in the hallways as he practiced with his walker.

Indeed, we were both lifted and buoyed in

so many ways by our friends.

One of my friends, Florence Isbell, called me and said, "I know people say, 'What can I do?' And they don't expect you to tell them, but I want to know what I can do. Do you need somebody to go shopping?" I thought about it, and I said, "Well, you know what I need is somebody to visit Floyd during the daytime and make sure everything is going correctly." And she did that so diligently for several weeks that a few of the nurses thought Florence was his wife.

Floyd became a very good patient because he wanted to get out of there. Justice Brennan, who by that point had retired from the Court, and his wife came to visit. They brought an embroidered cushion encouraging Floyd (and also me) to persevere. He was persevering. He was gaining weight, we could finally talk about his coming home, and I could not stop crying. The minute I would think about him or talk to anyone about him, I would start to cry. This was not the kind of crying where your eyes well up and you wipe away a tear or two; this was the kind of crying where once you start, you cannot stop. Finally, my mother said to me, "Nina, you need a brain rest." She suggested that I might also need some anti-depressants. This was the 1990s, and mental health was rarely if ever discussed. But I listened to my mother; I called the doctor who had helped Floyd and me with our early marital issues and told her what was going on. She said, "There are a lot of people who want antidepressants and don't really need them. You need them." She prescribed a low dose of Prozac — I keep an empty bottle in my closet to remind me — and said the drug would take about two weeks to kick in. Almost to the day, two things happened.

That morning, an empty plumber's truck hemmed me in on my street and I couldn't get out of the parking space. I had to go up the street looking for the plumber, and when he came out, he yelled at me, and I burst into a flood of tears. He drove off, scared, and I don't blame him. I would have been scared of me as well. But that night, my friend Valerie was in town from Boston, and we had drinks. For the first time in months, I felt not exactly happiness and certainly not contentment, but rather, very suddenly, a sense that I was in control of me and, more important, that I could do this. Somehow, magically, the crazy lady from that morning had vanished, replaced by someone who felt like I could handle what was in front of me.

Before Floyd was finally released, we sat down with the discharge specialist, and I was given a list of all the services that he would need. Cokie came to the meeting with me, listened to everything, and took copious notes. Nothing got by Cokie. When the insurers tried to cancel the morning nurse, who helped Floyd get up and ready for the day, she pulled out her notes and said, "Senator Haskell was promised morning care," and gave them the exact dates originally specified by the insurers. Whatever they had committed to, she made sure they held to it. That got us through the worst part. I hired two health aides to come to the house during the day. Between the two, they could cover the hours when I wasn't there. To afford it all, I started giving paid speeches. I was very fortunate that I was in such a visible profession and audiences wanted to hear what I had to say. When I had to travel overnight, my wonderful neighbors would send their teenagers to sleep over, so Floyd wasn't alone in the house.

Slowly, our lives seemed to be getting back on track. Floyd was growing stronger and gaining weight. He was bent over from calcium deposits that had settled on his bones, and he needed to use a cane, although he often tried to walk without it. Everything was progressing well when he went for a routine checkup and his doctor, Thomas Sacks, called me to say that Floyd had a lesion on his lung. He needed more tests, but it looked like both sides, cancerous, and very serious. Floyd needed surgery immediately. I hung up the phone, went into the bathroom, and cried my eyes out.

When the surgeon opened him up, he found that the cancer was only in one lung and the operation was deemed a complete success. Tom looked so happy when he came to check on Floyd in the hospital that night. For twenty-four hours, everything was great. The next day Floyd crashed.

From the euphoria that he might beat this, I was plunged into another medical siege, in some ways worse than his brain injury. He was in the ICU with a tracheostomy. He was partially conscious and aware but didn't understand what was going on; he would try to get out of bed, and eventually the medical staff had to use restraints to keep him in place. The nurses were wonderful, but he was locked in this condition for months on end.

A month or two in — time in these situations always spirals, twists, and turns in on itself — I was sitting at his bedside, and he

144

mouthed, "I need to go." I paused, thought for a second, and then I said, "Well, you know I love you, but if you do have to go, I'll be all right." And he said, "No, I have to go to the bathroom. Get me to the bathroom." He didn't realize that he had a catheter. That's the stuff of life: one person's literal statement of basic needs, "go," becomes another person's seminal moment of discovery. I had only a few seconds to think of what I should say to answer what I heard as his cosmic question. And I realized as soon as I said those words that I would in fact be all right. I had an enormous support system. In that period of such difficulty, it seemed that everyone I knew was a hand on deck, coming to the support and aid of Floyd and Nina.

There were some terrifying days when Floyd's life depended on them. He crashed multiple times during those months. And again, friends came to the rescue, among them lawyer Jamie Gorelick, whose husband, Richard Waldhorn, is a pulmonologist and was the chair of medicine at Georgetown University Hospital. Jamie had often asked me if I wanted Rich to see Floyd. I kept saying no, that I thought things were going relatively well at Sibley Hospital. Then suddenly Floyd was about to go into full

145

respiratory failure. I called Jamie in tears, and Rich appeared in half an hour. His assessment was that Floyd needed a different attachment for his trach tube, which Sibley did not have, so he got one from Georgetown. The attachment worked and suddenly Floyd was no longer at death's door. Still, we were not out of the woods.

In between the crises, I had a routine. Our friends Rob and Patty Liberatore lived near the hospital. Almost every night after work, I would drive to the hospital to see Floyd, stay for a half hour or so, then head to Rob and Patty's for dinner around their family table, which included their diverting teenage sons. I would then return to Floyd and sit and hold his hand; sometimes I would sing to him. Much of my life was now circumscribed by a hospital room, so my friends and family came to me. My sisters came, my parents came, Cokie and Linda came, and so did Val from Boston. Ruth offered her phone calls and invitations — and whenever I was feeling unsteady, I found myself replaying her sage advice, about preserving my own identity as I took care of Floyd. I could never have done it without all my friends, who to a woman, and a man, pitched in to keep me afloat. Most of all, though, it was the women in my life, my sisterhood as I came to think of them.

If there was a mother superior of the group, it was Cokie. At one point Floyd was holding steady, so I flew to Oklahoma to report for *Nightline.* Timothy McVeigh, the Oklahoma City bomber, was headed to trial and I was doing a piece on his defense team. A couple of times a day, I checked in with the nurses. Then, two days before I was to leave, I returned to the motel and called the nurse on duty. She said, "Nina, most people have nine lives. He has had twenty-eight, but I think he might be on his twenty-ninth. I don't want to lie to you, he's really not okay." I called the *Nightline* producer, Tom Bettag, asked him to find me the earliest plane back to Washington, and told him why. There were no direct flights, and I knew it was going to be a long trip. Very quickly, he called me back with instructions to be at the airport at 7:00 a.m., adding, "We've chartered a plane for you." I don't really remember how Cokie knew what was going on, but when I walked into the hospital bay in the ICU, Cokie was sitting with Floyd. Because that was Cokie.

I could never be as good as Cokie; few of us ever will be. With all that she did, she always made time to show up at the hospital, not only for me but for countless others.

Usually she would stay for only fifteen minutes. She always maintained that was the perfect length for a visit. People knew you cared, but you didn't overstay your welcome or tire out someone who was sick enough to be hospitalized.

After about half a year in the ICU, Floyd finally began to really get better, and even the nurses were shocked when he was moved to a step-down unit and then was discharged to go home. But it would still be a long slog, and our friends continued to care for us. Cokie and Linda would bring dinner a couple of times a week and, with their husbands, entertain us. Ruth and Marty, and other friends, did too. For me at least, those dinners were festive, and off-set some of the difficulties of taking care of my still very frail and sometimes disoriented husband.

When he returned home, Floyd was once again skeleton-thin. But he was valiant about getting better. He wanted to play tennis, but it had to be "safe" tennis. I took him out the first time and strapped a bike helmet on his head and hit balls to him as best I could. His balance was shot, so, to prevent a fall, he wasn't supposed to move much on the court. The saving grace was he had long arms and still had quick reflexes;

it was enough to make him feel alive again.

His tennis friends still rallied and came for terrible lunches of peanut butter and jelly or ham and cheese sandwiches. Fortunately, the food didn't matter because they simply wanted to be with him. Floyd was that kind of guy. He was captain of just about every team he ever played on, because his teammates so liked and admired him. After lunch his pals took him out to the courts to hit perfectly arcing tennis balls right to him, allowing him to actually play tennis.

Floyd disliked swimming, but on his own, he hired a high school swim coach to go with him once or twice a week to a pool in Southwest DC so he could swim laps and try to regain some strength and more co-ordination. He insisted on resuming driving, and I finally relented after he passed a driving test, although the prospect of him behind the wheel was terrifying. He spent his days writing the draft of a political thriller, and even though he never sold it, when I read the draft, I saw that it was pretty good. One night we were talking about persevering, and I told him how much I admired him. He always called me "Doc," and he said in his usual laconic way, "But, Doc, I want to stick around and be with you some more." Those words melted my heart. He did stick around for another few years.

He stayed very proud and wanted to take care of me, and my responsibility was to figure out a way for him to maintain his dignity to do that. From the time we were first married, he had always worried when I came home late at night. So now we made a deal: no matter how late it was, I would call him when I left the office, and if I couldn't find a parking spot in front of our house, he would come outside and stand watch, my fragile guard, determined to wait for me.

The end came when we were on vacation in Maine in August 1998. Floyd had a chest infection, and I took him to Blue Hill Hospital, where they diagnosed bronchitis and put him in their ICU, which was basically three beds with a nurse. His lungs were in terrible shape from the ARDS, the acute respiratory distress syndrome, that had besieged them after the cancer surgery. ARDS is what has killed so many Covid-19 patients, and once killed so many HIV patients. The hospital in Maine flooded him with massive doses of antibiotics, and the consensus was the treatment would either work or not. When he continued to get worse, I decided we should go home, so that his kids could come to say goodbye, because Blue Hill, Maine, is not an easy place to get to. One of the benefits on his credit card was an allowance for a medical transport plane, so I arranged for one, but bad weather delayed us for more than a day. Finally, the skies cleared. We took off from Bar Harbor, and he died over Augusta, Maine.

Under the FAA regulations at the time, his body had to be returned to Bar Harbor. So the pilot turned the plane around, and I asked him to call my father. My father, then eighty-seven, was thirty-five minutes away in Blue Hill, and I don't even want to think how fast he drove. He was waiting for me when the plane's wheels touched the ground. The local hospital called the funeral home in Washington, and that part was, mercifully, out of my hands. I came home alone to face all the tasks of death. Cokie — true, loyal Cokie — helped me with everything, as did wonderful Linda.

I had never been entirely responsible for arranging a funeral, and Cokie had arranged plenty. She knew which chapel to request at the National Cathedral, who to talk to, and what questions to resolve about the service.

We went to a fancy Northwest Washington funeral home to pick out the casket, and the salesman was like a character out of a Dickens novel. His face was ghoulishly pale, and he wore his dark hair slicked back. He was constantly wringing his hands and being overly solicitous. I was very up-front and said, "I just want a cheap casket." He kept showing me the fancy caskets that cost thousands and thousands of dollars, prompting us to repeatedly ask about plainer ones. Finally, after being worn down for nearly an hour, I started to give in. There was one model at the end of the "plain" row that looked a little prettier. The salesman said, "You husband was a tall man, wasn't he?" I answered, "Yes, a little over six feet." And in all seriousness, he said, "Well, I think he'd be much more comfortable in this one." Suddenly, out of the corner of my eye, I could see Cokie start to giggle — and I started to giggle. When the salesman walked away for a minute, leaving me to think about casket comfort, the two of us burst into quiet peals of laughter. And borrowing some of Cokie's spine, I bought the cheaper casket.

Floyd had wanted to be buried at Arlington National Cemetery. He had served in World War II, in the Pacific as a spotter and intelligence operator, rising to the rank of major. One of our favorite household expressions was "dig deep, puppy in bottom," a phrase he had heard when he stood in the chow line to get his portion of stew while serving with the Philippine guerrillas fighting the Japanese. He had been awarded the Bronze Star. But there was one big obstacle to being buried at Arlington: his military records had been burned in a government warehouse fire, and just months before his death there had been a scandal about high-level government officials being approved improperly for burial at the national cemetery. Cokie came to my rescue once again. She called a staffer in Senator Howard Baker's office, because Cokie knew everyone. Jan Vulevich figured out that Floyd must have filed proof of military service to qualify for his full government pension, which is based on years of federal service. Sure enough, when she went hunting through his personnel records, there was the proof of his five years in the Army.

We buried Floyd on a Friday and the memorial service was on Saturday. My father played the Bach Chaconne for solo violin, I spoke, and Floyd's friends and tennis buddies spoke as well. One of his tennis friends had been a private who served under him in the Pacific. Their unit was assigned a West Point colonel who was not exactly the brightest bulb, and Floyd judiciously suggested the colonel begin work on a mission that young Floyd had basically made up. The colonel went off and wrote his plans while Floyd and his pals planned the real operation.

I didn't sit shiva, the Jewish tradition, or hold a wake, because Floyd wasn't Catholic. But for five days, until the memorial service, friends arrived on my doorstep every night and the piles of food began to appear. One of my NPR colleagues, Bill Craven, and my intern at the time, William Tong (who would become the attorney general of Connecticut), arranged it all and brought it upstairs from the kitchen. Hundreds of people came that week, and we had a wonderful time talking about Floyd.

In 2011, I gave a commencement address at Washington and Lee University Law School. Commencement speakers impart many messages, often about going out and conquering the world. But every time that I speak to students, I save space for friendship. That June day I said, "Now, I want to talk briefly about your non-professional life — not exactly a traditional thing for a commencement speaker to do. But I would like, with a personal story or two, to show you, I hope, the value of friends and family. Yeah, yeah, everyone yammers about that . . . but most of you really haven't had to confront some of the toughest blows life has to offer.

"When my late husband fell on the ice more than a decade ago, nobody could have known on that morning that it would take three brain operations and four months in the hospital before he could come home, frail and learning to walk again. Nor could anyone have known that a year later he would return to the hospital and spend seven months in intensive care, reeling from one crisis to another. At the time, I really wondered if I was capable of doing all the things for him that I needed to. I managed in large part because of my dear family and friends. They wined me and dined me to keep my spirits up. They sat with me in hospital rooms, they went to doctors' meetings with me. They took notes at meetings with social workers and then read them the riot act if promised services were not delivered — and boy, oh boy, you do not want to have Cokie Roberts reading back to you from her notes like the Charles Dickens character Madame Defarge reading from her knitting.

"There is, of course, a lesson in all of this

besides friendship and family. It is a lesson that involves a rather old-fashioned word. Duty. When you come to a crisis in life, I think you will find that doing your duty will serve you rather well, whether it is your crisis or someone else's. The path is clear, the choices few, and there are no regrets afterwards. Indeed, there are rewards. You are a better person . . . for want of a better word, a deeper person . . . and able to accept life's blessings, too."

Six:
Friends of the Court

In the years between my wedding and my widowhood, I became moderately famous — or to some, infamous — due in part to my reporting on Supreme Court nominees. Ruth became truly famous as the second woman to sit on the Supreme Court. In an ironic twist, these parallel tracks helped nourish our friendship.

One reason was very basic: I understood her job. More than two decades of covering the federal court system had given me a special insight into the institutions where she worked, both the U.S. Court of Appeals for the District of Columbia Circuit, known primarily by its short-form name, the DC Circuit, and the Supreme Court. I had my own view of the pressures and challenges of the two courts and their dockets. And because it was my job, I was more than happy to talk about something else when I was off duty, as was she.

But there was another aspect of this glide path to the spotlight. Ruth and I knew each other long before other people were paying much attention to either of us. Much later, when Ruth became "The Notorious RBG" and everyone wanted a piece of her, that did not matter; we had decades of friendship between us already.

Two of Ruth's greatest strengths as a friend were her loyalty and her incredible timing. The woman with a myriad of obligations and demands somehow made space for those she cared about at just the right moment. It was not simply her seminal advice or her invitations when Floyd was so ill. It was the other small acts of thoughtfulness, the things she did when no one was looking.

In 1988, 110 years after its founding (and seven years after a woman was named to the Supreme Court), the Cosmos Club, a DC institution that prides itself on selecting members who are "distinguished in science, literature, the arts, a learned profession, or public service," finally voted to admit women. One of Floyd's friends belonged and wanted to nominate me. I wasn't much interested in a social club, but Cokie and Linda insisted I do this, so against my better judgment, I agreed to be nominated as one of the first female members. As it turned out, I was blackballed. I have been told that a committee decides who to propose for membership, and one or possibly several members of the Cosmos committee privately voted no. I was really hurt to be voted down, and at some point, I told Ruth about it.

Unbeknownst to me, after my rejection Ruth was invited to visit the Cosmos Club, and at the end of the tour of its lovely interior, her escort asked her to become a member. Ruth demurred, and either then or later said, "You know, I think that a club that is too good for Nina Totenberg is too good for me, too." It says everything about Ruth that she never told me about this; I heard the story from someone else. But she did fess up when I asked her about it.

She was fiercely loyal without being self-aggrandizing, and not just to me. There were legions of such stories after she died. One of her former law clerks, Joe Palmore, remembered that when he went to work for the justice, he and his wife were struggling to find a good day-care situation for their one-year-old son. He told his fellow clerks, but as he recounted to his law partners at Morrison & Foerster nineteen years later, he "had no idea that the Justice knew, much less that she would try to fix the problem."

As he later recounted, "One day, I accompanied the Justice to a speech at the Georgetown Law Center. Afterwards, we squeezed into an elevator with Court security officers and Georgetown personnel to depart. When the doors closed, the Justice asked, 'Where is the daycare center?' " That indeed was Ruth, asking the central question and economical with her words.

Palmore continued, "Baffled, one of the Georgetown escorts said it was in the basement. The Justice answered, 'I'd like to go there.' So, we did. We got off the elevator, and the Justice led me and the rest of the entourage into the daycare center. At the front desk, she announced, 'Hello, I'm Justice Ginsburg. My clerk Joe is looking for a daycare spot for his son, Simon. We'd like a tour.' The Justice and I then navigated the blocks, toys, and toddlers to check out the daycare center. Together." Problem solved.

I have to credit Ronald Reagan with being a proximal cause of some of the professional changes in both our lives. Ruth, however, credited Jimmy Carter. One moment came well into the 2010s, at a dinner party at my house. The usual suspects — Linda and her husband, Fred Wertheimer, Cokie and her husband, Steve Roberts, and Jamie Gorelick and her husband, Rich Waldhorn — were there. We somehow got on the topic of Carter, mostly lamenting his presidency and all the ways in which it had been a disappointment. Ruth sat there, listening, and then raised her hand, straight up in the air. As all our eyes turned to her petite frame, she intoned, with a mischievous grin, "I dissent!" She then proceeded to praise the man who had brought her to Washington and who more than doubled the number of women on the federal bench.

It was, of course, Ronald Reagan who was the first president to appoint a woman to the Supreme Court. He campaigned on that promise and made good on it the first chance he got, naming Sandra Day O'Connor. It was also under Reagan that the Court began a gradual sea change to the right, one which continues and accelerates, no longer gradually, to this day. Ruth and I, in very different ways, were caught in the resulting waves and undertow.

Sandra Day O'Connor's upbringing was the geographically polar opposite of Ruth's. O'Connor was three years older; her parents owned and ran a 160,000-acre cattle ranch in Arizona, with no good school nearby. She spent her school years living with her austere grandmother in El Paso, returning to the ranch in the summer. In her autobiography, O'Connor described life on the ranch, including a great story about her being charged with bringing lunch to the ranchhands who were working with her father many miles away. At the time she was about thirteen, and as she drove across this untracked landscape, she got a flat tire. With no one to help, she changed it by herself, using her full body weight to jump on the jack. Needless to say, she was a bit late when she got to the roundup, but she was very proud of herself. Her father was not, telling her brusquely, "You're late." She explained that she had had a flat tire. To which he responded, "Next time, leave earlier." RBG's mother wasn't so unforgiving, but her reaction to Ruth's one poor grade on a report card contains the same undercurrent of greater expectations, a higher bar to meet, which both women internalized from beloved parents.

Precociously bright, O'Connor left to attend Stanford University at sixteen. She graduated third in her class from Stanford's law school in 1952, at age twenty-two, one of only five women overall. (Future Supreme Court Chief Justice William Rehnquist graduated first.) Like Ruth, she made law review. O'Connor didn't have an academic background, or experience in a law firm; none would hire her after her law school graduation, except as a secretary. She would serve in various public-sector jobs until she was elected to the Arizona state senate, where she rose to the position of majority leader before becoming a state trial and then midlevel appeals court judge. She was unanimously confirmed by the U.S. Senate in 1981 to replace the retiring Justice Potter Stewart.

I was thrilled when O'Connor was appointed, as were most of the women I knew. And the Reagan administration understood the importance of the first female justice. Her Senate confirmation hearings were the first to be televised for a nominee to the Supreme Court. What few of us could fully appreciate was the immense pressure and scrutiny she felt as the first woman. Along with batches of homemade fudge in her Court mail, she received notes that said, "Back to your kitchen and home female!" and "This is a job for a man and only he can make tough decisions." Reporters dug through her trash and, paparazzi-like, chased her down at parties.

I never heard anyone discuss what Justices

William Brennan or William Rehnquist wore, but the commentary on O'Connor's wardrobe made it sound as if she moonlighted as a model for *Vogue*. Seven years in, the same year as my Cosmos Club debacle, legal journalist Stuart Taylor, writing about the relatively new Rehnquist-led Court in *The New York Times Magazine*, would sniff, "O'Connor in particular, whom Reagan seems to have chosen more for her sex than for her ideology." No wonder she later said that she knew if she failed, women lawyers and judges across America, few as they were, would pay the price. Of course, she did not fail, and instead there was an enormous growth in the number of women judges, particularly at the state level.

Understandably, the experience made her guarded. Perhaps my least successful dinner party with any justice was when I invited O'Connor and her husband to my house not long after she was appointed. I got a good sense of the direction of the evening when she walked into my tiny kitchen as I was carving my standard leg of lamb, observed me with the knife for an instant, and then said, without preamble, "You're cutting against the grain." For a third couple that evening, I had invited lawyer Joseph Rauh and his wife, Olie. He was a well-known civil rights advocate who had been a military aide to General Douglas MacArthur in the South Pacific during World War II and had clerked for two distinguished Supreme Court justices, Benjamin Cardozo and Felix Frankfurter. I thought she'd be interested in him, but instead his presence seemed to irritate her.

We still saw each other socially and I did interview her, but it took years before she loosened up with me — some of that had to do with Ruth's arrival on the Court, which took the burden of being the sole ambassador for a female judiciary off O'Connor's shoulders. By the end of her tenure on the Court, some two decades later, she was stoically caring for her husband, who was living with Alzheimer's disease. As his illness progressed, she would take him to her chambers for a few hours each day. "He would come and sit in her big office," their son Jay recalled in an interview published in *Forbes*. "She had a couch. She would do her work, and he just sat there and looked through the newspaper. If he did wander off, it would be harmless, because there always would be a guard nearby."

O'Connor announced her retirement from the Court in 2005 to care for him, but Chief Justice Rehnquist's death kept her on the bench until January 31, 2006, six months later. By then, as O'Connor biographer Evan Thomas noted, John O'Connor "could barely recognize" his wife of nearly fifty-five years, and she soon regretted her decision to step down. She was a vigorous seventy-five when she left, youthful by the standards of the time. O'Connor also could no longer properly care for her husband and had to move him into a care facility in Phoenix. There he grew interested in another woman. As Thomas wrote, Sandra Day O'Connor, less than a year after ending her service on the highest court in the land, "would come in and find her husband holding hands with this other woman, and with her characteristic strength she would sit down and take her husband's other hand."

I saw her not long after that. We were both featured at a November 2007 conference called The Presidency and the Court, held at Franklin Roosevelt's Presidential Library. I was moderating several panels and presenting, and Sandra was the keynote speaker. Having been a caregiver myself for so long, I could see the strain and exhaustion written across her face. She had recently broken her foot and was wearing clunky orthopedic shoes. As the conference's, concluding dinner dragged on,

Sandra, seated next to me, turned and asked in a low voice, "Do you think I could leave early?" "Absolutely," I said. "You look so tired. Go!"

Not long afterwards, I would be saying something similar to Ruth, who until almost the end of Marty's life, was his sole caregiver.

While Sandra, in hindsight, was a relatively obvious pick for President Reagan, the same could not have been said about Ruth in 1993. Many observers didn't think she had a chance. It was twelve years between the selections of these two women, while four male justices were confirmed in the interim — Antonin Scalia, followed by Anthony Kennedy (a third choice after two failed nominations), and then two picks by President George H. W. Bush, David Souter and Clarence Thomas.

Scalia's path was easy. He was a well-respected legal scholar and a judge alongside Ruth on the DC Circuit, and his confirmation has frequently been described as a "formality." He was unanimously approved by the Senate, an almost incomprehensible vote today for someone with such strongly held views. This vote was a reflection of an earlier era, the regard in which Scalia was held, and a fact little mentioned today: Scalia was the first Italian American nominated to the court. Not only was that a key consideration in Reagan's decision to pick him, but it was also a component in his easy confirmation; many Italian American groups let their senators know how important this nomination was to them.

President Reagan's next nominee, Judge Robert Bork, was also a colleague of Ruth's on the DC Circuit. He too was a conservative legal theorist with very strong views and a very long paper trail. But Bork, unlike Scalia, was nominated to replace the centrist Justice Powell, and his writings were different in fundamental ways from Scalia's. He had, for instance, written a lengthy article opposing the 1964 Civil Rights Act that required hotels, restaurants, and other businesses to serve people of all races. He also opposed a 1965 Supreme Court decision that struck down a state law banning contraceptives for married couples, and he had opposed Supreme Court decisions on gender equality too.

A bitter confirmation fight ensued. Known as a charming and witty man in private, Bork appeared dour and humorless in his public hearings. He was so overly confident that he had refused to do any practice sessions at the White House. He assumed not only that he could answer any question posed to him but that the public would support his views. But they didn't; a considerable number of Americans did not like what they heard. His answers seemed to play into the stereotype liberals were painting of a man who cared little for people whose lives would be affected by his decisions. When Republican Senator Alan Simpson of Wyoming pitched a softball to Bork, asking him why he wanted to serve on the Supreme Court, the nominee replied that "it would be an intellectual feast." The Senate ultimately rejected Bork, 58–42, a decisive margin and more than for any previous Supreme Court nominee. He later wrote a book in which he criticized the confirmation process and inveighed against premarital sex and working mothers.

More than two decades later, when I wrote Bork's obituary, I quoted Tom Goldstein, publisher of the popular SCOTUSblog, which extensively covers the Supreme Court. "The nomination changed everything, maybe forever," he said. "Republicans nominated this brilliant guy to move the law in this dramatically more conservative direction. Liberal groups turned around and blocked him precisely because of those views. Their fight legitimized scorched-earth ideological wars over nominations at the Supreme Court, and to this day both sides remain completely convinced they were right. The upshot is that we have this ridiculous system now where nominees shut up and don't say anything that might signal what they really think."

That is indeed, to a large extent, what happened although I would add one caveat. The Reagan administration overtly sought to move the Court in a dramatically more conservative direction. When it came to the choice of Bork to replace the more moderate Powell, the Democrats responded by aggressively attempting to block his nomination, never anticipating, I think, that Bork would turn out to be the most forceful witness against his own nomination. After that, when nominations did falter, it wasn't because of a misstep in the nominee's hearing; it was because the Senate Judiciary Committee and the White House had failed to do their due diligence. After the Bork nomination failed, I wrote a long piece in the *Harvard Law Review* about the confirmation process. One of my major points was that the Judiciary Committee was a disaster waiting to happen, because the committee did not really investigate a nominee's background. Case in point, the next nomination: Douglas Ginsburg, no relation to Ruth. He was just forty-one years old and had served in the Reagan administration before being nominated to the DC Circuit a year earlier.

Prior to his quick rise in the conservative Reagan administration, he had clerked for Justice Thurgood Marshall, the nation's first African American justice, and then taught at Harvard Law School. So I went to Cambridge to see what I could learn about him there. Rather quickly I discovered that he had occasionally smoked marijuana with students, and, to the displeasure of some faculty mothers, he had also smoked weed in front of their children.

Today it may sound crazy that having smoked marijuana would sink a Supreme Court nomination, but in 1987, this was a very big deal; in fact, the Reagan administration had a very hard-line policy on drug use and prohibited the Justice Department from hiring attorneys who had used marijuana after being admitted to the bar. Somehow, Ginsburg had been hired anyway.

But what to do with such revelations? I agonized. Ultimately, the answer was easy. These were corroborated facts. It is not up to me to determine someone's fitness for a position, but it is my responsibility to share information germane to a lifetime appointment. We broke the story on NPR's *All Things Considered* right after I returned from Cambridge. It would have been my preference to wait, but we were hearing that other reporters were beginning to "sniff out" the same information. So I wrote a series of questions for host John Hockenberry to ask me, questions so bland that he actually had me redo the interview for the second feed. He was right. I had buried the lede the first time around.

Still, at the end of the story, I kept the qualifier that it was unclear whether this in any way disqualified Ginsburg from an appointment to the Supreme Court. It turned out that it did; Republican senators in particular were horrified, and Ginsburg withdrew from consideration within a week.

On his third try, Reagan nominated Anthony Kennedy, who sailed through and was also unanimously confirmed.

At that moment, I wasn't considering the possibility of another Judge Ginsburg being nominated to the Court — or the possibility of being caught in a firestorm over another confirmation hearing. Within five years, both would happen.

Seven:
Friends and Confidences

Ruth had served on the U.S. Court of Appeals for the District of Columbia Circuit for more than a decade. In that time, she had watched three colleagues be nominated for the U.S. Supreme Court but only one be confirmed. Now, in the summer of 1991, a fourth colleague — Clarence Thomas — was being nominated to the High Court, this time to replace the retiring Justice Thurgood Marshall. He had been on the DC Circuit with Ruth for just over a year when he was selected, and I cannot remember her ever saying anything about him one way or the other. But when he was named to the lower court, it was clear he was being groomed as a potential Supreme Court nominee in the event of a Marshall retirement. When that expectation became reality, it would lead to the biggest story of my career.

The confirmation hearings began in September, and after eight days of testimony, the Senate Judiciary Committee was scheduled to vote on the nomination September 27. I did not expect anything unusual, but then something odd happened. The chairman of the committee, Delaware Senator Joe Biden, made a very cryptic statement before the committee vote: "I believe there are certain things that are not at issue at all, and that is his character or characterization of his character. This is about what he believes, not about who he is." With a warning tone in his voice, Biden added, "I know my colleagues, and I urge everyone else to refrain from personalizing this battle." Sitting there, I thought to myself, "What character questions?" As Biden was making his statement, I saw that all the committee members had been given large manila envelopes, and they were looking at the contents. The clear subtext was that this involved something that was perhaps highly inappropriate. I didn't know what was inside those envelopes, but I started kicking the proverbial tires. After Thomas had been nominated, on July 1, I had heard rumors about sexual harassment allegations, but I could not verify anything about them, so I gave up. This was, I assumed, "another good story ruined by the facts."

But after that Judiciary Committee session, I called up Democrats on the committee, starting with Howard Metzenbaum. And I asked, "What do you know about this?" In answer to my questions, he said, "Oh, Nina, this is no silver bullet. This is not a big deal." I wasn't so sure. I kept calling folks, and finally, I had a name: Anita Hill.

I began my own background check on Professor Hill, who was teaching law at the University of Oklahoma but who had worked for Clarence Thomas at both the Department of Education and the Equal Employment Opportunity Commission. Reliable conservatives gave her high praise and said she hung the moon. Both her current dean and the dean of the Oral Roberts University law school, where she had taught previously, spoke highly of her, calling her an outstanding professional and a woman of the highest integrity.

My next call was to Professor Hill, with an opening line about how I was writing a piece on Black law professors. She replied succinctly, "I know why you're calling." She said she would speak to me, but only if her name wasn't used. And I told her that I couldn't do that. In my view, I said, no one could make this type of accusation anonymously. That was especially true this late in the confirmation process, but any time as far as I was concerned. Professor Hill said she wouldn't talk to me unless I got a copy of her sworn affidavit.

I didn't know it at the time, but the Judiciary Committee staff had known about Hill for some time, although she had not been willing to come forward publicly. In September she reconsidered. As I reported when I broke the story, "By the time Clarence Thomas was testifying before the Senate Judiciary Committee the week of September tenth, Hill had contacted the staff of the Committee's chairman, Joseph Biden. She says that while Biden's staff seemed interested, it was not until ten days later, after repeated calls from her, that she was interviewed by the FBI."

On September 23, four days before the mysterious envelopes and Biden's statement, the FBI interviewed Professor Hill in Oklahoma. Hill provided the name of a corroborating witness, a friend in whom she had confided at the time, a friend she had known at Yale Law School, Susan Hoerchner, who was by then a worker's compensation judge in California. The FBI interviewed Hoerchner, as well as Clarence Thomas. Hoerchner, according to Senate sources who saw the FBI report, confirmed that Hill had told her contemporaneously about the harassment, but Thomas had denied the allegations. The White House examined the report for less than two days, declared it exculpatory, and told the Senate to move forward.

After the FBI meeting, Hill submitted her affidavit to the Judiciary Committee, so it would have her own words. (At the time, FBI interviews were not recorded or even transcribed verbatim. They were paraphrased from general handwritten notes taken by the agents during the interview. That was standard practice until 2014 and is still the case with many of the interviews the bureau conducts today.) She had also retained a high-profile attorney, Charles Ogletree of Harvard Law School. Ogletree may have told her I wouldn't be able to get a copy of her sworn statement, but by October 1, I had reviewed every word of it. I called Hill back, and she lived up to her promise to talk to me, on the record, and on tape. At the end I told her that she would be "the subject of great trauma and great controversy." I wanted to give her one more opportunity to say no. The decision to go forward, publicly, with the charge had to be hers. I also spoke to Susan Hoerchner.

Then I did something that would be impossible today: I held the story for one more day, while I tried to reach Biden and his staff for a comment. They refused to respond; only Senator Paul Simon would speak to me on the record, telling me that when Hill had first contacted the committee, he had said to her, "You can't have this kind of an accusation anonymously." Now, the accusation was no longer anonymous. So, on October 6, two days before the entire Senate was scheduled to hold its final vote on Thomas's nomination, NPR aired my report on *Weekend Edition Sunday,* laying out Hill's charges along with audio excerpts from my interview with her — and the information from the corroborating witness. That same day a *Newsday* reporter, Timothy Phelps, broke the story in print, identifying Hill by name but without any of the details about her charges. On Monday, Hill called a press conference and announced that she would testify in an open hearing if asked.

That morning, I was being interviewed by the host of NPR's *Morning Edition* and one of the questions I got was whether the Senate would vote on Thomas's nomination that week as scheduled. My response was that they would vote if the Republican leadership, namely Bob Dole, had the votes to confirm, and if they didn't have the votes, there would be a second set of hearings. It turns out, they didn't have the votes, but the subsequent hearings were very rushed, with enormous political pressures on both sides. The truth-seeking role was lost in the shuffle. The Thomas-Hill hearings, which riveted the nation and indeed much of the world (they received higher television ratings than that year's World Series), stretched from October 11 to October 14. But nothing was resolved. A few minutes after 6:00 p.m. on October 15, Clarence Thomas was confirmed for a seat on the Supreme Court by a 52–48 vote, the narrowest margin in more than a century.

That part of the story was over, but mine was just beginning. The Republicans were furious, and many saw my reporting as an attempt to derail Thomas's nomination and ultimately keep him off the Court. They believed that I was purposely sabotaging their nominee — even though Chairman Biden, under some duress, had directed the FBI to begin its own investigation before I ever asked my first question. Two days after my NPR report, Senator Alan Simpson and I argued about the story on *Nightline*. After the show had finished taping, he followed me to the hired car the network had sent to take me home, waving a journalistic ethics code in one hand and accusing me of "ruining Anita Hill's life." He held on to the car door and yelled at me until I got out and yelled back, using a few choice words, including, regrettably, calling him a "fucking bully." When my car finally left and had turned the corner, the driver pulled over, turned around, and said to me, "Lady, you better get a gun."

Simpson's fury was so profound, I desperately wished Floyd had been there. Instead, when I came home after that *Nightline* encounter, Floyd heard me and came down the stairs, in his pajamas and half asleep. He took one look at me, and I burst into tears, hardly the tough reporter I played on network television. Floyd was wonderfully supportive throughout. He was absolutely unlike his former colleagues, including the most liberal members of the committee, like Senator Metzenbaum, who had dismissed sexual harassment as a nonissue. While I was working on the story, before I had enough to go with, Floyd could not understand why this *wasn't* a big deal and why the committee didn't do something about it. The man who always wanted me to be home on time to make dinner kept saying, "You go do it. This is an outrage. This should be looked into."

What bothered me the most when I started digging was that neither side had fully investigated these allegations. It's much easier to investigate fully when charges are still confidential, before they are splashed across the nation as a huge news story. The fact is that no one ever disputed the truth or accuracy of my story, which was that a credible witness had made a serious allegation to the Judiciary Committee and those allegations, for all practical purposes, had not been examined. Hill's name had been forwarded to the committee weeks before, and the committee had dropped the ball.

Instead, I was put under the microscope. When I arrived at work, my voicemail would be full. I think it held thirty-six messages, and every morning, when I pushed the play button, almost all of them were abusive and awful (voicemail messages having been precursors of social media discourse). Once I heard the venomous talk, I would hit delete, delete, delete. It was incredibly unpleasant; my post-*Nightline* encounter with Alan Simpson was even written up in *The Washington Post,* having been leaked by Simpson's press secretary. Not certain where this was heading, a day or two later I destroyed all my handwritten notes that had any possibility of revealing information about my sources.

Nothing I'd ever done in my life, good, bad, or indifferent, went unexamined. Some of the attacks were withering. *Wall Street Journal* columnist Al Hunt, seeking to impugn my integrity, resurrected the nearly two-decades-old incident where I had borrowed quotes for my Tip O'Neill piece. "Purposeful plagiarism is one of the cardinal sins of journalism from which reporters can never recover their credibility," Hunt wrote.

I felt like one of Floyd's tennis balls being smacked back and forth between the opposing sides.

But suddenly the stakes were raised. In his defense of Thomas on the Senate floor during the final confirmation vote, Missouri Republican Senator John Danforth had delivered an impassioned speech, all but accusing Senator Metzenbaum's staff of leaking the FBI file. He said that the penalty for senators or staff who leak secret information is expulsion or dismissal. "That is how serious leaking an FBI file is," he thundered, as he fixed his eyes on the Democratic staffers sitting in the staff seats at the back of the chamber. Never mind that I had never seen the FBI file in question, or claimed to have seen it.

Inside the Senate, the controversy would not subside. On October 24, by a vote of 86–12, the senate passed a Democrat-sponsored resolution that gave the Republican and Democratic leaders the power to appoint a special counsel to investigate "the leak." He — it was always going to be a "he" — would have subpoena power and receive assistance from both FBI and General Accounting Office investigators. He would be given 120 days to complete his investigation and report back on leaks from both the Thomas-Hill hearings and the earlier Keating Five banking scandal, which had ensnared several prominent Democrats. Suddenly, I was not merely being excoriated in the press. I, along with Timothy Phelps, had been plunged into legal jeopardy. On December 6, Senate leaders George Mitchell and Bob Dole named Peter Fleming, a New York lawyer, as the special counsel. His investigation was slated to commence on January 1.

I insisted that NPR hire Floyd Abrams, a wonderful First Amendment lawyer, to defend me. He generously gave us a cut rate, and now I had two Floyds in my life. Special Counsel Fleming subpoenaed both me and Phelps. On February 24, I made my way to the Hart Senate Office Building, a white marble building with a massive black Alexander Calder half sculpture half mobile, *Mountain and Clouds,* dominating the atrium. I made my way to one of the closed-off rooms on the second floor for my interview.

To each question, I replied, "I respectfully decline to answer." I had given my word to the sources who helped me with the story, and to betray them not only would have been dishonorable but would also threaten my ability and the ability of the press in general to inform the public about the functioning and malfunctioning of government. As I explained first to Fleming and afterwards to a battery of cameras and reporters covering the subpoena, "I will not be a party to this effort, even if it costs me my liberty." I also told the special counsel that I would take the names of my sources to my grave, and I feel exactly the same way about that pledge today. No one will ever know.

The expectation was that, because of my refusal, the Senate Rules Committee would cite me for contempt, and contempt of Congress could mean jail. Floyd Abrams told me from the start that I didn't have a legal leg to stand on; the only thing I had was public opinion. He told me to do every media interview I was offered.

I was so nervous for the first interview, on the *Today* show, that he sat next to me. Fortunately for me, right-wing talk radio did not yet exist; there was no Rush Limbaugh show or Sean Hannity. That would have been far worse.

Fleming's next move was to subpoena my telephone records and Timothy Phelps's from September 23 through October 6. He also requested that we both remove any "personal calls" from the records. But, as Phelps's, lawyer, Ted Olson, pointed out, removing those calls would make it easier for the counsel's efforts to isolate and identify a source. Floyd Abrams was indignant, issuing a statement that called the subpoenas "dangerous assaults on the First Amendment," and saying, "Journalists must be free to use their telephones without fear of government surveillance." In the small world of Washington, the person who had signed the subpoenas was Senator Robert Byrd, Democrat of West Virginia, the president pro tempore of the Senate and one of my longtime sources. Byrd said he was required to do so by the terms of the resolution authorizing the special counsel investigation. He added that any objections should be raised with the Senate Rules Committee.

One member of that committee, Senator Daniel Patrick Moynihan, finally put an end to the spectacle. In a speech on the Senate floor, he declared that the special counsel was doing damage to the First Amendment, adding, "It's not as if any crime was committed here." More important, he said that if the matter came before the Rules Committee and anyone supported Fleming's tactics, "I'll guarantee there'll be blood on the walls of the committee room." Within a couple of weeks, the Democratic committee chairman and Republican ranking member had quashed the subpoena request. Just like that, my legal jeopardy was over.

But the ramifications, bad and good, have lasted a lifetime. In hindsight, I think I did really good work, and I'm very glad I did it. But at the time, I wondered almost daily if that one story was worth what was happening to me. I often joked that strangers had sent me flowers and candy, but I had to throw away the candy because first, it would make me chubby, and second, I didn't know if it had been poisoned. I was trying to keep up a good front, but in fact, I was using humor to state the truth. Many people deeply hated me and were not shy about expressing their vitriol.

As time passed, I realized it *was* worth it, even the awful parts. Part of what changed my mind was a small thing, a plane trip with Floyd. We had scheduled a quick vacation to the Caribbean before my special counsel interrogation, while the Court was on its February hiatus. On board, a flight attendant recognized me. She grabbed my hand and would not let it go, profusely thanking me for bringing attention to the issue of sexual harassment and helping to start a public discussion. And that was the thing. I, who had spent years gently fending off unwanted advances, had not fully realized what a festering wound this issue was for so many working women. When I reported the story, my first thought was that this was a very important political story. It never occurred to me that it was a sociological story as well, about a phenomenon that had gone largely ignored, and about which there was a volcano of experience and emotion ready to erupt.

Initially, I didn't know that women all over the country were sending thousands of faxes to offices on Capitol Hill. But gradually, I came to realize that many, perhaps even most women, had thought they were alone, that what happened to them had not happened to others. And I came to realize that I was one of them; I had for too long accepted the unacceptable.

I saw something else too. I saw how female members of the House, who walked to the Senate to ask for the hearings to be reopened, were denied access to the Senate floor and treated like second-class citizens. And eventually I also saw that women had real power at the voting booth. In November 1992, a year after the Thomas-Hill hearings, many women, mostly Democrats, were elected to office. The media dubbed it "The Year of the Woman." Indeed, Carol Moseley Braun in Illinois beat Alan Dixon, a fellow Democrat who had voted for Thomas.

I also developed a deeper level of gratitude for my friends. When I faced a withering onslaught, so many of them leaped to my defense, not only privately, but publicly. Female journalists who were colleagues, like Cokie, or even competitors, like Rita Braver of CBS News, put their good names on the line to support me. When Sam Donaldson of ABC News called to say that he wanted to do a story on me for the network's nighttime show, *20/20,* Cokie was sitting right there — our desks abutted each other. I looked in her direction and said to Sam, "Let me call you back." I sort of knew this might not be a good idea, and I had the good sense to ask Cokie. "Well for God's sake, don't do something that's just about you because it will be too contentious," she said. We ended up with a segment on Cokie, Linda, and me, and Diane Sawyer, not Sam, did the interview. Linda's husband, Fred, told me that "whatever they do, whatever they ask you, just smile, because nobody will remember what they asked you if you just smile." It was great advice, and I smiled my way through many interviews after that.

Remarkably, two retired Supreme Court justices, William Brennan and Lewis Powell, also came to my defense, allowing themselves to be quoted in *Vanity Fair*. Powell said to writer Ann Louise Bardach — in what she described as his "rolling Southern accent" — "I've known her [Nina] since I was sworn in, which was January 1972, and I generally have a high opinion of her. She takes great care to get the facts straight."

During one of our subsequent lunches, I also bemoaned to Justice Powell the fact that it was miserable to have so many people so angry with me, that I really liked to be liked. And he paused and said, "Really, Nina, you can't do what you do for a living and expect a lot of people to like you." Of course, he was right, but that didn't mean I didn't want to try.

On one level, I did succeed. Not long after, Alan Simpson and I became friends. I invited him to the Radio and TV Correspondents' Association Dinner, and we were the belles of the ball. Prodded, I think, by his wife and daughter, Simpson came to understand that burying the hatchet was in both our interests. He couldn't have been a better date, picking me up, and even bringing me a corsage to wear for the evening.

Of course, none of this would have happened without Anita Hill. If she had refused to talk to anyone, or said "I don't want to testify," the entire story would have gone away. If I had some tough moments in the aftermath of the story, it was a pittance compared to her. While my speaking fees went up, the nastiness that she faced in Oklahoma continued almost unabated, and after five years, she would resign her professorship at the OU law school and ultimately take a position at Brandeis University, where she still teaches. She paid an exceptionally high price for coming forward.

While our names have often been linked, I didn't meet Hill in person until 2022. My 1991 interview with her was over the phone, and what she said was pretty much the same as her subsequent Senate testimony. But the FBI's written account of their agents' interview with her is quite different, which argues that law enforcement should tape their interviews. I have no reason to believe that she would have said one thing to me and under oath before the U.S. Senate but something different to the FBI. It is more likely that the agents got something wrong or misunderstood her.

I did meet Clarence Thomas a few months after his confirmation. The Supreme Court press corps historically holds a welcome event to meet the new justice, and his welcome reception was scheduled in January. These events are opportunities to say hello and ask a few questions. I introduced myself, and we shook hands and exchanged pleasantries as if absolutely nothing had happened. But I also, unlike my usual self, did not ask a single question that afternoon. For understandable reasons, he's never granted me an interview, and when we attend the same social events, I keep my distance.

The next Supreme Court confirmation I would cover would be Ruth's.

Ruth and Justice Thomas had briefly served together on the DC Circuit before his elevation and then would spend more than twenty-five years together on the Supreme Court. After her death, Justice Thomas penned a remembrance for the Supreme Court Historical Society.

"Justice Ginsburg and I often disagreed," he wrote, "but at no time during our long tenure together were we disagreeable with each other. She placed a premium on civility and respect. This approach did not lessen her strong convictions, but rather facilitated a respectful environment in which disputes furthered our common enterprise of judging. Whether in agreement or disagreement, exchanges with her invariably sharpened our final work product."

He concluded that in her final years, "though frail in body, she remained intellectually rigorous and characteristically productive in her work. Despite her strength and perseverance, however, it was profoundly sad to see her physical suffering. Justice Ruth Bader Ginsburg will always have a special place in my heart and memory as a dear and wonderful colleague. It was my good fortune to have shared the bench with her for so many years."

The Ruth I knew and the Ruth her colleagues knew were very much one and the same. She did not, chameleon-like, change her bearings, her beliefs, or who she was depending on the setting. She was thoughtful about the small things and was always able to separate fierce intellectual disagreements from personal animus, though I must admit that a few times I could see she really was angry. Knowing there was no profit in that, though, she made it her business to get over her personal emotions.

What says the most about the climate of Washington over the last three decades is that on August 3, 1993, Mitch McConnell, Republican of Kentucky, was one of ninety-six senators who voted to confirm Ruth Bader Ginsburg to the Supreme Court. But in September 2020, then–Senate Majority Leader Mitch McConnell refused to grant a request for Justice Ginsburg's body to lie in state in the Capitol Rotunda. Instead, the first woman and the first Jewish person to be so honored had her casket placed in Statuary Hall, on the House of Representatives side of the Capitol. McConnell and his House counterpart, Representative Kevin McCarthy, refused to attend to pay their respects to the woman who was openly mourned by Thomas and all her colleagues on the Court, liberal and conservative.

Perhaps Ruth foresaw these things better than I did. In 2018, she wrote a short note to Anna Marie Hoover, a Columbia University master's of public health student, in response to her request for advice to a young woman just starting her career. The note began: "Concise advice: Stay strong and be resilient. It helps, sometimes, to be a little deaf when unkind or thoughtless words are spoken." That was the advice about marriage that Ruth's mother-in-law gave her on the day she married Marty. She often said that she occasionally applied that deafness to her colleagues as well. It's good advice.

EIGHT:
SUPREME FRIENDS

It's hard to fathom now, but when Justice Byron White announced his imminent retirement in March 1993, some two months into Bill Clinton's first presidential term, Ruth Bader Ginsburg was not at the top of anyone's potential nominees list. First, she was sixty years old, and the administration's preference was for someone younger, who likely would serve for a longer span of time. Even before Justice White had announced his retirement, I warned Ruth that the White House might not consider her because of her age. Her reply was "That's just silly," and she glared at me. (This is also probably why neither of us ever tried to give the other career advice!)

It does not say much for my long-term prognostication skills, but I did think that the Clinton White House would reject her because of her age. In addition, she was not a favorite of some women's groups, largely because of two lectures she had given that were critical of the reasoning employed by the Court in *Roe v. Wade.* *

Ruth's views about *Roe* had long been both more radical and more conservative than those of many of her legal peers. More radical, because she viewed abortion as a matter of personal autonomy, a woman's right to make decisions about her own body, just as a man does. She saw abortion for women as a question of liberty, rooted in the Fourteenth Amendment's guarantee of equal protection under the law, and thus far more than simply a matter of personal privacy, which was the basis of the argument advanced by Justice Blackmun in his majority opinion.

But, at the same time, she also thought the Court would have been better served to take a more incremental approach to establishing reproductive rights. Instead, it essentially legalized and regulated abortion through one decision, creating a nationwide framework that permitted the procedure during the first two trimesters in every state

* The University of North Carolina William T. Joyner lecture in 1984 and the James Madison Lecture on Constitutional Law at New York University in 1993.

in the union. "My criticism of *Roe* is that it seemed to have stopped the momentum on the side of change," and "gave opponents a target to aim at relentlessly," she said in 2013 at a University of Chicago symposium on *Roe v. Wade.*

She may have been right that *Roe* gave opponents an easy target, but the pro-choice movement's legislative successes before 1973 had been relatively limited. In 1962 the American Law Institute, which represented, then and now, the gold standard in writing model laws, proposed a model abortion reform bill, recommending that states legalize abortion in cases of rape, incest, fetal abnormality, and to protect the life or health of the mother. Colorado was the first to adopt this proposal in 1967, and soon twelve additional states had adopted it, including some more conservative southern states and states with Republican governors. In California, Governor Ronald Reagan signed the bill into law.

But on the ground, little changed. In a state like California, the legislation translated into only a few hundred legal abortions each year. Abortions remained very expensive and were obtained to a large extent by well-to-do white women. By the early 1970s, only four states had legalized abortion completely — New York, Hawaii, Alaska, and Washington.

When the Supreme Court handed down the *Roe* decision in 1973, much of the momentum toward legalization had, in fact, already begun to falter and even be reversed, according to University of California Irvine law professor Mary Ziegler, author of four books on the history of abortion in the United States. The pro-choice movement had suffered some major setbacks, losing reform referenda in several states. In New York, the state legislature had gone so far as to vote in favor of recriminalizing abortion. Only a veto by the state's Republican governor, Nelson Rockefeller, kept abortion legal in the state. And the pro-life movement was on the march.

RBG may have been overly optimistic in her assessment of the odds for achieving change through the political process in the 1970s, but she was spot-on in her view that *Roe* wasn't the best case to use to establish abortion rights. She preferred a case she had worked on in the early 1970s, a case the Supreme Court agreed to hear in 1972. I think it was one of her greatest regrets as a lawyer that the case fell apart because the other side caved. She thought that if the Court had ruled on her case, not only would the legal doctrine have been on firmer ground, but the political ground would have been firmer as well.

In typical Ginsburg fashion, Ruth had picked a case that illustrated both sides of the abortion coin. Her client was Susan Struck, an Air Force captain who became pregnant while serving as a nurse in Vietnam. At the time, the U.S. military had a rule that required pregnant servicewomen to have an abortion, usually on a foreign military base, or be discharged. Struck, a devout Catholic, didn't want an abortion, nor did she want to give up her military career. So, she sought help from the ACLU.

Representing her, RBG sued the Defense Department, arguing for the right of a woman *not* to have an abortion. The principle was the same as guaranteeing a woman the right *to have* an abortion. The point being that under the Constitution's equal protection clause, it is the woman's right to make the decision. Ginsburg lost in the lower courts but won a stay preventing Struck's discharge pending appeal. In 1972, two years after Struck's baby was born and adopted by friends, the Supreme Court agreed to hear the case. But the Defense Department, understanding that this was a political hot potato — and probably a loser

— changed its policy and agreed to let Struck remain on active duty. Thus, the case was formally declared moot by the High Court. Shortly thereafter, the justices ruled on *Roe.*

Ruth's views regarding the reasoning in the *Roe* decision gave pause to some women's groups in 1993; the nuances either escaped them or more likely any criticism was considered problematic.

So when Senator Daniel Patrick Moynihan proposed Ruth's name to President Clinton, Clinton reportedly replied, "The women are against her." Moynihan immediately let Marty Ginsburg know, and behind Ruth's back, Marty began a quiet campaign on behalf of his wife.

Reminiscent of that binder of letters he had solicited for Ruth's fiftieth birthday, Marty began collecting a binder of letters in support of his wife's nomination, and that was just the beginning. Pulling strings wherever he could, he facilitated calls to the White House from members of Congress, campaign donors, and anyone who could help.

Meanwhile, a parade of male candidates was identified — and almost all of them were political figures: New York Governor Mario Cuomo, Senator George Mitchell,

Interior Secretary Bruce Babbitt. But each either did not want the job or in Babbitt's case, Senator Orrin Hatch, the ranking Republican on the Judiciary Committee, told the White House that he couldn't be confirmed. (Remember, this was still the era when the filibuster existed for judicial nominees.) Women's groups, however, continued to be hesitant about Ruth, in large part because of those lectures about *Roe,* where she had suggested the Court had gone too far too fast, and that the legal underpinning of the decision should have been more focused on the idea that laws forbidding abortion discriminate against women, denying them the equal protection of the law and their personal autonomy.

For a long time, Ruth was not really in the mix, as President Clinton continued his search for the perfect nominee. After nearly three months, he finally met with short-lister Stephen Breyer, an encounter that did not go well. Breyer was recovering from a serious biking accident, in which he had broken several ribs and punctured a lung. He had to travel from Boston to Washington on the train because he wasn't cleared to fly, and he was in considerable pain; his lunch with the president in the Oval Office was not his best performance.

The last person to be invited to the White House was Ruth. But she was somewhat mortified by her attire. As she later told me, White House Counsel Bernie Nussbaum called her on a Saturday to ask her to a meeting with the president. She was in Vermont for a wedding and asked if the meeting could wait until Sunday. Fine, said Nussbaum, "You'll go right from the airport to the White House."

That presented a wardrobe dilemma for the ever-elegant RBG, who protested that "I'll be wearing my 'traveling clothes,'" which for Ruth likely meant a slightly more casual skirt and top. As she told the story, he assured her that would be okay because the president would just be coming off the golf course. "So, I arrived in my clean clothes and in comes a very handsome president wearing his Sunday best because he had just come from church."

Clinton didn't seem to care; when their meeting ended after ninety minutes, he was smitten. Every White House aide I talked to later told me that he fell for Ruth, "hook, line, and sinker."

Later that night, Ruth was taking a bath when Nussbaum called and told her that Clinton was going to nominate her to the

Supreme Court. It was one of the few times in her life when her emotions betrayed her: she started to cry. In all the years I knew Ruth, I never saw her cry, really cry. But, as Marty later told me, this was one of those rare times.

Ruth herself later said to me, "It was one of the happiest moments of my life. I was absolutely on Cloud Nine and then the president [came on the line and] said tomorrow morning we will have a little ceremony in the Rose Garden, and we'd like you to make a few remarks. So, I had to come down from the cloud and sit at my writing table.

"I liked the remarks," she observed wryly. "It was the only time in that entire episode when there was no time for White House handlers to go over what I was going to say," and that allowed her to speak, "my own words, unedited."

Ruth used the formal nomination announcement to talk about her mother: "I pray that I may be all that she would have been, had she lived in an age when women could aspire and achieve, and daughters are cherished as much as sons."

The stars had truly aligned for Ruth. It helped that all the political people had dropped out of consideration and the White

House was forced to pick a prominent judge. It also helped that Ruth was widely respected in the legal world, not just by liberals but by conservatives, like Orrin Hatch and Antonin Scalia. As Scalia said puckishly years later in an interview that I did with the two of them onstage, "What's not to like about her, except her views on the law?"

I switched to my reporter mode as soon as her nomination was announced. In fact, I actually distanced myself from my old friend. I had no role to play, except as a reporter. It would be inappropriate to celebrate the moment with her or to advise her in any way. Even to spend time with her. Our roles were obvious to each of us, and they were entirely separate. My recollection is that whatever tiny bits of color I got during the process came from Marty, and believe me, they were sparse.

For every Supreme Court nominee, the confirmation process is an arduous, uncertain path. And while Ruth would prove a good student in the mock hearings, known as "murder boards," at the White House, Clinton aides often found her unyielding and pigheaded in what she would and wouldn't agree to do and say. But her confirmation hearing, in public at least, was a triumph, as the documentary *RBG* captured with great clarity. She was incredibly focused and well prepared. For years Republicans have claimed that her answers set the standard for saying nothing artfully. In fact, though, she said quite a bit, especially when compared to nominees in confirmation hearings today. Although she noted in her opening statement that she would not give "any hints" about how she would rule in future cases, she was quite clear about what she considered settled law. She answered extensive questions about her legal writing as a lawyer and scholar, including her view that the Constitution recognizes a right to privacy.

As she put it, "The right to determine one's own life decisions" including "the right to marry, the right to procreate or not, the right to raise one's children — the degree of justification the state has to have to interfere with that is very considerable."

She didn't even shy away from discussing *Roe v. Wade*. Asked whether the decision to terminate a pregnancy is a fundamental right, she noted that in both of the Supreme Court's major abortion decisions, two decades apart, the fundamental question was: Who decides? In *Roe,* she said, "the answer comes out: the individual in consultation with her physician . . . somewhat of a big brother figure next to the woman." But in the Court's 1992 decision, she said, "Whatever else might be said about it . . . the woman decides."

By the time she finished testifying, Ruth had answered questions about affirmative action, gender discrimination, single-sex education, the limits of congressional powers, even "Indian" treaties and government funding for the arts. Indeed, a recent study showed that she was among the *most responsive* nominees ever to appear before the Judiciary Committee.

I don't know that I ever sat down to contemplate what it might mean for my wonderful friend to become a sitting Supreme Court justice or how or if it might change our friendship. The funny thing was, I actually saw her more because I covered the Court and sat in the press gallery during the arguments, which was something that I did not do with any regularity at the DC Circuit Court of Appeals.

At the Supreme Court, I thought she would never notice when I was or wasn't in that courtroom, but she did. And occasionally she would bring up an exchange and say, "What did you think of that?" What's more, unlike most of her friends, I very much understood her job. Watching the sessions month after month and year after year gave me a grasp of the Supreme Court's complex interpersonal dynamics, of the workload, of the effort to balance opposing forces and points of view, of how difficult it was to achieve consensus, even of the distinct role of being one of the more junior justices on the Court. That appreciation only deepened over time. And I'd like to think that it helped me get the nuances right in my reporting.

We didn't discuss the particulars of the Court, but we always maintained a mutual respect for each other's work. In a decision in a 2016 immigration case, for instance, Ruth wrote the majority opinion, holding that U.S. citizenship determinations must be applied equally to the children of unwed mothers and unwed fathers. The decision overturned an existing law that allowed a child born abroad to an unwed American mother to automatically become a U.S. citizen if the mother had previously lived in the United States for at least one year. But in contrast, a child of an unwed American father could not become a U.S. citizen unless the father had lived in the United States for a continuous period of *five* years, two of them when he was over age fourteen. Ruth's opinion struck down the discrepancy as violating the equal protection clause. But she also wrote that until Congress made a modification to the law, children of unwed mothers would have to adhere to the stricter citizenship standard applied to unwed fathers. Much of the commentary about the decision complained that she had not delivered a full-throated embrace of women's rights by making it ultimately harder for children of both single males and single females to attain citizenship. But as I reported, while it might not have been what immigration and women's rights advocates wanted, it was obviously all she could get and maintain a majority opinion. The next day my phone rang, and it was Ruth, saying four words, "You got it right."

Moments like this I truly enjoyed because, for the most part, if we talked shop, it was about the Court's published opinions, or what had actually happened in the Court during oral arguments. As for the Court's non-public deliberations, they are supposed to remain secret. And they almost always did — until the spring 2022 leak of Justice Samuel Alito's draft opinion in *Dobbs v. Jackson Women's Health Organization,* the Court's recent landmark abortion case.

The need for boundaries and a break

forced us to seek out other topics of conversation. At the same time though, I could know, without her telling me, when there was a rough patch and when the workload was the most consuming. She might look exhausted or roll her eyes when I asked her why a particular case was taking so long, but that was it. Still, the shared rhythm of our professional lives led us to be more personally in sync. And we both knew, appreciated, and respected the other's drive and need to work.

For the first time in her life as a judge, Ruth was also part of a genuine sisterhood. She had served on the DC Circuit with Patricia Wald as the chief judge, but I got a quiet sense that there was a bit of competition there. The Supreme Court, however, was the last professional stop. There was no higher rung to climb, and Sandra Day O'Connor was thrilled, after twelve years, to no longer be the only female justice.

It's difficult to overstate the role of tradition at the Supreme Court and the adherence to ritual and repetition. Rulings from the Court carry a weight outside of legislation and executive orders because they set precedents, and they can be modified in the future only by new cases and new rulings.

The pressure to get it right is enormous. In her first years on the Court, Sandra Day O'Connor was very cautious. She knew she was a role model and that any misstep would affect other women judges. For twelve years, she was not just the first, but the only woman on the Court, so she was extremely careful in how forcefully to advance the cause of women's rights. Ruth's arrival changed some of that dynamic, and the two of them became very close — not close in the sense of doing a great many things together outside of the Court, but close in terms of being a mutual support system inside.

Ruth repeatedly called Sandra "the most helpful big sister anyone could have." (And around the conference table, due to her seniority among the sitting justices, Sandra always spoke much earlier than Ruth.) In September 2019, during an interview with me at the Clinton Presidential Center, Ruth recalled, "She told me just enough to enable me to navigate those early weeks. She didn't douse me with a bucket full of information — just enough to get by." With a smile Ruth also recalled the first change that accompanied her arrival at the Court, and how pleased O'Connor was. "Justice O'Connor was the lone woman on the

Court for twelve years. In our robing room, there was a bathroom and it said 'men.' For Justice O'Connor, when the need arose, she had to go all the way back to her chambers. When I came on board, they rushed a renovation. They created a women's bathroom equal in size to the men's."

Justice O'Connor's advice began in earnest with Ruth's first opinion assignment from Chief Justice Rehnquist, an assignment that, to understate matters, did not thrill the new justice. It involved a complex employment law case. Ruth was writing for the majority, and Sandra was dissenting from the decision. But Sandra was happy to help, telling her forthrightly, "Just do it and, if you can, circulate the draft before he makes the next set of assignments. Otherwise, you will risk receiving another tedious case." When it came time for Ruth to deliver the Court's ruling from the bench, Sandra passed a note down to Ruth. It was written with O'Connor's typical no-nonsense formality: "This is your first opinion for the Court. It is a fine one. I look forward to many more." The note made such an impression that Ruth did the same for Justices Sonia Sotomayor and Elena Kagan when they joined the Court.

Neither Kagan nor Sotomayor would feel

the same kind of isolation that O'Connor did for twelve years, and that Ruth did in the three years after O'Connor retired.

In her years as the only woman, Ruth would occasionally find herself sitting in the weekly conference with her colleagues, men she had worked with for more than a decade. She would make a comment, and it would go entirely unremarked upon. Fifteen minutes later, a male justice would make the same point, and the response around the table would be "That's a good idea." The day-to-day dismissal of a smart woman's voice — which so many women have experienced — happened even on the Supreme Court. But it never happened when *both* Sandra and Ruth were seated at the table. Despite being very different people, they really were a team.

One thing that happened repeatedly when they served together — and that always floored me — was how many lawyers, including experienced lawyers, men who had argued frequently before the Court, confused Ruth and Sandra. Time after time, lawyers would call one of the two by the other's name. I could understand doing that with a row of balding, bespectacled white men in black robes, but that never seemed to happen on the male side. The two women, of course, looked nothing alike. Sandra was tall, raw-boned, a plain-spoken woman of the West with a nasal twang, while Ruth was diminutive in size, wearing owlish glasses, her brown hair pulled back in a scrunchie, and her low voice marked by a Brooklynesque accent. But they were somehow interchangeable in the minds of some male advocates.

Indeed, early on, the National Association of Women Judges gave them T-shirts imprinted with I'M SANDRA, NOT RUTH and I'M RUTH, NOT SANDRA. I think it occasionally amused but more often irritated them. Ruth had already been on the Court for about four years when in 1997 veteran lawyers Laurence Tribe (a Harvard Law professor) and Walter Dellinger, who was the acting solicitor general at the time, both addressed the female justices by the wrong name. O'Connor replied, very much unamused, "She's Justice Ginsburg. I'm Justice O'Connor." Dellinger would later tell me that he couldn't account for the mistake. The minute he said the wrong name, he knew it and just wanted the floor to open as an escape hatch.

Years later Ruth put it as diplomatically as she could, explaining during an interview at the University of Chicago, "When I was a new justice, people had become accustomed to there being a woman on the U.S. Supreme Court. And that woman was Sandra Day O'Connor, who was the lone woman for twelve years. So, every now and then when I asked a question, the response would be 'Justice O'Connor.' And then Sandra might say, 'I'm Justice O'Connor, she's Justice Ginsburg.' We don't look alike. We don't talk alike. But they heard a woman's voice." She ended with her own exclamation point: "It's not that way any longer, because I've been there so long, I sit next to the chief."

Perhaps the greatest testament to the strength of the bond between the two female justices was O'Connor's tolerance for Ruth's driving or, more precisely, her parking skills. For most of my time covering the Court — until the threat level increased markedly — most justices drove themselves to work. So for most of her tenure, Ruth was at the wheel when she pulled into the Supreme Court garage, where the parking places are very tight. Our Ruth, it turns out, was not a great parker; indeed, as far as I know the only test she ever failed was her first driver's test. Her less than stellar parking skills put something of a strain on her relationship with Justice O'Connor, who had been driving since she was thirteen. The two justices had parking places side by side, and Ruth once told me that perhaps the worst moment in their friendship was when she had to tell Sandra that she had scraped her car in the garage. O'Connor was not amused because she had just repaired the previous Ruth-inflicted scrape. Not long after that, Ruth stopped driving to the Court, and then she stopped driving entirely. Either Marty or her protective detail drove.

Ruth also was not the first female icon on the Court; that position belonged to Justice O'Connor, who was constantly traveling and making appearances. Still, when Ruth arrived, O'Connor was unfailingly gracious. Indeed, in 1996, when Ruth was still quite a junior justice, O'Connor did something incredibly generous. The occasion was a landmark case, *United States v. Virginia,* challenging the Virginia Military Institute's all-male admissions policy. John Paul Stevens, as the senior justice in the majority, assigned the opinion to O'Connor. But she demurred, saying, "I really think Ruth ought to write this." The ruling was 7–1, with Rehnquist concurring, Scalia dissenting, and Thomas recused, because he had a son enrolled at VMI. When Ruth announced the decision, she pointedly cited a 1982 precedent, written by O'Connor, which held that it was unconstitutional to exclude men from a state-funded nursing school in Mississippi. O'Connor had written that the female-only admissions policy was based on "archaic and stereotypic notions" of the "proper" roles for men and women.

Now, as Ruth read the VMI decision, she looked up, turned her head to one side, gazed down the long bench at Sandra, and gave her a nod. O'Connor kept her gaze straight forward, but to me, sitting inside the chamber, it was possible to see her tiny smile.

The sea change produced by these two women, and indeed by the times, was contained in that one unspoken communication. As Ruth would later tell reporter Joan Biskupic, "As often as Justice O'Connor and I have disagreed, because she is truly a Republican from Arizona, we were together in all the gender discrimination cases."

RBG and SOC, as they were known inside the Court, changed the dynamics of the institution in ways large and small. Both had adopted the practice of sending notes of congratulations to former clerks on professional and personal accomplishments. They sent wedding presents and baby gifts. (When Ruth sent a note of congratulations to one of her clerks who had a same-sex wedding, I remember hearing from other people, "Oh, that's it. Things are going to completely change.") They were both sensitive to wording from their male colleagues that might have been perceived as offensive but which did not trouble the men. Ruth felt that the two of them had different, as she put it, "perceptions," than the men.

Ruth wasn't incensed often, and she tried to maintain the highest level of respect and affection for her male colleagues, but there was one time when, even from the press section, I heard her truly lose her patience. The case was argued in 2009 and involved a thirteen-year-old girl in Arizona who had been falsely accused by a classmate of illicitly distributing prescription-strength ibuprofen. Although she had no prior disciplinary issues and nothing was found in her bag, Savana Redding was told to remove her clothes and allow herself to be strip-searched by the school nurse. Specifically, the nurse instructed her to strip down to her bra and panties and then hold them away from her body so the nurse could conduct a thorough inspection. The school justified the search on the grounds that it had a zero-tolerance policy on drugs. When nothing was found, school officials left Savana sitting alone in the hallway outside of the vice principal's office for more than two hours.

The ACLU helped Savana's mother sue the school board, arguing that her daughter's Fourth Amendment right to be free from "unreasonable search and seizure" had been violated. A district judge dismissed the case; the Reddings appealed and eventually won, leading the school district to appeal that ruling in the Supreme Court.

I remember the day of the argument well. All the women in the press section, including a couple who were fairly conservative politically, sat there shaking their heads and saying, "What?" It was clear that the male justices did not understand the importance of what had happened to this girl. Ruth was listening to an extensive back-and-forth about whether Savana's classmate — whom they called "the tipster" — had received any punishment for making a false charge, and a discussion of body cavity versus strip searches and who should conduct those.

Ruth interjected to ask about the "reasonableness" of the school administrator's behavior: "In addition to not following up with Glines ['the tipster'], after Redding was searched and nothing was found, she was put in a chair outside the vice principal's office for over two hours and her mother wasn't called. What was the reason for . . . putting her in that humiliating situation?" No one answered her question.

Her colleagues still didn't seem to get it. And not just the conservatives. Justice Breyer asked on several occasions how this search was somehow different from changing clothes for gym in a locker room or putting on a bathing suit. "I'm trying to work out why this is a major thing to say strip down to your underclothes, which children do when they change for gym, they do fairly frequently," versus this situation where "there are only two women there. Is, how bad is this, underclothes? That's what I'm trying to get at. I'm asking because I don't know."

I'd been watching Ruth as the argument unfolded, and I could almost see the steam coming out of her ears. Finally, at that moment and with those words, she broke. She seemed to all but shout that boys may like to preen in the locker room, but girls, particularly teenage girls, do not. She didn't even allow Savana's lawyer to answer. Addressing him, her fury barely contained, she asked, "Mr. Wolf, one thing should be clarified. I don't think there's any dispute what was done in the case of both these girls [another girl was similarly strip-searched the same day]. It wasn't just that they were stripped to their underwear. They were asked to shake their bra out, to — to shake, stretch the top of their pants and shake that out. There's no dispute, factual dispute about that, is there?"

It was a truly memorable moment because she was so clearly angry. After that question, which was really a statement, the entire chamber fell silent. You could have heard the proverbial pin drop. And suddenly, the whole tone of the argument changed. I could see the male lawyers and the justices, who previously had been up on their high horses pontificating and theorizing, suddenly say in essence, Okay, better back down. If we just climb off this ledge quietly, maybe nobody will notice that we were up here in the first place. Ruth, however, remained furious. And she did something very rare, breaking her silence on the case during an interview with *USA Today* before the opinion was handed down. Referring to her fellow justices, she said, "They have never been a thirteen-year-old girl. It's a very sensitive age for a girl. I didn't think that my colleagues, some of them, quite understood."

Ultimately, the Court ruled for Savana on the question of her Fourth Amendment rights, but it split the difference by refusing to allow her to receive any monetary damages. The Court majority said that because the school officials couldn't have known at the time that the search was illegal, they had "qualified immunity." Ruth wrote her own opinion, disagreeing that the adults who authorized this search should be immune from consequences. As my colleague Dahlia Lithwick wrote in the essay collection *The Legacy of Ruth Bader Ginsburg,* "It was almost as if something had finally snapped in the sole female justice. As if she had grown tired of laughing along with the guys after a lifetime of ignoring the laughter." Ginsburg had spent her life being a good girl, and she had finally decided she wasn't going to be a good girl anymore, Dahlia theorized.

Linda Greenhouse of *The New York Times* had a similar view, writing that after Justice O'Connor retired and was replaced by conservative Justice Samuel Alito, Ginsburg, now the lone woman on the Court, had found her voice. Sociologist Cynthia Fuchs Epstein, a longtime Ginsburg friend, described RBG's switch this way: "Her style has always been very ameliorative, very conscious of etiquette . . . She has always been regarded as sort of a white-glove person, and she's achieved a lot that way. Now she is seeing that basic issues she's fought so hard for are in jeopardy, and she is less bound by what have been the conventions of the court."

My view is that the justices are like partners in a dysfunctional marriage, bound together for the rest of their lives. Whether you agree with your colleagues or not and whether there are things about them that you really don't like, you cannot look forward to the day when you have moved on to your next job. Instead, this is for life, or as long as you want to remain in the job. Bottom line: if the justices want to work effectively with each other, they simply have to get along as best they can. And that was definitely Ruth's approach. When she couldn't find something that she really liked, she survived, but survival no longer meant she would play the role of the good girl.

In my conversations with Ruth, both public and private, we tried to get at how often men, frequently inadvertently, treat women as invisible or inferior. Women of a certain age and generation stuck together and helped each other because there were so few of us. That's what Sandra Day O'Connor and Ruth Bader Ginsburg did, despite some very pronounced ideological differences. It's what I was fortunate to do as well with my female friends in the press or, as we are called today, "the media."

Sandra and Ruth saw each other every day the Court was in session, but those of us in the media had to make time. A small group of us — Cokie, Linda, me, and Lesley Stahl of CBS News — used to meet for lunch about once a month at Morocco's, a family restaurant on M Street, NW, around the corner from the CBS and NPR offices. We were the core group, but there were other women journalists and women in politics who floated in and out. We called it the "Ladies Who Lunch," which was a bit of joke, because none of us had all that much time for lunch. But in newsrooms and workplaces that were dominated by men talking sports, and, more to the point, frequently talking over us, this was a refuge. We could have smart talk and girl talk.

One of our semiregulars was Dotty Lynch, who had worked as a pollster for both George McGovern and Jimmy Carter. She sat down one day and told us that her job at the Democratic National Committee had been eliminated. By the time we left that lunch, everybody had an assignment for people to call, and by the end of the week, she had a job working for the CBS News election unit. It was a demonstration of the old girls' network — which we didn't quite understand that we had. At NPR, I had submitted Cokie's CV, and Linda and I both advocated for her to be hired. I did something similar for Mara Liasson. In 1989, stuck in the newscast unit at NPR, she took leave for a Knight-Baghot fellowship, and was in Europe when a congressional reporting spot at NPR was announced. Linda, Cokie, and I were pretty sure this was an effort to place one of the "old boys" in the job while Mara was away. I tracked her down and told her to fax me her résumé and her application, and I would make sure it went into the mix. She got the job, and the rest is history.

Why did we go to such lengths? The answer is much the same reason that Sandra and Ruth pointedly acknowledged each other, even in the awkward moments. Ruth would tell the story of how she, on one occasion, thinking that Sandra was finished speaking, had started to ask a question, and

Sandra piped up, "Just a minute, I'm not finished." Ruth apologized, and Sandra replied, "It's OK, Ruth. The guys do it all the time, they step on each other's questions."

Women were "stepped on" in many situations. I remember taking my good friend and bridesmaid at my wedding to Floyd, Valerie Bradley, out to celebrate when she won her first consulting contract. Val worked as an advocate in the disability rights field, and the $100,000 grant to conduct a major study was huge for her small business. She, I, and one or two other women went to a fancy Italian restaurant on K Street in downtown Washington for dinner. It was a restaurant that thrived on expense account business, and most of the diners were men in groups of four or more. Our group was totally ignored. The waiter couldn't have been less interested in us, and by the end, we were really pissed off. The owner came over and said, "I hope you had a lovely meal," and Valerie said, "No we didn't because our waiter treated us like second-class citizens."

Still, we thought we were lucky to have just enough of a chance to get started and build a life. We almost expected it to be lonely and were surprised and grateful to discover that it often wasn't, that our work world could be inhabited by friends.

For many years, Cokie, Linda, and I were not only a trio of friends but also the unofficial HR department at NPR when it came to gender discrimination. Younger women came to us all the time with serious complaints, and some less serious ones too. This role originated in part when we intervened to help Mara Liasson get that congressional reporting job. She was the best qualified and absolutely deserved the job.

National Public Radio then was half the size that it is today — indeed, probably even smaller. I knew almost everyone in the News Department back then, and we weren't spread hither and yon by a pandemic. That is far from true today. What's more, I am painfully aware that I have reached an age when many of the young women who work at NPR view me as everything from a fuddy-duddy to a role model, with the emphasis these days maybe on the former. There are reasons for that. For instance, I know that I am viewed as a grammar Nazi. That said, however, we all share the journalistic values that I learned as a young reporter. They are particularly important in these times: make sure both sides get their say, try to keep your personal opinions out of the story, and learn as much about the topic as you possibly can — while still meeting the inexorable deadline.

Over the decades, I have sometimes been a mentor, and sometimes a mentee. Nothing has pleased me more than helping my niece Emily Green, who now is a seasoned journalist herself. Not only has she already won an Emmy Award, Emily has also won a Pulitzer Prize. She was one of two investigative reporters to win the prize for long-form pieces about the Trump administration's "Remain in Mexico policy," which aired on *This American Life,* winning the first ever Pulitzer for audio reporting. I have won neither an Emmy nor a Pulitzer! Just saying!!!

Emily and I first bonded journalistically in 1991, at the time of the Clarence Thomas–Anita Hill hearings, when she was about ten years old. She wrote an essay, which I have framed on my desk. It begins, "My heroine is my aunt, Nina Totenberg . . . She taught me how to fight for my rights (not that I am being treated unfairly). She also taught me not to do the same thing my friend[s] want to do (usually I don't get persuaded by my friends). This is why my aunt Nina is my heroine."

Now Emily is often *my* heroine. Her

mother, my sister Amy (a.k.a. federal judge Amy Totenberg), probably planted the journalism bug in her when she required her daughters to read one article in the newspaper every day. It didn't matter what article, but they had to read one. Emily chose the ongoing 1990s soap opera involving the attack on figure skating champion Nancy Kerrigan, an attack that was orchestrated by the ex-husband of Kerrigan's rival, Tonya Harding. Em devoured the tale daily and has never stopped reading the newspaper. This training is also a tribute to my mother, who was always fascinated by the news, worked in political campaigns as a young woman, and read the newspaper front to back.

Like me, her granddaughter Emily had to work incredibly hard to master journalistic writing. I taught Em how to write a good lede, especially for radio; when she was a freelancer, I taught her how to use sound to make a piece more interesting and more alive; and, by God, when there was a major earthquake in Mexico City, where she lived, she was the first on the air, despite her bleeding bare feet. When she was covering city hall for the *San Francisco Chronicle,* I taught her to stand her ground with city council members and staff, even if that meant some of them didn't like her.

What I didn't and couldn't have taught her was how to be brave, really brave, covering the southwest border, and lots of other tough stories in Latin America. She is fearless, and that is something you can't teach. She is beyond persistent; and her accomplishments are hers alone.

Over the years I have had more than one hundred interns, including NPR's Ari Shapiro, fresh out of college. As a group, "the Totenterns" as they are known, have done very well. Some have even been elected to statewide office. And all, in one way or another, have taught me something important. Tom Goldstein, the founder and publisher of *SCOTUSblog,* set up the system I still use today to be ready for the train wreck of Supreme Court opinions that arrive each June. Not just Tom, but his wife, Amy Howe, and also his sister were my interns — all selected, I promise you, on merit. Really! I was beaming when I learned that Tom and Amy named their first child after me.

The interns have been my connection to different generations, and to technology. Rebecca Buckwalter-Poza even taught me how to write a tweet that is interesting enough for someone to click on the link to my story. Timur Akman-Duffy helped me write a correction to a story involving Native Americans and their land rights, something very subtle and tricky. And all have, at one time or another, been my third arm when all hell is breaking loose with a deadline approaching.

I have learned from them too that the young person I see, usually in their early to mid-twenties, is not the person I will see years later. People learn, they gain confidence, they change. When I first met Erika Dean, a University of North Carolina law student, in 2009, I couldn't imagine her doing what she said she wanted to do — try criminal cases. In fact, she didn't end up doing that. She ended up as a real force in business. And when she sent me a video of one of her presentations, I saw a totally different person — confident, smart, "out there." She is now in charge of developing new product strategies for YouTube.

These days I don't have to tell new interns everything about their jobs. In 1990 one of my interns, Jessica Horrocks, began something she called "The Guide to Nina." As you might imagine, it has changed dramatically over the years, as technology, platforms, and lots of other things have evolved. But one thing that has not changed for a very long time is a line buried somewhere in "The Guide." I don't know which intern put it in there, but I find it funny, touching, and maybe true.

"Ignore what you may hear from other people in the building about Nina. She is wonderful to interns. The fact that she is so feared works to your advantage because everybody thinks you must be a saint, and they scurry to do your bidding." I suppose that comes from the fact that I have a low tolerance for fools or laziness. But I have learned over time that snap judgments are not always correct. It's been decades since that passage was written. I hope I have learned to be more tolerant since then.

Nine:
Male Friends

Some of my best friends — and Ruth's — were men. This stemmed in part from the fact that so much of our lives revolved around work. My work, my family, my friendships are who I am, and Ruth would have said the same thing. I cannot imagine a life without work, and neither could she. And we both worked with and around men.

Ruth developed close friendships with both Justice Antonin Scalia and Justice John Paul Stevens, two ideologically opposite people, but that was of no consequence to her. She appreciated the depth of their minds but also the breadth of their hearts and their ability to make her laugh. She truly loved to laugh. She was also very close with Justice David Souter, who had the unique role of being the one to pinch her if she started to nod off on the bench after a late night of work.

Stevens became Ruth's friend after she

joined the Court, but she could trace the origin of her friendship with Scalia to a brief stint, for her, at the University of Chicago Law School in the 1970s. The recipe for their friendship was simple: they really liked each other. Yes, Scalia made Ruth laugh (he made me laugh too). They were two fierce minds who enjoyed sparring intellectually and spurring each other on. They had the greatest respect and affection for each other.

Scalia loved people. I can't begin to count the number of people I've invited to dinner who were totally and unexpectedly charmed by him after a few hours in his company. He was just a delightful human being and so much fun, an amazing combination of interesting and hilarious. No one could tell a joke better. His timing was, quite simply, impeccable.

Ruth said on more than one occasion that while she disagreed with a lot of what he said, she was "charmed by the way he said it," and that he "said it in an absolutely captivating way." Their professional paths would cross on the DC Circuit Court of Appeals, where the judges would hear cases in panels of three. "He would sometimes whisper to me during oral argument, and what he said was so funny I had to do all I could do to keep from bursting out into hysterical laughter," she said.

For his part, Scalia joked that their friendship was a "mutual improvement society," and in many ways, it was. Ruth saw in Nino, as he was known, someone who was equally dedicated to his work and to his craft. "We also cared about not only getting it right as we saw the right, but writing an opinion that at least other lawyers and judges could understand." Both worked very hard on their opinions, but as she put it, "Our styles were not at all alike. He was a fine grammarian. So, every once in a while, he would stop by chambers or call me on the telephone and say, 'Ruth, you committed a grammatical error. I don't want to embarrass you by circulating my comment to the Court, but you should fix it.' And I in return would sometimes say, 'This opinion is so strident. You will be more persuasive if you tone it down.' And that advice, he never took." But she did take his. They were in many ways each other's best editors. In the Virginia Military Institute case about the exclusion of women, Scalia came to her chambers one Friday afternoon as she was about to leave for a judicial conference in New York. He said he wanted to give her a chance to see his dissent before it circulated to the other members of the Court. Ruth often said that getting that draft dissent "ruined my weekend" but that it ultimately made her opinion much stronger.

That said, the footnotes in the final opinion and dissent were a furious ping and pong back and forth, with one zinger after another, down to sparring over her reference, quoting a lower court opinion, to "the University of Virginia Charlottesville campus," which Scalia called "careless" because there is only one UVA and it is located in Charlottesville.

The two justices had many similarities — both were New Yorkers, both were somewhat outsiders. Scalia grew up during a time when anti-Italian and anti-Catholic prejudices were still prevalent; Ruth was both Jewish and a woman. Scalia, however, preferred to talk about their shared background as academics, as well as their joint love of opera and family. To be fair to the record, Ruth was more of a lifelong academic, not necessarily by choice, but because no one else would hire her, while Scalia had worked in the Nixon administration, which is where I first met him, and in private practice before becoming an academic.

It is perhaps now hard to understand how much Scalia's deep personal and professional respect and admiration for Ruth's intellect, his view of her as an intellectual equal who made his own work better, and his forthright public acknowledgment of all of this, would have meant to someone who had spent the start of her career being repeatedly rejected and limited solely because of her gender. But outside of Marty, Scalia was one of Ruth's greatest champions. They also had that rare friendship in which they loved each other's spouses too.

Ruth and Nino were the ultimate happy warriors, playful with each other, maintaining an almost sibling-style banter, each tweaking the other for being "wrong" — even though Scalia maintained that they agreed on a great many things, including the legal rights of defendants. What they also agreed on was their approach to their work. They both worked unbelievably hard, before they were famous and after. They were both very meticulous when it came to "legal procedure," going back to their time on the lower court. Stuff that bores me to tears did not bore them.

And they were particularly focused on writing. Scalia was quite open about the fact that he had his clerks write a first draft of most opinions, essentially just to get it down on paper, but as one former law clerk told me, those original drafts came back almost entirely rewritten. (Ruth was much the same. Once, in returning a draft, she circled "the," which apparently was the only word that had survived unchanged.) While Scalia's language, of necessity, was often limited when he wrote majority opinions, his dissenting opinions were something else. As one of his early clerks, now Judge Roy McLeese III, wrote, "The Justice loved few things more than a good argument." For a dissenting opinion, Scalia would sit at his computer, typing away and, as another former clerk recalled, "feverishly" working, until he would hit the print button and say, "Got 'em!"

For Ruth's tenth anniversary on the DC Circuit Court of Appeals, Scalia, by then a Supreme Court justice, was invited to speak at a roast held in RBG's honor. After regaling the crowd with a litany of gentle Ruth jokes, he ended this way: "That's all I have to say by way of roasting, but I will conclude with a few earnest comments. I have missed Ruth very much since leaving the court of appeals. She was the best of colleagues as she is the best of friends. I wish her a hundred years."

I don't think Ruth found the Supreme Court lonely, but likely, to a degree, Scalia did. He was frequently a lone dissenter, and he suffered from having been passed over for Chief Justice by George W. Bush, who named the more Ivy League style, and younger, John Roberts instead. In later years, it probably got harder and more frustrating for him because he lost a lot of battles, unable to persuade some of the Court's conservatives to adopt his harder line.

For Ruth, it was exhilarating when she could pull one out of the fire, because the Court, with some notable exceptions, was not a liberal Court. But for Scalia, who was often pushing the envelope, that tendency often meant he wasn't winning, although on paper the conservatives were a majority. From opposite ends, they both had their moments with the Court and recognized how difficult it was for them to convince their colleagues.

Even as Scalia's views became more conservative — some would and did say more extreme — their friendship never wavered. Not only did they share dinners together, they also both appeared together as "supers" — amateurs who play bit parts in productions — at Washington National Opera performances. And they traveled together on judicial exchanges. Along with the Mark

Rothko and Jasper Johns paintings in her chambers, a photo taken on one of those trips, in India, held a prominent position. She described it as "the two of us riding on a very elegant elephant. My feminist friends commented, 'Why are you sitting in the back of the elephant?' And I said, 'Well, the driver said it had something to do with the distribution of weight.' " Scalia, of course, mischievously maintained it had something to do with "seniority."

But there was more to it than that. I loved Scalia too. Although I met him when he served in the Nixon administration, I didn't really know him early on. So when he was appointed to the federal bench, I made it a point to get to know him well. We would meet for lunch. It was always the same terrible restaurant, not far from the courthouse. I remember sitting there one day, noticing a couple of cockroaches crawling up the wall and saying to myself, "Okay, you can't say anything because this is where he loves to eat lunch, and *this* is where we're going to eat lunch." At one of these midday meals after he was appointed to the Supreme Court, I asked him what the new job was like. "Well, there are just a whole bunch of questions I had actually never thought about that come here [meaning the Supreme Court] and didn't come before the DC Circuit," he said. "And I don't know what I think about them." After a few years, he did know, but I never forgot that he didn't arrive quite so certain.

It was easier to get to know Scalia than it was to get to know Ruth because he didn't hold back; all his emotions, including occasional grouchiness, were on display. On the bench, he could sometimes be a bit of a bully. Once or twice in the courtroom, spectators literally gasped because he had said something so politically incorrect or insensitive. In 2004, in a case testing congressional power to require access to vote for the disabled, Scalia took on his former law clerk Paul Clement, who as the Bush administration's deputy solicitor general was defending the law. The plaintiffs in the case had to crawl up the stairs, or be carried if someone was willing, in order to vote in a county courthouse. There was no wheelchair-accessible place for them to vote. But Scalia had little sympathy, asserting that an "inaccessible voting place proves nothing at all. It just proves that the state did not go out of its way to make it easy for the handicapped to vote, as it should, but as it is not constitutionally required to do."

Although Scalia could sometimes sound

totally unsympathetic and intolerant, at his core, he was a mensch. He was a born extrovert, full of charm; he loved people, and if you liked him, chances are he would like you. Ruth, the quintessence of decency, also had a real connection to people, but hers was covered by her quieter reserve, while his was covered by that tough-guy outer shell. Underneath, however, he had a tremendous heart. Inside, as I came to see, he was frequently mush.

When Scalia's son-in-law died suddenly at the young age of forty-two, my husband and I went to the viewing before the funeral. Scalia looked utterly ravaged, his eyes were bloodshot. Instinctively, I wrapped my arms around him. Somehow it seemed totally natural when he put his head down on my shoulder and wept. He said simply, "I've lost a son."

He had what can only be described as a tender soul. After his death in 2016, Judge Jeffrey Sutton, one of Scalia's favorite former law clerks, described one of his last visits to Scalia's chambers. On the justice's table were two dozen red roses, and he explained that they were for Ruth, for her birthday (by this time, she had been widowed for nearly five years). Sutton joked about the lavish bouquet, asking, "What good have all these roses done for you? Name one 5-to-4 case of any significance where you got Justice Ginsburg's vote."

"Some things are more important than votes," Scalia replied.

After Scalia died, Ruth, speaking about their relationship during a public interview, referenced the comic opera that had been written about them. It was entitled *Scalia/Ginsburg,* and she was explaining why, as in the elephant-riding photo, Scalia's name appeared first, this time deferring to his explanation. "Because seniority really matters in our workplace, and he was appointed to the Court some years before I was. So, I miss him very much. Our conferences are not as lively as they were when he was with us." She did miss him, as he would have missed her.

The beauty of friendship is that it is by nature retrospective. The longer it lasts, the more experiences you have to unravel in the process of working your way back to its origin. I remember that first phone call with Ruth; she recalled a lecture given by Nino; and for another deep friendship, I remember a lunch I had during the early months of the Reagan administration with a Justice Department official named Ted Olson, who at that time was the assistant attorney general for the Office of Legal Counsel.

In the early 1980s, nobody paid much attention to NPR, which had the effect of making me a very tough little cookie. I would not take crap from anyone, because I was afraid that if I gave any hint that I could be pushed around, I would never be taken seriously, never get the truth, and everyone would dismiss me — and NPR. (I still think that sometimes. There are moments when I am quite sure that I am being lied to and if I don't push back, I will be lied to consistently.)

This attitude clearly helped my journalistic pursuits because I was scoring a lot of exclusive stories during the late 1970s. Most are not particularly worth remembering now. They were significant only in that week or at best that month, but at the time they mattered. And so, when the Reagan administration came into office, I began to hear from career lawyers in the Justice Department who were upset with some of the policy changes, particularly in the Civil Rights Division. What especially galled these lawyers was that, in their view, changes were being made by sleight of hand. Typical was a case involving Bob Jones University, which had previously had its tax-exempt status revoked by the IRS because of the school's policy banning interracial dating. The new administration sided with Bob Jones when the case reached the Supreme Court. Reagan White House Counsel Fred Fielding later told me it was his fault. After receiving the recommendation to support the school's position, he had advised President Reagan to sign off on the change. Fielding didn't have much history in the world of civil rights, and he didn't appreciate the implications of such a policy reversal until the career deputy solicitor general refused to sign the government's Supreme Court brief.

That and other policy changes prompted a meeting between the lawyers in the Civil Rights Division and their new boss, Assistant Attorney General William Bradford Reynolds. I found out about the impending meeting ahead of time.

Back in those days, it was possible for almost anyone to walk into the Department of Justice, wave to a guard, and head straight to someone's office. On the day of the meeting, that's what I did. Nobody in the administration knew who I was. I walked into the meeting and sat down in the back of the room. I got away with it for about fifteen minutes, until Charles Cooper, a political appointee in the Civil Rights Division who had been a clerk for William Rehnquist on the Supreme Court, spotted me. I saw him animatedly talking to Reynolds and gesturing at me. Soon thereafter someone very discreetly came over and told me that I was not supposed to be there, and I should leave. I stood up, but before I walked out, I said to the folks around me, "My name is Nina Totenberg, I work for National Public Radio, and I've been asked to leave this meeting. But if you want to talk to me afterwards, call me." I may have even given my phone number. I would never have the gall to do that today. Never. That's why it pays to be young.

Of course, I started getting phone calls, which led to stories, and the head of the press office was furious. That was a problem for me. If you were a reporter who covered the Justice Department, which I did, you were totally dependent on the department callouts to alert you to impending news or to invite you to a briefing. There was no email, no texts, not even many fax machines, because a single fax machine cost around $20,000 in 1982 and it took about three minutes to transmit one page. The only way reporters received word was when their landline phones rang, with someone from the press office on the other end. My phone was silent.

It didn't help that one of the few times I was at a briefing, the press office announced that we could not use the briefer's name; it was all on background — we could use the material but not disclose what official was providing it. As is often the case in such briefings, there was no reason for the secrecy. It annoyed me. I stood up and this time I said, "I'm leaving. I'm not agreeing to the ground rules for this," and a bunch of other reporters also stood up and followed me out. Afterwards, I called up the reporters who had stayed; they were generous about sharing the information from the briefing, and I used the material and included the briefers' names — which made the press office even angrier.

I became persona non grata at the Justice Department. I wasn't being unfair or spilling state secrets, I was simply not willing to essentially reprint the department's press releases. And in retaliation, the department press office froze out both me and by extension NPR. For weeks I would read a relatively routine but still interesting story in the newspaper about the Justice Department that I should have known about but didn't because I was no longer on the call-out list. It was becoming embarrassing. There was little I could do, because the Justice Department press office held all the cards. And the press office could get away with it because I was not someone important, and NPR was still in its relative infancy.

I was frantically looking for a solution when someone told me that I needed to meet Ted Olson, adding, "He's in the Office of Legal Counsel and he's a very sensible person and believes in journalists' rights, so you should get to know him." I took the advice, called Ted, and asked him to have lunch.

I met him at Morocco's, the place I frequented with Cokie and Linda and the other Ladies Who Lunch, and I explained what was happening, adding, "I don't expect you to like everything I write but I expect to have equal access to my competitors." Ted was surprisingly outraged and said he would see what he could do. He returned to the Justice Department and took my complaint to Attorney General William French Smith (fondly referred to as "Frenchie" behind his back. It helped that Ted was one of Frenchie's protégés). As Ted would later tell me, the AG "simply said this is not the way we do business." The message was conveyed to the press office, and the deep freeze ended. I was now on the regular call-out list. I got treated if not well, then at least reasonably.

But something else happened as a result of that lunch. Ted and I became friends and have remained friends to this day. It was not an intuitive pairing — a feisty, often undiplomatic reporter and a conservative lawyer. But it was based on mutual respect for each other's work and professionalism, even when our views were different. Ted, in addition, has always been a vociferous defender of the First Amendment right to freedom of the press, counting several journalists among his many illustrious clients over the years. In 2000, he successfully argued on behalf of George W. Bush in *Bush v. Gore,* putting the Texas governor in the White House. As the Bush administration's solicitor general, he strongly and successfully defended the McCain-Feingold Campaign Finance Act because that was his job — when you're the government's lawyer, your job is to defend laws enacted by Congress. But when he returned to private practice, he argued his conscience and took the opposite stance, fighting against laws that limit campaign contributions. His view is that money is speech and is thus protected by the Constitution's guarantee of free speech. I don't share that view, but as my mother used to say, that's what makes horse races.

Ted has also been a leader on gay rights for a very long time and believed same-sex marriage should be legally recognized long before I thought it was possible to happen in the courts. Indeed, in the early 1980s, when I first heard of the idea, I remember thinking it was, well, preposterous that it would even be considered by the Supreme Court. So, in 2010 I asked Ted why, as a conservative, he had for so long been an advocate for legal recognition of gay marriage. "We're talking about an effect upon millions of people and the way they live their everyday life and the way they're treated in their neighborhood, in their schools, in their jobs," he said. "If you are a conservative, how could you be against a relationship in which people who love one another, want to publicly state their vows . . . and engage in a household in which they are committed to one another and become part of the community and accepted like other people?" He also talked about his "searing" experience as a college debater in the 1960s, when he traveled through the South and restaurants would not serve his team because one of their members was Black. I've often thought that Ted should have been on the Supreme Court, appointed by a conservative president because he is a conservative on most things. He is also a quintessentially interesting person who thinks not in lockstep, as his varied career has shown.

Ted did something very important for me in making my professional case to William French Smith when there was no obligation for him to get involved, and I've never forgotten his fundamental decency and help. Those beginnings gave us both a special level of trust.

His wife, Barbara, was killed on board the plane that hit the Pentagon on 9/11 — she called him at his desk at the Justice Department just before impact. When he began dating again, he brought his lady friend, actually named Lady Booth (it's a family name) to our house very early on in their relationship, knowing we would be a safe and welcoming place. Usually, our dinners together are small, just us and maybe another couple. But I have been to his home from time to time for Federalist Society picnics, big events for hundreds of young people, plus some conservative glitterati. I mention this only because of a hilarious incident at one of these events. I was standing in line for dessert — Ben & Jerry's ice cream — when I heard two law students behind me debating whether it was ethical for conservative Federalist Society members to eat ice cream made by liberals. I quietly rolled my eyes.

Sometimes in life, if you are lucky, you can pay back a good deed. Decades after Ted got me unpurged at the Justice Department, he suffered a serious bike accident on vacation in Portugal. My second husband, David, a trauma surgeon, helped get him flown back to DC, where Ted and Lady were met at the airport by an Inova Fairfax Hospital ambulance and taken to David's personally coordinated "dream team."

All's well that ends well. A couple of years later, when the Covid-19 lockdowns lifted, Ted and Lady were part of our first dinner party; it was just David and me, Ted and Lady, and two other couples. It was a late night; no one wanted to leave.

It's been some four decades since our first lunch, and in the fullness of time, I realize how important someone like Ted has been in both my professional and my personal life. We have, after so many years intersecting with each other, developed a deep fondness. I realize "fondness" is an old-fashioned word, but it is very much the right word. It's not the same as loving Cokie or Ruth, but it reflects a deeply personal friendship as well as a professional one. I'm grateful that I can feel that way about many people who are on different points of the political spectrum — liberal, conservative, and in-between. I've come to realize that I have friends like this all over Washington and thank God that I do. One of the saddest parts of Washington today is we all — and I include myself — can be so suspicious of each other's motives.

In our current climate, could a Ruth and Nino, a Nina and Nino, or a Nina and Ted friendship ever take root and thrive? And what does the answer to that question mean for all of us?

TEN:
FRIENDS IN JOY

At age fifty-four, I became the very thing that I had worried about twenty years before: a fairly young widow. I knew that I did not want to be alone for the rest of my life. But wanting and having were two very different things.

Floyd had died in August 1998. In November, my eighty-nine-year-old father was slated to give a major recital in Boston. I said to myself, "He's eighty-nine, how many more of these are there going to be?" And I decided I had better go. The concert was beautiful. Every seat was taken, and I stopped counting how many encores he played. One was a Niccolò Paganini Caprice, and while my father coaxed the beautiful notes and devilishly difficult passages from his violin, the student orchestra seated behind him watched, transfixed. Two of the young violinists wept as they took in the sight of this elderly artist playing as if he were thirty and with a passion like there was no tomorrow. People in the audience roared their approval and threw dozens of floral bouquets onto the stage.

Afterwards, we stored the flowers in a bathtub to arrange the next day and then sat down for tea, heaping praise upon the maestro. His eyes sparkling, he looked at us, and opined, in that distinctive Polish accent, "You know, one of the advantages of living so long is that when you can play very well at a very young age, the audience screams and yells, and when you are very old and can still do it, they scream and yell. I," he said with a mischievous smile, "have been lucky enough to hit it at both ends."

During the concert's intermission, a man I did not recognize walked up to me and said, "Hello, Nina, remember when we met?" I faked it and pretended I did. Meanwhile, I was frantically scrolling through my mental Rolodex trying to recall who exactly he was, and please God, what was his name? As he talked, I finally remembered that he was a doctor, and that my mother had sold a house to him and his wife. My mother, as I recalled, had been very fond of his wife, who had been recovering from breast cancer treatment when she was house hunting. Blessedly, I remembered his wife's name.

Gail. "How's Gail?" I asked. He told me she had died, and then asked me, "How's Floyd?" I answered that he too had died. They had died within a month of each other. And my mother had died almost exactly two years before.

I didn't think much about our chance encounter until I received a letter from David Reines. I'm someone who keeps almost nothing, but I kept this note. It's been in my desk drawer for almost a quarter century. In his wretched doctor's handwriting (which he later told me he had labored to make decipherable), he wrote out what he recalled of the poet Mary Elizabeth Frye's words:

Do not stand there at my grave and
     weep,
I am not there, I do not sleep.
I am a thousand winds that blow;
I am the diamond glints on the snow.
I am the sunlight on ripened grain;
I am the gentle autumn's rain.
When you awaken in the morning's hush,
I am the swift uplifting rush
of quiet birds encircled flight.
I am the soft star that shines at night.
Do not stand at my grave and cry.
I am not there; I did not die.

He closed by saying, "If you are in Boston or just need to talk to someone unrelated, feel free to call. The people we know in common were uncommonly terrific. Sincerely, David." With his phone number at the bottom. I replied with a rather generic note of my own, written in a very formal way, basically saying thank you for your lovely letter.

There is no way to transition to this next sentence, dear reader. But every time I took my seat in the Supreme Court chamber before a big argument, I would look around and think, "There's not one man in this entire chamber I would want to go on date with, much less kiss." I certainly did not think of going out with David that night when we re-met, but I told my friend Patty Liberatore about him, and she said, "You should practice on him." So I decided to ask him out on a quasi date when I was next in Boston. Which turned out to be two months later, in February 1999.

One of my father's former students and her husband — Mira Wang and Jan Vogler — were giving an afternoon concert with a reception afterwards. I called David, and invited him. He asked where he could pick me up, and I told him I'd meet him at the concert hall. I watched for him from my seat until the lights dimmed. Periodically, I'd raise my head to look at the back of the hall, where latecomers stand, and finally I saw him. At the end of the first piece, I waved at him, and he came down to sit with me, my father, and some other friends. He apologized and said he was late because he had been finishing up a case in the operating room, known to all TV watchers and surgeons as simply "the OR." After the concert, my father's friends Saul and Naomi Cohen held a large reception at their house. As David and I stood there chatting, I suddenly realized I was flirting with this guy. I hadn't flirted with anybody in years.

Soon we began talking on the phone. During one call, after I had returned from an assignment in New Orleans, I started to cry. David asked what was wrong, and I told him that on the trip, I had lost an earring from a pair that Floyd had given me. I could have it duplicated, I told him, but it would be the first real jewelry that I'd had to buy for myself. It was a bit of a non sequitur, but he said, "Would you like me to visit you?" And I said, "Yes."

We had a great time. But if this is the point in the story when most people would assume that two professionally successful, widowed individuals in their fifties, with decades of marriage between them, might enter a sensible, drama-free romance, well, most people would be wrong. It is possible to revert to being a hapless teenager at almost any age, and we were living proof. About two weeks after that first weekend visit, David told me, "You don't really want to be dating somebody like me. It's too soon after Floyd's death." Never mind that his wife had died at basically the same time, less than a year earlier. He added, "You need to be dating a lot of other people," which to me sounded like "On second thought, never mind."

I was stunned. I called my sister Jill in New York. She's the tough one of the three of us, and she said, "Oh, he's a conceited Jewish doctor with too many women after him. Dump him." (She was right about the women. David had been dating — a lot.) Then I called my sister Amy in Atlanta, for a second opinion. She said, "Nina, he doesn't know what he wants any more than you do. Just ignore it." I chose to take Amy's advice.

Apparently, David did too, because his words notwithstanding, we started seeing more of each other. Almost every weekend, one of us would travel to either DC or Boston.

Beyond Cokie and Linda, there was one other person I told about David, very early on. Ruth had invited me to an event with Marty. She and I were walking side by side down a hallway, and I said, "Ruth, I'm dating somebody." She stopped, and it was as if her head swiveled around. She looked at me very intently and said, "Details. I want details." Who could possibly refuse that summons? I told her all about David, but I added that I had no idea where this was going. After all, he was the first guy I had really dated in more than two decades, and in my conscious mind I was just "practicing."

Ruth wasn't the only one who wanted details. For twenty-one years, I appeared as a panelist on a weekly television talk show, *Inside Washington.* I was the only woman, and one day I showed up on the set, and the first thing that all the men said to me was "So, we hear you're dating somebody." I had been spotted at a restaurant with David, and the follow-up line from fellow panelist Charles Krauthammer was "You gotta hold out." I looked him in the eye and replied, "Too late, Charles."

Just as the weather began to turn warm, the program's host, Gordon Peterson, and his wife, Ann Fleming, had a party. When I arrived with David, I quickly realized that whatever the excuse for the party, the real purpose was for the guys and their wives to get a look at David.

Months before, I had planned a late spring trip to Europe with my father. We were going to the Czech Republic, where I knew the U.S. ambassador, John Shattuck, and his wife, Ellen Hume, a fellow journalist. We were to stay at the U.S. embassy and my father would give a small concert. From there we would go to Italy. As our departure date grew closer, I asked my father how he would feel if David came with us. And my father, with a twinkle in his eyes, said, "Oh, that would be a good idea. Then I don't have to amuse you all the time." We had a fabulous time, down to a cherry pit spitting contest between my father and me in Venice, with David as our photographer.

Compared to Floyd, David was easy because he is my age — he is actually a couple of years younger — and we'd been through all the same things, particularly long illnesses with our spouses. We had good friends who had stood by us during those difficult years, and they were thrilled that we had each found somebody. One of David's closest friends, Bob Taraschi, and his wife, Kathy, told me they were so relieved to meet me and discover that I was a normal person. (Apparently, some of his earlier dates were not!) We dated through the summer of 1999. David had told me that he wouldn't move from Boston; I had told him that we didn't have to get married. "We're grownups," I said. "We can have an affair forever." And I meant it when I said it. But then a series of things shifted. Among them, Ruth was diagnosed with colon cancer.

She started having symptoms during the summer, when the Court was on recess and many justices travel abroad. She had gone to Crete and was teaching as part of a Tulane Law School program. At first, she was misdiagnosed, but in September, the cancer was found. She underwent surgery on September 17, 1999, twenty-one years and one day before cancer would ultimately claim her life. But of course, there was no way any of us could have known that then.

About ten days later, I was scheduled to receive the first Toni House Award, named for a longtime Supreme Court press secretary who had died suddenly of lung cancer. The award recognized a body of journalistic work and was given by the American Judicature Society during an event in the East Conference Room at the Supreme Court. The presentation was scheduled for 5:00 p.m. on a Monday, and when I arrived, I was stunned to see that Ruth was there to preside. Only when I hugged her did I realize how much weight she had lost. I received my second shock when David walked in. We had been together that weekend, but he had already flown home to Boston for work, never letting on that he had organized his surgical day so that he could turn around and fly back to DC for a couple of hours. In that moment, I realized that neither of us was practicing anymore. This was real. I was not the only one whose heart had been revived by a new love.

Our grand affair had one small problem, however. Ultimately, I discovered that I'm very traditional, if you will, and I wanted to get married. I suspected that deep down, so did he.

On one of my early visits to Boston, I went directly from the airport to a downtown restaurant. It was cold and snowy, and David arrived bearing boots and a warm fur coat that had belonged to his late wife. There was a funny story surrounding the coat — I had tried it on years before, on the day that my parents and I went to their house for lunch. At the time, it was a recent gift from David to Gail, and as women will, my mother and I tried it on too. But now, the coat had returned, and I wore it regularly when I came to visit, so that I didn't have to drag my own heavy wool coat back and forth from Washington. One day, I was wearing it when we were walking David's dog, and he looked at me and said, very matter-of-factly, "That coat's too big for you. We are going to have to have it altered." And I thought, "He's going to ask me to marry him." You don't alter a coat for somebody you're not going to stay with.

But nothing happened. Weeks passed, and we both came down with terrible cases of bronchitis. I was sicker than David and still had an awful cough, but it was my turn to travel for the weekend, so I trekked to Boston. I followed our usual routine. I met him at the hospital, we picked up food for dinner, and he bought flowers, as he sometimes did. I started to carry the forks and knives to the kitchen table, where we always ate, and he said, "No, we are going to eat in the dining room." He had set the table with beautiful Rosenthal china and the good silver and the good glassware.

Trained observer that I am, nothing occurred to me.

After dinner he pointed to the cookie sitting on my bread and butter plate and said, "Why don't you open your fortune cookie?" I broke it in half, but I couldn't read anything without my glasses, so I handed the slip of paper to him, and asked him to read it to me. His answer was "No, go get your glasses." Glasses on, I picked up the tiny paper, and saw that in his terrible handwriting, he had written, "Will you marry me?"

David had used his surgical skills to make a small incision, delicately removing the old fortune with tiny forceps, and replacing it with his handwritten fortune — which looked like "Will you mally me?" Then he had resealed everything, including the cellophane wrapper. After I read it out loud, he got down on one knee and asked me again. "Of course I'll marry you. I love you," I croaked. It was as simple as that. And then I called up the world and told everyone.

Many months later, David and I were lying in bed, and I said to him, "Do you think this is just good luck or what?" He laughed and said, "No, my wife and your mother got together, and then they went to Floyd, and he finally said, 'Oh, all right.' "

But we've often said that we would not have been a good pair when we were younger. As David puts it, he could be an insufferable surgeon, and he had a temper. I too had a temper, but over the years, we've both learned not to let our tempers explode (although I've let myself lose my temper a few times with management during union negotiations at NPR). Losing your temper is not good for dealing with people, and it's not good for you. The person who feels the worst afterwards is usually you.

Most of all though, what binds us is that we have a wonderful time together, even if we are just doing dishes while we talk. David takes very good care of me, and in different ways, I take very good care of him. We know each other profoundly in all possible ways, the passionate ones and the dispassionate ones too. As I read this paragraph I realize it really says so little about the life-changing meaning of a deep love affair, but there is no way to explain it or describe it. It is something that just is.

Being with David also changed my friendship with Ruth. For many years while Floyd was so diminished, she had been a refuge, the friend throwing me a lifeline, the person who reminded me not to lose myself. Now the dynamic shifted; David and I and Ruth and Marty could be a foursome because it turned out that we were incredibly compatible. For starters, like Marty, David is a wonderful cook, and he does almost all the cooking at our house. I am no longer carving the leg of lamb against the grain. After Ruth and Marty had come to dinner a couple of times and realized that David was a good cook, the two men would divide things up. Marty would bring a fabulous dessert and his famous baguette, and David would prepare everything else. That way there was no competition. If there had been, as David said, Marty would have beaten him "consistently."

Sometimes it would be just the four of us, or sometimes one or two other couples, but it was always raucously fun because Ruth would be the straight person. She'd say something, and Marty would chime in with a hilarious follow-up, maybe slightly off-color but never too much. It helped too that David was not in political life; he was easy with Ruth and undaunted by her quietness. He has the inquisitiveness of a reporter and could always find something to talk to her about. One of their frequent early topics was opera. Ruth could even discuss a contemporary performance versus a performance from twenty years before.

Gradually, David came to fill a role for Ruth that I could not. Washington tends to be a city where the higher your stature in public life, the fewer true confidants you have. The Supreme Court conference is

266

hardly the place for justices to share personal issues, nor can they do so with their young clerks. Work and outside obligations leave them with few opportunities for the type of personal friendship that others depend upon. Yet their stature does not insulate them from the complexities and challenges of ordinary life; think of Sandra Day O'Connor bringing her husband, John, into her chambers to keep him safe and try to look after him as he began to struggle with the ravages of Alzheimer's.

Ruth built her own relationship with David regarding health and medical issues. Always a very private person, she came to trust him as someone who could offer her counsel and who would never violate a confidence. It was a relationship that he did not share with me, and I never asked about what they discussed. I was grateful that he could share his expertise with her. Periodically, the two of them would retreat to the kitchen or even the closed powder room to speak. He could explain the complications from her colon cancer surgery and why the radiation and chemotherapy treatments too often created additional complications. (She later candidly explained that the surgery had led to a stricture or narrowing in her colon on the left side, and the radiation and chemo treatments made it worse, frequently causing blockages and other problems in her bowel. She endured those for the rest of her life.) It became common over the years that when Ruth came for dinner, she and David would briefly and discreetly slip off and in his words, "talk about what was going on with her."

When it came time for us to make it official, there was no doubt about who we would have perform the ceremony. It could be no one other than Ruth. The only person who was not happy when they found out was David's mother. She began by asking him what synagogue we were getting married in, and he had to tell her we were getting married in a hotel. I had a very specific hotel in mind because I wanted Charles Krauthammer to come, and Charles was a quadriplegic from a diving accident years before. He needed a location where he could roll in and roll out and didn't require anyone to try to carry his motorized wheelchair up any stairs; he wouldn't allow that. (Even then, not as many venues were completely accommodating to anyone with a disability.) My future mother-in-law's next question was "What rabbi is marrying you?" David said, "Well, we're not being married by a rabbi. We're being married by a judge." His mother was, quite simply, horrified. "You're not getting married by a rabbi? Oh, my God!" David answered, "It's a Jewish judge, it's Ruth Bader Ginsburg." The reply was fast and furious. "I don't care who it is!" But ultimately, she had to live with it.

Fortunately, by the time you reach your fifties, you can make the choice for yourselves — although David was nervous about whether Ruth truly had the legal authority to marry us — so much so that he called her up and asked her!

A little-known fact about Ruth is how much she loved to perform weddings. It was a gesture of affection for people she cared about. Law clerks, judicial assistants, me, other friends, opera and arts friends, friends' children, all of us were the beneficiaries. I think she put almost as much thought and effort into writing our wedding ceremony as she did into a Supreme Court opinion. Well, maybe that's an exaggeration. But Ruth was not someone to show up and pull out a frayed three-by-five index card. Every element was meticulously planned and choreographed.

She began by asking me what I wanted her to say and what I wanted to say, and she also sent me the drafts of some wedding ceremonies she had performed in the past, so I had a template to work with. I responded by writing a draft, including some of the passages from prior weddings that she had sent me. But Ruth was even more detailed. She wrote out every word and every direction for the event — such as "processional music," "Chuppah is opened," and "Bob hands David the ring" — also for David and me — David says, and Nina says — and for herself. She even scripted the jokes — and they were funny. "A resident of Massachusetts, David was uncertain of my authority to officiate at this ceremony." It was as if she were blocking an opera, and she was determined not to leave anything to chance. What I did not know until later was that she almost didn't make it to the service.

My father played a couple of short pieces as part of the ceremony, and Cokie, Linda, and my sisters were my "bridesmaids," although they didn't wear matching dresses. Months before the wedding, Cokie, Linda, and I had gone to the movies, as usual, with our significant others (their husbands and my almost-husband.) At dinner afterwards, we began talking about the wedding and either Cokie or Linda asked, "What kind of a chuppah are you having?" I said, "I don't know that we'll have a chuppah." Neither

Cokie nor Linda is Jewish, but they both said, "You have to have a chuppah." And they volunteered to make it. When it was unveiled, it was a beautiful sort of golden silk brocade creation for David and me to stand under during the ceremony. The only problem was that the wooden legs that held up the canopy started to slide on the slick floor, so it kept sinking, like a tent collapsing in slow motion. And as she read her script, Ruth added a quip about "this chuppah, the likes of which we'd never seen before." We made it through the entire ceremony without a complete collapse, as Cokie, Linda, and my sisters valiantly worked to keep it aloft. (Cokie always maintained that my sisters were not really competent at their assigned part of the job.)

I can honestly say I've never been at a more joyous wedding. It was particularly joyous because we had both survived such difficult, long losses, and then we had somehow found each other. As Ruth put it, "When you turned fifty, I told you the decade ahead would be the best. I was wrong in that prediction. For a time you were not, as you usually are, filled with joie de vivre. Then, one day, the bright smile returned. You had encountered David, an acquaintance of some years, a man then adjusting, as you were, to a tragic loss. What started as companionship in melancholy magically became a love youthfully vibrant, yet deepened by your life's experiences."

She continued, "Nina and David, all who witness this marriage rejoice in the happiness and strength each of you brings to the other." Before we broke the glass, a central part of a traditional Jewish wedding, Ruth noted that this "symbolic step reminds us, at the very time we celebrate the construction of a marriage, of the fragility of relationships and of life. We break the glass too as an audible, tangible reminder of those who are not with us to share our joy, but whose voices we can hear and whose presence we can feel. We think of all those we have loved and still love, and it is the eternalness of that love that brings them to this place at this time. Our remembrances do not detract from our joy but reinforce it."

And indeed, it wasn't just our joy. It was the joy of all our friends and family, some 140 of them, who had been through hell and back with us and who were so happy for us. We tried to go to every table to speak to each guest, but eventually, I went upstairs and changed out of my beautiful but discreet champagne-colored dress into a black dress with a fur collar — David's favorite —

changed out of my gold shoes, threw my hair up into a big barrette, and reappeared to dance the night away.

At the end of dinner, Ruth took me aside and asked if it would be all right if she left early. "You know, Nina," she said, "I had a blockage last night, and I was briefly in the hospital." Except I didn't know. She had sworn Marty to secrecy so nothing would spoil our wedding. "I'm kind of tired," she admitted. I immediately told her to get out of there and go home. She started to thank me, and I interrupted to say that I should be thanking her. Ruth had a particular grit about her. She would never abandon a commitment; she was determined to fulfill it above and beyond. She could have easily left, and no one would have thought anything of it. But I'd like to think she was glad to be there.

I can look at our wedding pictures now, and Ruth, smiling and happy, appears fine; she is wearing her black judicial robe and a decorative collar. She looks healthy. But she was also able to compartmentalize. She was a master at stuffing everything down and trying to present her best face. Her health issues were a decades-long reminder that life is fragile and not fair. She had learned that lesson early on, in a household where daily life was an economic struggle and where her mother had been dying and in great pain for many years. Ruth's adult life was different. She had met Marty when she was seventeen. His family became her new family. They were well off, and I don't think Ruth and Marty ever really had to worry significantly about money. From that standpoint, it was a fairly privileged life. Even when Marty got sick during law school, they could afford to pay for a babysitter for Jane.

But from her early struggles and her later ones, she understood better the plight of people who were less fortunate. Nothing came easy in her life — not getting a job as a lawyer, not even becoming a judge, and for two decades there were constant health challenges. Nothing came easy, except for her brains, intellect, and curiosity.

I don't know if any of these obstacles helped to make her a kinder person, but the entire time that I knew her, she was truly and deliberately kind. It must have been innate. Ruth had the same instinctive ability as my father to make connections to people. He had legions of students who loved him so much because he was able to respond to and care about them, just as Ruth did with her law clerks and others around her. I do think it's an ability that must be partly genetic or encoded in some fundamental part of who we are — or are not. My sister Amy has it; I see it in all the ways that she deliberates as a judge, how she considers what sentences to hand down, how she thinks about the impact her decisions will have on people's lives. My father's mother was also like that. My sister Jill, born with a heart of gold but a tough exterior, has learned it. It's a skill that I wish I were better at.

Perhaps having Ruth officiate at our wedding sprinkled kindness on my marriage to David. The honeymoon was a different story. Let's say it was fortuitous that I had married a trauma surgeon.

We had chosen a getaway on the Caribbean island of Anguilla. The first two days were bliss. On the third day, David and I went snorkeling. I was about thirty feet from David when I heard a boat engine but didn't see that the boat was coming directly toward me. And the fisherman did not spot me in the water. David tried to scream, but it was too late. The twenty-foot craft ran right over me. David heard the thunk and dove down, expecting to find me at the bottom. I was able to get myself to the surface, but there was blood streaming down my face. I thought I had been knocked over by a strong wave and had a nosebleed. Instead, I had been hit by the propeller. I started to feel dizzy, and David was trying to swim and drag me to shore. He had traveled about 150 yards when he spotted a motorboat pulling a group of kids on a tire. He started yelling for help, and the boat swung around. I was hauled on board, and we raced to shore.

At the hospital, David scrubbed in. The regular surgeon was already in the operating room doing a gallbladder procedure, so they called another doctor to come sew me up. David held the light and walked him through every step. At first, David asked the nurses not to shave my head because "she's on TV," but after he got a good look at the wound, he grimly told her to "Shave her head!" Fortunately, the nurse did it strategically. After they had dealt with the massive head wound, they moved on to the rest, including the huge clean cut under my arm, with the artery visible. I'm very fortunate the propeller didn't sever my arm.

The hospital insisted that I stay overnight, but they wouldn't let David stay with me because I was in the women's ward. Finally, the minister of health arrived, undoubtedly alerted by Cap Juluca, the hotel where we were staying, and David was permitted to sleep in a hard chair next to my bed. He knew what could have happened to me, all the possible ways that this could have been much, much worse. When we were alone, he broke down in tears before I did.

The next day we paid our hospital bill and returned to the hotel. As we left, David joked that the entire hospital bill was less than one night at our hotel. The fisherman who hit me had no idea what had happened; he learned about it because his wife worked as a maid at the hotel. As it happened, she was the maid in charge of our room. They came to see me with their children, all looking utterly terrified, and I told them that what had happened wasn't anyone's fault. It was just a horrible accident. I also insisted that David track down the children who had been on that tire and had seen me get hauled in. I wanted them to see that I was okay. That night I went to dinner at the hotel restaurant to prove to my sweet husband that I would survive, and to prove something similar to the folks at the hotel. The really hard part was rinsing the dried blood out of my hair. It hurt.

Word of my accident got out, and Ruth was one of the first people to call us in Anguilla to make sure that I was okay. David still wanted to get me checked out, so we left the island and flew straight to Boston, where the head of neurology at his hospital examined me and said that once the injuries healed, I would be just fine.

Once I was cleared, David told me, "You need to go back to work." We had scheduled our wedding for November 19 so that it would be after the presidential and congressional elections, when everything was usually quiet in Washington. But this was 2000, the year of *Bush v. Gore,* and the election recount was still going on. In fact, it was headed for the Supreme Court.

I was covered in bruises and stitches, but David put me on a plane to DC. I went back to work, and Ralph Green, Amy's husband, called to say, "I'm coming to stay with you. I can cook and I can take you wherever you need to go. You shouldn't be driving." On the morning of the Supreme Court argument in *Bush v. Gore,* I did a live shot for NBC's *Today* show on the steps of the Court. At the end of the segment, cohost Matt Lauer said on air, "Nina, let me ask you about something else. You were run over by a boat on your honeymoon. And you look just fine," or something to that effect. And I answered, "Matt, it's a triumph of makeup and drugs."

■ ■ ■ ■

Ruth was so angry after *Bush v. Gore.* I could see it in her face; she looked ferocious every time she glanced at some of her colleagues on the Court. She had wanted to write a longer and more important dissent, replying to the majority's decision to end the recount, which effectively meant that Bush would be declared the winner of the election then and there. And she particularly wanted to reply to the chief justice's separate opinion. But Chief Justice Rehnquist in essence told her, You don't have time. Give me what you've got by tomorrow. Years later, I learned she had felt blindsided.

From an analytical perspective, one of the interesting aspects of the *Bush v. Gore* decision was that the two sides flipped. The side that usually argued on behalf of states' rights, the conservatives, said this is a federal matter and the state of Florida should defer to the federal court. And the side that usually argued for federal control, the liberals, argued for states' rights and wanted to defer to the state courts. There was also basically no way to separate the legal outcome from the election outcome. I've been told by someone who knows

Sandra Day O'Connor well that she eventually regretted her vote, but we will probably never know for sure. Ruth remained angry for a while, I think, but in the final analysis, every justice understood that the only way to get the business of the Court done was to get along.

Getting along isn't measured by simply eating lunch together or sharing a few birthday cakes. It entails discussing issues in a forth-right way, for months if necessary, to reach some consensus, if that's possible. On a court that is functioning well, justices engage in a give-and-take; they soften and narrow their opinions. Justice Scalia once described it to me as "the price of admission." Getting along is also arguably easier to do if there is a center to the Court; it's far less difficult to draw in people who reside on the ideological edges of the center rather than to draw them together from the more extreme edges, whether that outer edge is on the left or the right.

I think it's fair to say that my scars from that snorkeling accident healed far faster and more cleanly than Ruth's scars from that judicial season. This was not something that she ever said to me directly, but it was something I sensed very clearly, after knowing her for nearly thirty years.

ELEVEN:
NOURISHING FRIENDSHIPS

Ruth. Nino. Ted Olson. Lewis Powell. It's tempting in retrospect to look back and say, "Oh, look at Nina, she made such wonderful friends." But I have had some failures, a sad loss, and one very dear friendship that required a decade of patience to nurture.

As a young reporter, I tried to interview every sitting justice. Some were not at all eager to sit down with me. In 1971, Justice Hugo Black wrote, "Dear Miss Totenberg: I am so sorry that I cannot fix a specific date to see you. Two weeks ago [sic] I went out to the Naval Hospital for my annual check-up and found that I had developed a headache that the doctors have not yet been able to alleviate. They do say that it is nothing serious and that time will get rid of it. For that reason, therefore, I would prefer not to fix a date to see you during the week of August 9–15." I'm not sure I've ever had anyone else decline to meet me due to a

281

headache. At least Justice Black did not infer that I was the proximate cause.

But by far the least inclined to meet with me was Justice William J. Brennan, Jr., the same Justice Brennan who would later so eloquently and publicly come to my defense after the Anita Hill events. In the 1970s, requests to meet with the justices were sent via typed letters, and then I would await a typed reply. It was a slow, deliberate process of mailrooms and letter openers to slice the envelopes, and secretaries taking dictation and then threading a piece of stationery into the typewriter roller and lining up the margins before they began to type the reply. Justice Brennan minced no words when he tersely wrote on June 3, 1974, "Dear Miss Totenberg: Thank you for your letter of May 22. I must decline. I'd not be able to adhere to the policy if I made any exceptions." I obviously pushed back, because he wrote me again on June 19, taking a firmer tone, "I don't understand your reference to an exception. I have made none. And, as I told you, I am going to adhere to the policy and so I must decline your renewed request." I did not succeed in getting an appointment, an "exception to the policy" if you will, until the early 1980s. Initially, I saw that as a reflection on me, but I was wrong.

Only long after did I come to appreciate that Justice Brennan had spent fifteen years rushing home each day late in the afternoon to care for his wife, Marjorie, who was ill with cancer. As I reported in 1976, Chief Justice Warren Burger didn't fare much better when he summoned Brennan to a late afternoon meeting but was absent from his chambers when the associate justice arrived. "Brennan didn't wait long," I wrote. "Without seeing Burger, he stormed out of the building, leaving rage everywhere he went in his wake." Brennan's stated commitment was to pick up his granddaughter at school, but in retrospect, it seems it was most likely Marjorie who required his attention. Brennan himself was treated for throat cancer two years later, leading some to speculate that he would retire and allow Jimmy Carter to name a replacement. (He did not; he served until 1990.)

Marjorie Brennan died in December 1982, and in March 1983, after a brief time dating, the justice married his secretary of nearly twenty-five years, Mary Fowler. They wed in private, and Brennan subsequently dashed off a note to his fellow justices that read, not unlike his earlier letters to me: "Mary Fowler and I were married yesterday, and we have gone to Bermuda." Not long after, he agreed to sit down with me.

Whatever terrible experience he anticipated must not have materialized, because he eventually agreed to a long series of interviews, each one taped early in the morning, which was his favorite time of day, though not mine. And equally important, he was willing to allow me to get to know him as a person. For the rest of his time on the Court, I made it my business to see him at least once a term.

I also invited Brennan and his new wife for dinner with Floyd and me, and I selected a date when my sister Amy and her husband would be visiting from Atlanta. Amy, like many in the legal profession, greatly admired Justice Brennan. The day before, she had also learned that she was pregnant, so she and Ralph arrived brimming with excitement. Justice Brennan was very kind, asking Amy about her work and her life, and thrilled at her news. Many months later, as the term ended, I stopped by the justice's chambers to say goodbye for the summer. He piped up, "Nina, that baby should be coming pretty soon, shouldn't it?"

"That baby," I replied, "was born two weeks ago." Brennan responded with a big smile and an "Oh my." He reached for a pen and paper and immediately barked out,

"Name? Address?"

A few days later, a letter arrived in Atlanta, addressed to the baby: "Dear Clara, Welcome! Welcome! Welcome! It's a great world if you will make it so. Enjoy every minute of it. Love, William J. Brennan, Jr." That letter was Bill Brennan in five quick sentences, his wonderful warmth of spirit, his eternal optimism, his joy in living, and his firm belief that things will turn out well if one just tries to make it so.

This five-foot-six, rather impish justice, son of an Irish immigrant coal shoveler turned commissioner of public safety in Newark, New Jersey, was born before women received the right to vote. He rose to be among the towering justices of the twentieth century. He was a brilliant man, with a pragmatic streak. In 1986, one of Brennan's law clerks shared the justice's description of how to win and preserve a majority. It remains about the best, most sensitive, and shrewdest description of how the Court works, when it works well, in the fewest words. Brennan said, "It really isn't very mysterious or complex. After debating the issues and the merits, when it comes time to write, in our chambers, we discuss the various possible approaches. We ask about some of the approaches. Will this be rejected by Lewis Powell or Harry Blackmun? Will Thurgood agree with this? Has John Stevens written any cases which may suggest how he is thinking and about which we should be aware? What does Sandra think? You try to get, in advance of circulation, a sense of what will sell, what the others can accept. And you write it that way, and when it works out — and maybe you have suggestions that come in and perhaps you make substantial revisions — but when it works out and you have a Court, you are delighted."

Brennan never wanted to retire. During my last interview with him as a sitting justice, I asked him if he was going to retire, and he thundered, "ABSOLUTELY NOT," instead demanding to know if I was going to quit. But a stroke in June 1990 led him to step down. Soon after, the *Harvard Law Review* asked me to write a tribute. I talked about his history, his judicial philosophy, and his rulings, which frequently worked to overturn discrimination, whether on the basis of race, or sex, or even acts of political patronage in low- and midlevel government jobs. But I also wrote, "In Washington, where cynicism is often justified, it is quite an amazing thing to learn more and more about a 'great man' and to find that he really is great, that his beliefs are genuine, that his work is his life, that his soul is a gentle one, and that he has a rare gift of perception and tolerance of others, even when their beliefs threaten his." I could not have known any of that if Bill Brennan had not finally given me permission to get to know him.

After Brennan retired, I visited him quite often. At first, he was vigorous, but gradually his health began to decline. In November 1996, he fell and broke his hip, and he never fully recovered. He was moved to a nursing home in Arlington, Virginia. With Floyd stable, I would try to visit every couple of weeks, until the justice passed away the following July at age ninety-one. Sometimes, he was mentally sharp and wanted to be told all the Court gossip that I could offer. Other times, he was just an old man sitting in bed. I would scoot my chair close, hold his hand, and sing "When Irish Eyes Are Smiling" and every other Irish song I knew. (Justice David Souter, who had replaced Brennan on the Court, would also drop by to do much the same thing, though probably not sing.) There was no story, there was no reporter, no subject, no questions, just a visit between two longtime friends.

Not all friendships take. Sometimes the chemistry is not right or there is too much wariness. Sometimes spouses do not get along. And sometimes a single moment can damage, even irreparably, years of affection. We live in the opposite era from the months-long back-and-forth between me and a sitting justice. Today, everything is about the quick reaction. I once ruptured a dear friendship over a tweet that my intern mistakenly scheduled for p.m. instead of a.m. The result was that news of a judicial retirement got out before the judge had planned, and he was justifiably furious.

If there is one trade secret that I have found for making and keeping and nurturing friendships, it is the act of sitting down together for a meal. For decades Washington has been an event city. Before Covid-19, there were multiple galas to attend almost every week, if you were so inclined. The same with large-scale parties. Every year, the late *New York Times* columnist William Safire hosted a large, famous break-fast to mark the end of the Jewish holiday Yom Kippur. Cars would line up around the block. Early on in our romance, I took David to a Safire break-fast, which typically featured a who's who of Jewish Washington. At the end of the evening, as we walked out, David shook his head and said, "I can't believe I just had breakfast with more than a hundred Jews, and I was the only doctor."

Dinner, a small group around a table, is different. It is a lovely way to spend time and get to know people well. Washington, at its best, is very much a dinner party town. It is hard to be acrimonious when you are surrounded by food and wine and especially when you are looking at the person next to you, rather than communicating through a small Zoom screen. Those dinners David and I had with Ruth and Marty really cemented our friendship. They were where Marty told David that it was time for him to be inducted into the somewhat mythical "Denis Thatcher Society" — named for British Prime Minister Margaret Thatcher's husband and designed for men who are married to prominent women.

It was also where Ruth was able to be her authentic self. She truly enjoyed people, but she did not welcome the role of facilitator, which is one of the reasons I loved seating David next to her. He had an uncanny ability to draw her out. When she was at our table, she never, ever raised her voice.

Instead, the rest of the table would have to cease talking to hear her. She spoke very slowly, and often there would be a pause, but that did not mean she had finished all that she planned to say. Instead, the rest of us needed to wait. Once she had made her point, she stopped. Would that the rest of us had that restraint.

Ruth did not believe in small talk, she spoke only when she had something to say, and most often when she did interject, it was to say something neat, smart, or incisive — although she loved good gossip, and she knew plenty. She didn't break confidences on her own Court, but if there was something happening on a lower circuit court, such as a big fight between two judges, she would say, in almost a whisper, "I hear they're at each other's throats." She even knew which judges were dating other judges. And she knew everything about the lives of her clerks, although she kept their confidences too.

We were always very firm on the ground rules with guests; nothing about current cases before the Court. I remember once we did have a dinner guest who started to ask Ruth a question about a case that was pending, and David and I jumped in and said, "That's against the house rules."

Ruth certainly would give a big hug when one was needed, or when she was congratulating you, but she wasn't generally outwardly demonstrative, especially when compared to someone like Marty or Justice Scalia. She was perfectly happy to sit back and enjoy the social play unfolding before her. She would remember an entire evening, almost from start to finish. She was also an incredibly slow eater, the slowest eater I have ever known. David, my resident chef, learned early that when cooking for Ruth, it was important to time the clearing of plates. She needed at least five minutes, often more, beyond the rest of us to finish the course in front of her, and despite her birdlike appearance, she ate everything she was served. She also never spoke with her mouth full and was happy to work her way through her plate and leave the majority of the talking to Marty.

One thing we did not do was mix Supreme Court justices at our table. Doing so would have made a dinner too much like work, and each friendship had a different flavor. We had an easy, roll-up-your-sleeves bond with Stephen Breyer and his wife, Joanna. Before we were married, they invited David and me to dinner at their home in Boston.

There were six of us around the table, and David offered to help clear. He was shocked to see Breyer hop up and tell him, "No, no, no," and proceed to stack plates and silverware.

Justice Breyer does enjoy talking about theories and fine points of the law, and some years ago he gave David a copy of one of his books, which explained his judicial philosophy. David slogged his way through the first chapter, which was packed with footnotes, and found it terribly dense, while the rest of the book was much more readable and approachable. At our next dinner David ventured, "Stephen, I really enjoyed much of your book, but I couldn't understand the first chapter." To which Breyer replied: "Aw, you should have just skipped it."

Joanna, a clinical psychologist who spent her career primarily with children diagnosed with cancer, worked at the Dana-Farber Cancer Institute in Boston, so we would regularly invite Steve for a casual Sunday dinner in our kitchen, knowing he had many Sunday nights alone when Joanna had returned to Boston. Possibly our most memorable evening occurred the first time we had the Breyers to our house. It wasn't just the four of us. It was four couples, a genuine dinner party. David had started the dishwasher before the guests arrived in order to clear the kitchen, but in his haste, he dumped in liquid dish soap, the kind you use to hand-wash plates and pots and pans, not the dishwasher liquid meant for a machine.

Suddenly, it was as if we were part of an *I Love Lucy* episode. An avalanche of tiny, shiny soap bubbles was gurgling out of the dishwasher and spilling all over the kitchen floor. I grabbed rags and mops, and at that precise moment, the doorbell rang. Steve and Joanna were the first to arrive. I dashed to the door and explained we had a small kitchen disaster, but instead of staying in the living room, they followed me. Once they saw David trying to contain the mess, they asked for more mops and helped to clean up. Fortunately, by the time our other guests arrived, the cleaning team of Breyer, Reines, and Totenberg had prevailed.

No justice produced more laughter around the table than Antonin Scalia, a.k.a. Nino. And some of the dinners with him produced new friendships. At one of those gatherings, we had the justice and his wife, Maureen, along with two of our doctor friends, Guillermo Gutierrez and his wife, Marian

Wulf-Gutierrez. Guillermo, then chief of the intensive care unit at the George Washington University Hospital, was complaining about a recent speeding ticket. Nino's immediate and vociferous advice was "Fight it. Go to court and stand up for yourself." So Guillermo went to traffic court, waited all day because his was the last case to be called, and lost. Guillermo had made his case, but the judge replied, "I understand, and you may be right, but that's not how the law works. You will have to pay the fine."

The next time we were all at dinner together, I brought up Guillermo's court experience. Scalia was horrified, roaring, "What? You took my advice? You took a federal judge's advice? You took a Supreme Court justice's advice about a traffic ticket? Never take that advice! That's crazy!"

The closest we ever came to legal commentary was after Scalia's ruling in the landmark case *District of Columbia v. Heller,* a challenge to a DC law that banned handguns. In a 5–4 ruling, Scalia prevailed, declaring that the city's law violated the Second Amendment's guarantee of the right to bear arms.

Just days after the decision was announced, the Scalias came over for a long-scheduled dinner. There were eight of us, and David, who has operated on hundreds of gunshot victims in the course of his career, bought eight plastic squirt guns and put them in the empty soup bowls, so when everyone sat down, that was what they would immediately see. When we got to the table, everyone burst out laughing, including Nino. That's not the end of the story, however. Scalia's opinion in the *Heller* case contained a much-quoted line saying one of the advantages of a handgun is "it can be pointed at a burglar with one hand while the other hand dials the police." So, after soup, David reached under his chair and pulled out a massive Super Soaker, pointed it at Scalia, and asked, "Should I still call 911 with the other hand?" That brought down the house. We gave the squirt guns to Maureen for their grandchildren, and she sent a thank-you note saying that, as she was writing, the grandchildren were outside playing with the squirt guns, while "his Honor" was inside, cleaning the real ones.

Scalia was even willing to debate the legal philosophy of originalism, which essentially argues that the Constitution is a fixed document, not open to multiple interpretations as society changes, a document that should be interpreted as the Founders intended. At dinner, David responded that medicine has changed one of its most fundamental definitions, that of death. When he started out, death was defined as when the heart stops beating. Today brain death and lack of brain activity are the accepted legal definitions of death. Isn't that, he asked, sort of the same thing? To that, Scalia responded with his usual certainty, "Death is Death!"

A different version of death was on the dinner menu at the Scalias' after Nino shot a wild boar on a hunting trip. Maureen ultimately cooked the deceased animal into a delicious meal, but we had to be careful not to crack a tooth on one of the many buckshot pellets left behind.

Hunting was a passion for the Queens-born-and-bred Scalia. He decorated his Court chambers with the head of an elk he shot in Colorado (he named it Leroy). He was fearless about most everything, except perhaps Maureen. One night after an event at the Supreme Court, he invited David up to see his new chambers. Inside the office, with just the two of them, Scalia pulled out a pack of cigarettes. On the spot, David decided to invoke the law rather than medicine, and said, "I didn't think you were allowed to smoke in federal buildings." Undaunted, Scalia replied, "I'm a Supreme Court justice. I can do what I want." But when Maureen appeared at the door, he quickly hid the cigarette from her gaze, quietly snuffing it out.

Scalia loved good conversation, good food, and good wine. His favorite was the sweet, after-dinner Sauterne. He even coined a word for lingering in the front hallway at the end of a happy evening — "vestibuling." No one enjoyed drawing out the moments of friendship and fun more. Ruth was hardly the only one of us who would miss him in their lives.

Twelve:
Friendship and Hardships

I know exactly when I did not show up for one of my dearest friends. To this day, I could go back and circle the weeks on the calendar. In June 2002, Cokie found a lump in her breast. It was cancer. She had surgery in July but wanted to control the narrative, anticipating that someone would see her when she was at chemo and word would get out. In early August, she minimized the situation, telling Lloyd Grove of *The Washington Post* that the cancer "was caught early," and she expected "a clean bill of health after six months of chemotherapy." Grove dutifully reported that Cokie also told him the treatments wouldn't "cause any major interference with my work," adding, "The doctors tell me there are different effects for different people, and that I am likely to feel crummy for a day or so after every treatment. . . . This is pretty standard." Cokie finished by saying that Supreme Court

Justices Sandra Day O'Connor and Ruth Bader Ginsburg, both cancer survivors, "are awfully good role models for me."

They certainly were, and Cokie had the same grit. For all her efforts at a cheerful and confident exterior, though, she faced very serious odds. In fact, she didn't have anything like a simple, isolated tumor. She had nine positive lymph nodes, meaning that the cancer had spread. When David heard that, he warned me that Cokie might have only a couple of years to live, and while I heard him, I simply couldn't accept it. It had been only four years since Floyd's death. David and I had been married for less than two years, and I felt in many ways as if I had just climbed down from the ramparts following a nearly five-year medical siege. Cokie was fifty-eight. This, I told myself, was not going to happen. And anything I could do to help, I would do. I did everything I could to make sure that we could still act "normal," as we had before, sharing a lot of laughs and now, a few tears. But I ducked about one big thing. I couldn't bear to take Cokie to chemo, and bless her, she didn't ask. Two decades later I still feel terrible about my failure to even offer. Instead, Linda, bless her, went with Cokie every time. Cokie, in her typical fashion, insisted upon driving herself; her one concession was that she would pick Linda up.

Cokie hated being defined by her cancer, so I chose to believe that somehow everything would work out, and it did for more than fourteen years. After her diagnosis, Cokie was able to participate in a clinical trial at the National Institutes of Health; there was a range of choices, and she and Steve were able to pick. It drove both Cokie and Steve crazy that one trial director they met with, a male, addressed only Steve as he described his project, until Steve finally exploded, telling the scientist, "She is the one who is sick. Don't you think you should be talking to her, not me!" The cocktail of medications that she received — from another doctor — is a standard treatment now, but it was brand new and experimental then.

It was around this time that we established a tradition: Cokie and Steve, Linda and Fred, and David and I reserved most Saturday nights for a movie and dinner. Our default location was the DC suburb of Bethesda, close to Cokie and Steve, and our usual restaurant was the Pines of Rome, owned by one of their neighbors. David and I didn't go every week, often begging off for a concert or opera at the Kennedy Center.

And there were longer breaks in the summer when any of us went away, but we regularly set aside many of these nights to be together.

Like sitting with Ruth in a darkened opera house, there was something about being in a dimmed movie theater, having to suspend our thoughts and share in a particular moment, that braided us together. It was not simply the ritual and routine; it was the implicit statement that we would reserve that time for each other, and we loved being together. Then too, there was the dilemma of what movie to watch. Cokie and I had rather different tastes than Linda and the men. We didn't like violence; we didn't want to be scared; and, if at all possible, we wanted a happy ending. They loved terrifying thrillers with lots of gore, and dead bodies, but they deferred to us, almost always.

When a book was written about the early years of NPR and the women involved, including Cokie, Linda, me, and Susan Stamberg, several reviewers speculated that there must have been some private competition among us, some darker side that we didn't talk about publicly. But in fact, there wasn't. We saw each other through enough "stuff" — and tough stuff — outside of work that there was no space for anything adversarial. We recognized that we needed each other. Had we been dropped into an actual jungle, rather than the metaphorical jungle of Washington, we would have been each other's survival packs.

Cokie, who sometimes knew me better than I knew myself, no doubt recognized my inherent limitations. She never asked me to do what I was not equipped for. After Floyd's long illness and death, sitting with her during chemo, as the poison was pouring into her veins, and with uncertain results, was more than I could do without breaking down in tears, and that was definitely *not* what the moment called for. So Linda was the heroine then. I would try to redeem myself later.

True friendship is also sustained by a certain level of humility. On some level, we know what we are capable of, both our strengths and our limits. We cannot be everything to everyone. I learned this from David, or more precisely, I watched him, and I learned.

There is a tendency, particularly in this century, to view people as their public personas. When people can curate their lives on Instagram, or give "revealing" behind-the-scenes glimpses in TV interviews, we leave with a false sense of intimacy. I'm guilty too — my voice is in your kitchen, your car, your headphones, how could you not feel as if you know me? I've talked about my life in interviews, I'm talking about it now. But less remarked on is this other, private world, where people have relationships, where they have real struggles, and they show up for each other in all kinds of quiet ways. It's where we are vulnerable rather than invincible. Those are the stitches that weave together a complete life.

I often think about this in the context of my friend Jamie Gorelick. We can't even remember how we met — that's the way of long-time friends, sometimes the origin stories grow hazy or disappear altogether. Her career has been illustrious; she was general counsel at the Defense Department, then deputy attorney general in the Clinton administration when Janet Reno was the attorney general. I have a picture from her swearing-in ceremony, back from before Floyd fell, when we were all still women in our forties — and from the vantage point of today, young. Ruth was there too, to swear in Jamie. This usually is a fairly perfunctory performance where the official doing the honors leaves quite quickly. But not only had Ruth written extensive remarks — with a commemorative copy for Jamie — but she stayed at the party, and truly celebrated the swearing in of a female second-in-command at the Justice Department, marking the first time that both the attorney general and her number two were women. Jamie would go on to other prominent roles. She was appointed to the 9/11 Commission, where she was a workhorse, a combination of serious commission member, who participated in interviews and sifted through reams of information, and behind-the-scenes staffer. She would lock herself in the security vault, the oversized room that held all the classified documents, take notes, and write up memos.

One day, in the midst of Commission hearings, Jamie and her husband, Rich Waldhorn, came home to find a package sitting on their front doorstep. At that time, package tracking was rare; there were no texts or emails alerting recipients to shipping, let alone delivery. This particular item arrived the day after they had received a phone call threatening to blow up their house and their children. The package had no identification or markings, it was just a plain brown box. But after the attacks of 2001 and the anthrax packages sent to the

Department of Defense and Capitol Hill, there was no longer any such thing as an innocuous plain brown box. Jamie phoned the FBI and made sure everyone was out of their house.

There was an extensive search; the full bomb squad and many emergency vehicles clogged their narrow suburban street. When the bomb squad finally opened the package, they discovered that it contained an order placed by Jamie and Rich's son — for a gumball machine! But for several hours, they did not know if they had been sent a toxic chemical or if their house was going to blow sky high. Jamie remained, as she has always been, very stoic, but Rich, a doctor who was not ordinarily in the public eye, was undone.

That weekend they hosted their annual outdoor summer party for about fifty friends; they didn't cancel. David and I came — at this point, we hadn't been married long — and I remember watching through the window as David walked outside with Rich, who had been so frightened, not for himself, but for his wife, for his children, and for their longtime housekeeper, who had been in the house when the suspicious box arrived. As I looked out into the yard, I saw David putting his arm around Rich, which is not the kind of thing that you see men of their generation do for each other very often. I think we've always been a different kind of friends, as two couples, since that moment. We were family. It was not something we ever spoke of, but that ability to lean on each other — as Rich and Jamie had done for me with Floyd, when Rich took such exquisite care of him. And now, the way we could care for them in the aftermath of this peril, which in those post-9/11 years seemed to stalk us in such personal ways in Washington, changed the underlying foundation of our friendship. But I saw too that David could provide something to Rich, and Jamie by extension, which was different from what I could. It is possible to be a great friend by doing some things, but not attempting to do everything.

I would learn that lesson even more strongly with Ruth in the years to come.

Long, thriving marriages have some of the qualities of an orchestra. They can, at intervals, showcase soloists, and certainly there are leads, but for the orchestra to thrive and soar, the musicians need to collaborate. The harmony that we hear arises from each one playing their part, together. Ruth and Marty Ginsburg had that symbiotic harmony. Marty was her stalwart champion, and she, in return, receded and let him perform. It is almost impossible to overstate how incredibly supportive Marty was, particularly for a man of his era. Of her first judicial appointment, which required him to leave the tax law orbit of New York and move to Washington, he often quipped, "My wife got a better job. So, we moved." But he had helped facilitate it, enormously. He both luxuriated in and I think the best word is the Yiddish word *kvell*[ed] in Ruth's success. He was probably one of the three or four best tax attorneys in the United States, and yet he was nothing but proud and supportive of her and was never threatened by her accomplishments. Instead, he did everything to make them possible.

Marty wasn't just her legal champion. Harry Edwards, a judge on the DC Circuit, laughs when he remembers golfing with Marty and Ruth. Ruth was sporty; she rode horses, she loved to water-ski, she even parasailed, and she could read legal briefs while working out on a NordicTrack. But her golf skills apparently left a bit to be desired. As Harry described it, Ruth would hit the golf ball and it would go bumping along, "dit, dit, dit," and Marty would say with great enthusiasm, "Ruth, that's wonderful!"

Gradually, though, the golf stopped. Marty remained as engaging and charming as ever, but with less and less stamina, and more and more trouble moving. He had back surgery for a disc, and the hope was that it would resolve the issue. In the summer of 2007, they traveled to Venice to teach at Wake Forest Law School's summer abroad program. When they arrived, they stayed in a lovely hotel, in a nice room, until the moment Ruth walked across the lobby and a woman screamed, "OH MY GOD, IT'S YOU!" The Italian hotel staff previously had no idea who Ruth Bader Ginsburg was, but suddenly an American tourist was telling them how famous and important Ruth was, and about thirty nanoseconds later, Ruth and Marty found themselves and their luggage transported to a room with a balcony overlooking the Grand Canal. Marty would sit on the balcony and read while Ruth explored parts of Venice. He couldn't take the walking. When they went out together, he needed a car, or in this case, a boat, to transport him. It was what would be a wonderful summer, but in retrospect, the last of its kind for the two of them as a couple.

I noticed a striking change when Ruth was honored by the Woman's National Democratic Club. I was asked to emcee the event, but was concerned because it was a partisan club for Democratic women. I asked my boss at NPR for permission, and his response was "Ooh, for Christ's sake, you can do that." So I stood on the podium and presided. Marty was the main attraction, and when he spoke, he was fabulous, hilarious, and completely on point. But he needed a lot of help getting inside and up onto the dais. Each time I saw him, he had deteriorated a little more, and nobody seemed to know why. He looked okay, but he was clearly in pain and able to do less and less physically.

Since her first bout with colon cancer, Ruth had come to seek David's advice and confide in him about medical issues. I never knew what they discussed; and neither of them told me. It was a thorough separation, both professionally and personally. David and Ruth were such excellent compartmentalizers that they could duck into a private space, talk, and return to carry on a perfectly normal evening. As a follow-up, Ruth's doctors insisted that she be scanned each year, and from 2000 to 2008, her scans were normal. But in January 2009, during her annual checkup at the National Institutes of Health, the CAT scan found a one-centimeter tumor on her pancreas. Pancreatic cancer is one of the deadliest, in part because it is rarely detected until it is quite advanced. Ruth's was caught almost by accident. One of her first calls was to David.

In early February, when the Court had a brief recess, she underwent surgery at Memorial Sloan Kettering in New York. Dr. Murray Brennan removed the lesion and her spleen, in case anything had spread, even though a splenectomy makes the patient more prone to infections. The surgery was major and painful, but while most of us would be lying prone, in agony, Ruth forced herself to sit up and began working on the draft of a speech. She couldn't deliver it herself. That task was left to a former law clerk, but she was determined to write it herself. As for the pain, she just worked through it.

Marty and their daughter Jane were fiercely protective and determined that Ruth would beat the disease. They spent days researching and found a study of some three hundred people in a Scandinavian country where chemo had helped prevent recurrences. Marty brought it to David, who gently told him that the chemo course was incredibly potent and more likely to be fatal than the disease. Her cancer surgeon was opposed too. But it's very difficult, when it is someone who you love, not to want to do everything possible. Ruth had one treatment, but she was physically too petite to tolerate it — 105 pounds and about five-one, though she claimed to be taller. As David has described it, "She was sicker than hell," and she vetoed having any more. It was rare for Ruth to make a decision like that. Up until then, she had deferred to her husband and her children, who were desperate for her to do whatever was possible. She was devoted to them, and they were devoted to her. But when she decided no, that was it.

Ruth recovered, fully. It was Marty who did not. When he'd had those many months of terrible back pain and surgery, the doctors missed the fact that he also had a tumor in his spine. It later became clear that the tumor was located below the field where they had originally operated. By the time the doctors made the correct diagnosis, the cancer was too far advanced for surgery. It was terminal.

There are some life moments that you

absorb in a friendship, moments of deep vulnerability that you bundle and carry, because no one, no matter how stoic, can walk with every burden alone.

I'm of the generation that makes phone calls, and I called Marty just to check in. I could hear in his voice that he was really not doing well. So I picked up the phone again and called Ruth. I asked her if David and I could bring over something to eat. And Ruth, in her typical way, said, "Oh no, that's not necessary. There's plenty to eat here." And I don't know why I uttered the next words, but I said, "Would you like to have David take a look at Marty?" Her voice soft, she quickly said, "Oh, I'd be so grateful." We packed some food — a baguette, even though Marty made incomparable ones, some soup, and an artichoke soufflé that we had picked up at the weekend market near our house. It's amazing how you remember those small details.

Ruth was waiting for us with a look that I recognized, that look when you have crossed the threshold to a place beyond exhaustion and are simply wrung out like a dishrag. She looked and sounded like she had been up all night. I was there as a friend, but I didn't go upstairs with David and Ruth. I had no role to play there, and it would have been intrusive. Instead, I sat in the living room. I had brought the newspaper, and I tried to read, to keep my mind off whatever was happening on the floor above. Whatever they felt comfortable sharing, I knew I'd find out afterwards, more or less, from both of them, likely at different times. I knew if there had been something that Ruth didn't want David to tell me, as much later there would be, he would not say a word. And so, she trusted me. She trusted us.

It was June, the busiest month at the Supreme Court, when the most important opinions are usually being passed around and fine-tuned before being released in a slow-motion flurry. Some years there are more opinion pages than snowflakes that land in Washington. But inside Ruth and Marty's Watergate apartment, it was quiet. They had lived there for forty years. It was a very elegant but comfy two-floor apartment. The living room was dominated by an expansive deep beige sectional. There was artwork everywhere and all kinds of interesting objets d'art that people had given them or that they'd purchased on various trips. On the coffee table, Ruth had placed a large decorative plate and on it she had perched a tiny wooden snake. The serpent was realistic enough that if someone had set it on my pillow, I probably would have shrieked and thrown it across the room. That was Ruth's (and Marty's) wry wit for those who might put their wine glasses down on the table.

Where there wasn't art, there were books. The main living room wall was lined with books, an eclectic assemblage, including one book that was also in my father's collection: a compilation of the letters between Wolfgang Amadeus Mozart and his father. The living room fed into the dining room, which had modern chairs with padded seats and a rectangular glass dining table; if it had been in my house, I would have spent hours worrying about how to keep it clean.

The kitchen was tiny, far more of a New York apartment kitchen than a Washington one, or else a kitchen designed for someone who did not cook. It was a wonder to contemplate the magnificent meals that Marty produced in that space. He had installed a pegboard to hold an assortment of his most-used pots and pans; in fact, if you happened to turn left when you entered the apartment, you would run straight into Marty's pegboard. Aside from the sweeping views of the Potomac River, it was a bit like one of those New York apartments where you walk in and immediately know that an intellectual lives there because there are so many books and so many interesting pieces of artwork, and yet nothing is very flashy. There was nothing to impress you simply because it may have come with a high price tag. Indeed, it may not have. But in the incredibly mixed-media context of their apartment, everything together was beautiful and whimsical.

A curved staircase led upstairs, which had a study with a pullout couch, a small guest room, and Ruth and Marty's bedroom. And that's where David was, while I blindly turned the pages of the newspaper and waited. I could think back to my years caring for Floyd, and I easily surmised from the amount of time they were gone that things were bad.

The late stages of cancer spare no one, and spinal tumors are particularly insidious. Marty was in tremendous pain, and I don't think he could walk. Ruth had been changing their bed, giving Marty sponge baths, and cleaning up everything, without any professional assistance. She saw it as preserving his dignity. David stepped in as the kind but candid surgeon he had trained to be. He told Ruth, "You need help here. You need to get hospice or palliative care — I have Medicaid patients who have more help than you have right now." The next morning, she would call for help.

When she and David came down, I busied myself with Ruth, pulling out the food, and I paused, almost just trying to make conversation, and asked her if she knew how to heat up the soufflé dish. She answered confidently, "Yes, I'll just put it in the microwave." The soufflé was wrapped in aluminum foil with cardboard across the top. I immediately said, "No, no, no. You can't put that in the microwave because it will short out everything in the house," to which she said "So, I put it in the oven?"

I walked her through taking the cardboard top off and as I was turning to leave David asked, "Do you know how to work the oven, Ruth?" And with total candor, she answered, "No." So, standing in Marty's treasured kitchen, in which he would never cook again, my sweetheart instructed Supreme Court Justice Ruth Bader Ginsburg on how to use her oven, and they practiced turning it on and off a couple of times. He wouldn't leave until she could show him that she knew how to do it.

I felt nothing but love for these two people standing before me, and for Marty upstairs, who wanted his wife to succeed without impediment or reservation. And for the knowledge that sometimes we all, even Supreme Court justices, need someone to show us how to work our actual, or metaphorical, ovens.

Ruth took Marty to Johns Hopkins Hospital later that week, and she called us from there to say Marty was dying. What should she do? David said, "Bring him back so he can die at home." And that's what they did.

When she was sick Marty wanted to do everything possible that could be done. Every single thing possible. But he did not wish the same for himself, and he said so in his last note to Ruth, which she found beside his bed at Hopkins. I saw Ruth betray her emotions only a few times. One of them was when I interviewed her several years later and asked her to read Marty's last letter. She had not looked at it in a while and had forgotten to bring it to the interview. One of her judicial assistants raced to her chambers and found the sheet of yellow-lined paper. When you know you're going to perform, you can steel yourself, but she had not steeled herself, and as she spoke Marty's written words, she started to cry.

6/17/10

My dearest Ruth —
You are the only person I have loved in my life, setting aside, a bit, parents and kids and their kids, and I have admired and loved you almost since the day we first met at Cornell some 56 years ago. What a treat it has been to watch you progress to the very top of the legal world!!

I will be in JH Medical Center until Friday, June 25, I believe, and between then and now I shall think hard on my remaining health and life, and whether on balance the time has come for me to tough it out or to take leave of life because the loss of quality now simply overwhelms. I hope you will support where I come out, but I understand you may not. I will not love you a jot less.

Marty

THIRTEEN:
FAME AND FRIENDSHIP

Ruth had now entered the sisterhood that I had joined twelve years before, when Floyd died. Widowhood after a long, debilitating disease is often a bit different. Perhaps the only good thing about having someone you've loved very dearly die after an extended illness is that you are ready for the death. You're never as ready as you think you are, but you can see it off in the distance, you know that it's coming. The time you spent managing care and making accommodations is transferred over to funeral and memorial plans. There is a mountain of paperwork and busyness that engulfs you. What is new is the quiet, particularly at night. Every blast of air-conditioning or heat, every cycle of an appliance, every creak of a floor or squeak of a hinge is somehow amplified. TV, radio, stereo, nothing quite overcomes that underlying layer of silence.

And there is the stuff. People are very different about how they handle their loved one's belongings after death. When Floyd died, I wanted everything out of the house except for a couple of things that smelled like him and felt like him, one denim shirt and one sports jacket. I think the jacket may be gone now. I haven't looked in quite a while. But I still have the shirt.

As for everything else, I saw no reason to have sweaters and pants and suits hanging in a closet only reminding me over and over that there's nobody here who still wears those clothes. I donated the rest of his things. I was also still a relatively young woman, and I wanted to move on with my life. I had taken really good care of him for almost five years. I had loved him and done my duty, and cried when he got hurt, and cried for him at his limitations and how hard he had to fight against them. But I recognized that I had many years stretching ahead of me, and I had to live them.

So, in her own way, did Ruth. But she kept the physical world she had shared with Marty — their apartment — largely intact. His kitchen stayed, including the pans carefully hung on the pegboard, and his books.

Two months after Marty died in 2010, Ruth

traveled to the Tenth Circuit Court of Appeals Judicial Conference. Marty had been scheduled to deliver a speech on the historic joint case that he and Ruth had argued before the Tenth Circuit. He had written the speech before his death, and Ruth delivered it — with an aside to offer her own dissent that, unlike what Marty had written, her study in their New York apartment was *not* bigger than his. She sounded very much like Marty when she spoke, capturing his cadences and especially his trademark humor about tax law, and about most everything else. It was an amazing performance and so funny that it was almost possible to miss the poignant final line: "Ruth and I are truly delighted to be back with you in the Tenth Circuit again," and the very slight catch in her voice as she said, "again," which she quickly covered with a glowing smile. Because, of course, now it was Ruth alone.

I was there because I had been asked, as part of the event, to interview Ruth and the chief justice of Canada, Beverley McLachlin, on the differences between the U.S. and Canadian judicial systems. Ruth, however, was the main attraction. Her own familiar spunk and sense of humor were on full display during the conversation. She had a unique ability to recite the minute details of a case, much as if she were a second-year law student presenting in class, but to do it in a way that was witty and relatable.

She started off by a discussing a "silly" Oklahoma law that allowed girls who were age eighteen to buy low-alcohol beer, while boys had to wait until they turned twenty-one, "so, the thirsty boys at a fraternity in Stillwater, Oklahoma, brought this case." When she discussed why the plaintiffs' lawyers, including her, did not make it a class action suit, Ruth said it was because the fraternities had an "endless supply of eighteen-year-olds." That case, however, became a landmark. It produced the ruling in which the Supreme Court, and Justice Brennan, declared for the first time that laws that discriminate on the basis of sex must be viewed with "heightened scrutiny." This was a new and more difficult standard to meet. In describing the litigation, Ruth deadpanned that at the time, "we wished the Court had chosen a less frothy case."

With the benefit of hindsight, I see that two truths converged at this moment in Ruth's life. She had begun to step more fully into the spotlight back in 2007 with her blistering dissent in the *Ledbetter* pay discrimination case. Sandra Day O'Connor had retired. And Ruth was the only woman on the Court. The *Ledbetter* case particularly galled her. By a 5–4 vote, the justices ruled against Lilly Ledbetter, who had been repeatedly discriminated against in wages, as well as subjected to harassment, while working for nineteen years at the Goodyear Tire & Rubber Co. in Alabama.

Summarizing her dissenting opinion from the bench that day, Ruth spoke slowly and deliberately, drawing out every word for maximum impact: "The court does not comprehend, or is indifferent to, the insidious way in which women can be victims of pay discrimination." She ended her *Ledbetter* dissent noting that Congress had previously corrected the Supreme Court's interpretation of this very statute, adding that "the ball again lies in Congress' court." She was very proud when the first piece of legislation enacted after President Obama's election amended this statute to clarify that its protections applied from the time the workplace discrimination began, not from the time the legal complaint was filed.

By 2010, Ruth was no longer the only female justice. Because she was now the elder stateswoman of the three women on the Court and the senior member of the Court's liberal wing, Ruth's words carried even more weight. She was also writing far more dissents, and her dissents were getting noticed. Oral dissents are relatively rare at the Supreme Court. Prepandemic, the tradition was that the author of an opinion would summarize the decision on the day it was handed down. And, on rare occasions, a justice who disagreed strongly would summarize her or his dissent.

Ruth used that oral dissent tradition as a mechanism to call the public's attention to any decision she thought was profoundly wrong. In 2013, she dissented from the bench when the Court gutted a major provision of the Voting Rights Act. Writing for the conservative majority, Chief Justice Roberts said essentially that times had changed since the law was enacted, in 1965, and there was no longer any need for its extraordinary provision requiring state and local governments with a history of discrimination to clear any changes in their voting laws with the Justice Department. Ruth, in her dissent, said that "throwing out preclearance when it has worked and is continuing to work to stop discriminatory changes is like throwing away your umbrella in a rainstorm because you are not getting wet." For some reason, Ruth did not include that "money quote" in her oral dissent. When I told her that years later, she was both surprised and horrified. But her predictions of racially motivated changes were rapidly proven true as legislatures in states with discriminatory histories immediately began to enact changes that made it more difficult to vote.

Ruth was also becoming more public and more visible. During their married life together, Marty had been the main attraction in social settings, while Ruth was far more content to sit back. But now, she seemed to intuitively understand that she needed to step up a bit more. She knew herself well enough to realize that it was important she not sit at home. And she certainly wasn't interested in cooking for herself. She also genuinely liked the theater, the opera, all kinds of events, so she accepted numerous invitations to occupy her time. Rather like the energy one draws walking down the crowded streets of Manhattan, the bustle of a theater, the snippets of conversation, the visual stimuli of so many people in one space, gave Ruth bursts of energy. It's not that she couldn't be alone. Quite the contrary, sometimes when we knew she was working very hard, especially during the last month of the Court's term, David and I would all but insist that she could take an hour off if we brought dinner. We would arrive with the meal already prepared, or ready to make, do the final cooking, set the table, and call her down, first for a glass of wine and then for dinner. After she took her last bite, we would scoot her upstairs to work while we cleaned up, and quietly let ourselves out.

Invariably, she would sigh as she headed upstairs, and say, "You were right, I did need a break and some social interaction. I didn't realize how isolated I was." We, of course, were thrilled to perform this mitzvah, and we joked with her that she should start calling us "the couple," a reference to the term sometimes used by the rich and famous for their married household staff.

At the same time, Ruth's professional star was rising. Within a few years, coinciding with her eightieth birthday, she had become an icon. That status truly began to take hold in 2013, twenty years after she had been appointed to the Court, largely thanks to a blog appearing on the now mostly forgotten Internet site Tumblr. Entitled *Notorious R.B.G.,* a play on the name of the late rapper the Notorious B.I.G., the blog was started by a Columbia University law student, Shana Knizhnik, as a celebration of all things Ruth. In its first year, it had

250,000 visits. *Notorious R.B.G.* was sparked in part by Ruth's dissent in the voting rights case. Suddenly, in the vernacular of popular culture, the woman who wore white lace collars (and a jet-black collar for dissent days) with her black robes was "cool."

Ruth explained that one of her law clerks had originally told her about the blog. The clerk, she added, "also explained to me what *Notorious R.B.G.* was a parody of." Giggling, she continued, "Well, my grandchildren love it, and I try to keep abreast of what's on the Tumblr." (This was a stark contrast to the time one of her grandchildren decided to unfriend Ruth on Facebook.)

This popularity — to some, it was merely notoriety — had a bit of a double edge to it, however. Because Ruth received so much more attention than the other members of the Court, even the chief justice, people thought that she was fair game for their own version of "strict scrutiny." Some of her colleagues were no doubt put off by her new celebrity, and some academics thought it was unseemly, but ultimately, she understood that she had become an important role model for women — young and old. And none of the other justices could have done that in the same way.

Sandra Day O'Connor had accepted that

role before Ruth. For as long as O'Connor had been on the Court, she was its most famous member. And because of her centrist position on the Court, she was dubbed "the most powerful woman in America." There was even talk of her as a potential presidential or vice-presidential candidate.

During those years, Ruth remained largely in O'Connor's shadow; she wasn't that famous until her own time came — and then, as a sign of the social-media age, it was a very all-encompassing fame. Or as I wrote when the blog became a book in 2015, "Supreme Court justices are generally robed and mysterious figures. Their faces are not emblazoned on T-shirts, painted on fingernails, tattooed on arms and shoulders, and their characters are not parodied on TV programs ranging from *Saturday Night Live* to *Scandal.* At least not until Justice Ruth Bader Ginsburg became a cultural icon at about the same time she turned eighty." As Irin Carmon, who coauthored the *Notorious RBG* book, told me, "I think the Internet has given young women the opportunity to choose our own heroes." And they chose RBG because "There's this desire on the Internet to find something that feels authentic, and real and raw."

■ ■ ■ ■

I came to fully recognize this new chapter for Ruth at an event that I did not attend. In the summer of 2013, David and I were invited to the wedding of Kennedy Center President Michael Kaiser to John Roberts — no not that one — an economist at the Commodity Futures Trading Commission, who shared the name of the chief justice of the United States. The ceremony was scheduled to take place in the atrium, and the guest list included opera stars, Broadway marquee names, and philanthropists, including Jacqueline Mars, heir to the candy fortune, who to this day works incredibly hard on all things Kennedy Center. But it wasn't just the guest list and the grooms that made this a significant night. Ruth was going to officiate at the wedding, the first time a sitting Supreme Court justice had ever married a same-sex couple. She had waited until the Court made same-sex weddings legal. I was really looking forward to the evening, but the day before, I broke my foot, badly. I couldn't get out of bed. When I called to tell Ruth, her first words were "Oh, no! Can't you come?" I promised her that David would be there.

David and I had already been designated as her "dates" for the evening; now David was seated in the front row, which he found somewhat intimidating. He says he will never forget when Ruth reached the end of the ceremony and spoke the words "I now declare you husband and husband." He held his breath.

But it was at the dinner that followed that he (and later I) came to realize what a rock star Ruth had become, as actors, singers, and stars from every walk of life appeared at the table to speak to her. Ruth could barely finish a couple of bites of food because the crowd was so substantial. People looked at David sitting next to her and subtly, or unsubtly, conveyed the question, Who the hell is this guy? Ruth would graciously say, "Oh, do you know my friend Dr. David Reines?" They would perfunctorily shake David's hand and then pivot back to Ruth. She was the biggest star in the room. She had broken through the glass ceiling to a whole new level.

Now when she arrived to watch an opera, often wearing a babushka to hide her hair, the audience was not fooled. Even if she sneaked in through a side entrance, a rolling wave of applause would start as soon as she reached her seat, until everyone was on their feet, giving her a standing ovation. The outpouring was immediate and visceral. She would smile and offer a slight wave. But that was all. She always kept her reaction to the accolades controlled. Ruth attended because she loved the opera. She often told me that if she were to be anything other than a Supreme Court justice, her "other" first choice would have been to be an opera diva. Alas, she couldn't carry a tune.

But it wasn't just events that she attended. It was events where she was the attraction. The interview chats that she and I had started doing in the early 2000s, beginning with the Ninety-second Street Y in New York, were suddenly multiplying and sold out immediately. A few of my Supreme Court reporter colleagues occasionally referred to these Ruth-chats with veiled criticism, whether I was the interviewer or not, seeing them as conversations geared to her fans.

People certainly didn't go to the trouble of getting tickets to watch Ruth be skewered, but if I could get her to talk about an unusual or different topic, or about her early life, or a news topic, I would try. I learned that it was better if I shared the topic with her in advance. It gave her time to think about it, and almost always she would have things to say that were interesting. Sometimes her answer was a revelation to me, such as when I asked her if she'd ever had a MeToo harassment moment. But if I ambushed her without warning, it didn't work; she was very good at deflecting. All the justices are, it's part of their job.

She also became a star of stage and screen; in addition to the opera written about her relationship with Justice Scalia, her life and work became the subject of both an award-winning documentary, *RBG,* and a movie biopic, *On the Basis of Sex.* There were major premiere events for both. And she was invited to the Virginia Military Institute in February 2017 to give a talk about her famous opinion. At the event a 2003 graduate gave Ruth her steel combat ring. A graduate of the class of 1967 had also sent Ruth the Keydet pin given by the school to his mother when he graduated. In her speech, Ruth said, "He wrote to me that this pin was given to the mother of every man in the graduating class and when his mother died, he thought I might like to have the pin — he thought she would be proud if I would wear it."

It was thrilling to see Ruth elevated to this iconic status, something which her work and her life richly deserved. But her new fame also came with new challenges. Her security detail, once rather minimal and content to remain in the background, became far more of a visible presence. Once, when Ruth asked to go to the movies with us, David and I arrived at the theater only to discover that her detail had blocked off the entire back two rows, which ended up calling more attention, rather than less, to our little party. The other patrons were constantly swiveling their heads to look at the justice, and a few assumed we were famous too. Ruth's fame made the divisions between public life and private life far more pronounced, brightening the boundary between our home and the outside world.

One of the first things David and I do when someone is relatively newly widowed is to invite them over for dinner. We usually do this after a few months have passed, because that's when it really hits you that you're alone. Even if your spouse has been sick for a very long time, as was true for both David and me, you find yourself realizing that a whole part of you is gone. After Ted Olson's wife, Barbara, was killed on 9/11, we invited him to dinner in our kitchen. And we started doing that with Ruth, not only dinners at home but sometimes parties, festive occasions that we thought she would enjoy, much as Ruth had reached out to me month after month when Floyd had been so ill.

We had her for birthday parties and anniversary dinners, and each December holiday season, David and I hosted an interfaith party. The invitees include David's surgical residents and my current and some former NPR interns, with an additional mix of doctors, journalists, politicians, lawyers, and judges. We always try to introduce people who might not naturally talk to each other, so I would walk up to a group and say, "Excuse me. You're all journalists and you're talking to each other." I would then start introducing them to other people, because along with my theory that any guest should make time for the oldest person in the room, I believe it's fascinating to talk to people you don't know and people from different walks of life. We welcome parents *with* their children and have Hanukkah and Christmas gifts for them, and our tree has a Santa Claus on the top and a smattering of Muslim ornaments on the branches. We light the menorah too. My favorite photo shows a couple of Palestinian children, the daughters of a surgical resident, lighting the menorah with the Jewish and Christian children.

The party starts at five and Ruth knew to come about seven-thirty, when we'd be down to thirty or forty people at the most. She liked a lot of activity, but not so much that she would be mobbed or overwhelmed. We always saved food for her, so she didn't have to think about dinner. She would sit at our dining room table, with a paper plate, and she would eat in her incredibly slow way. I would sit next to her, and gradually, people would gather around — often about fifteen women, usually David's surgical residents and attendings, and my interns, and I would essentially chat with her in front of them and ask her some questions. In the beginning, it was just a personal conversation, but by the second year, I realized the two of us could have a conversation that was inclusive of everyone else. And as Ruth realized that she had an audience, she enjoyed the format too.

It may not be what most people would expect of a holiday party with heavy hors d'oeuvres, but Washington parties are often different. Many have a purpose; even the dinners can be performative, with either topics for discussion or a somewhat gentle interrogation by the host. This was more of a spontaneous, inclusive conversation. We would start talking and people would start gathering. In a significant way, the conversation made her more approachable. While she often seemed to shrink when in a crowd, this wasn't a big group, and I could show her off, while she in turn could reveal bits about herself and be quite funny. David took a few candid pictures over the years of our young female guests, standing around in absolute awe of this tiny woman, and the effect is very touching.

We would often simply make small talk, about places where she was planning to travel, operas on her calendar for the summer (at our Not July Fourth party). About as much as she would say about the Court was something to the effect of "This wasn't my favorite term" or "It was very arduous, but we did quite well, didn't we?" Sometimes too, a small topic would lead to a gem of a revelation. We were talking once about the portrayal of Washington on television, and I mentioned something about the popular show *The West Wing*. Ruth said that the actor Martin Sheen had been in her Lamaze class when she was pregnant with James. She told me that she always referred to him as "Perfect Martin Sheen" because he appeared so picture-perfect and handsome. And he would jokingly reply, "I am all yours, Ruth," so now she called him "My

Martin Sheen." At the time of their Lamaze classes, her Martin Sheen had just achieved his first big acting break in a Broadway production, and I asked her if she remembered what play. Without missing a beat she replied, *"The Subject Was Roses."* David was shaking his head in disbelief, but he Googled the name, and sure enough, she was correct. Ruth had a truly incredible memory, which was part of the reason an ordinary conversation with her never stayed ordinary.

It was different when we were outside the house. I could not fully protect Ruth from her occasionally overzealous fans or interlopers, whereas Marty would have. So David sometimes took on that role. I understood the instinct to meet her or to take a picture, but increasingly strangers thought nothing of interrupting her during dinner or as she was arriving or departing. They thought they were entitled to a piece of her. What Ruth knew was that I didn't need a piece of her. Nor did David. So more and more she wanted us to be her table companions. For years, at opera galas and other events, Ginsburg, Totenberg, and Reines were a trio.

I have had a small taste of that treatment, but in my case the most you could say is that periodically I have been quasi-famous. When I was on the weekly public affairs TV show *Inside Washington,* people recognized me all the time, but they often didn't know how they knew me. Was it from a PTA meeting? The grocery store? Gordon Peterson, the host, taught me that when you go through the airport or any crowded place, don't make eye contact, just look straight ahead. You aren't being rude, but you also aren't engaging. That, however, was far, far easier for me than it was for Ruth. Not only in Washington, but even in a big city like New York. One evening after an event for the movie *On the Basis of Sex,* we decided on the spur of the moment to go to dinner. It was a Saturday night, we had no reservations, and we were a group of eight.

So my sister Jill's husband, Brian Foreman, called in a favor at a small Italian restaurant that he often frequented. "We are bringing a special person, so please give us a nice table," he told the restaurant's host. And they did, but still, it was a restaurant, with fairly open spaces. Almost immediately after we sat down a woman came rushing over, and David, who is six-three and imposing when he wants to be, intercepted her and said, "We're having a private dinner; please let the justice have some time by herself." It set the tone, so the next time someone approached with a cellphone for a photo, Brian stood up and said, "The justice is trying to have some private time. Please respect that." Eventually, the interruptions stopped, and we had a wonderful evening. Another patron very kindly sent over a bottle of wine. But it was a reminder of how on display Ruth always was.

There were other ways in which we treated Ruth differently. Her lifelong penchant for working until 4:00 a.m. meant that, in all the years I knew her, I never called her before noon, or later, on a weekend. It also meant that she was prone to napping. Marty had been the one to ensure that her internal clock stayed reasonably in sync. After he died, if we were having her for dinner on a Saturday or Sunday, we'd call about six o'clock to make sure she was awake. The one time we didn't, the occasion was my birthday party. She called me, apologetic, and said, "I've overslept, can I still come?"

In much the same way that Ruth, and also Ruth and Marty, had scooped me up and whisked me off to events and activities when Floyd was so desperately ill, I wanted to make sure we did the same for Ruth. That led to some unintentionally memorable moments. It is easy to forget, but Ruth was a very good athlete. She not only waterskied but went parasailing. And when white-water rafting, she refused to be consigned to the rear of the boat, explaining dryly, "I don't sit in the back." Ruth also particularly liked sports and activities with a bit of an adrenaline kick. Over the years she had become a very proficient horseback rider and had accrued a full set of riding gear — helmet, boots, jodhpurs, all of it.

When we were slated to attend the Tenth Circuit annual conference in Colorado Springs in 2010, Ruth asked David and me beforehand, "So, what's there to do in Colorado Springs?" David replied, "Well, you can go horseback riding," and suddenly her face lit up, and she said, "Oh, I'd love to do that. I have all the equipment." Directly behind us, another voice chimed in, saying, "I want to go." David turned around, and it was Justice Sonia Sotomayor. So now my husband, who loved to ride but knew it could be dangerous, was responsible for arranging a horseback outing for not one, but two Supreme Court justices.

David's daughter, Alissa, was joining us. I don't ride. I am a total chicken when it comes to horses. So it was David, his daughter, Ruth and Justice Sotomayor, and two or three members of the U.S. Marshals

Service for protection. David made reservations for seven riders. The Chief Marshal was not pleased. When David arrived, his first words were "Why'd you do this?" And David replied, "Justice Ginsburg wants to go. Both justices want to go."

He said, "Well, we need twelve horses. I need two people with backpacks to save their lives and I need another couple for security." When the marshal paused, David asked him, "Can you ride?" His reply was to stare at David.

As she had promised, Ruth arrived in her full riding gear, while Justice Sotomayor rented her equipment. With such a large group, the guide changed the original route and opted instead to travel through the Garden of the Gods, a gorgeous place but quite rocky. The Chief Marshal had decided that he would lead the riders, so he was first, Ruth was second, and David was behind Ruth. Midway through, Ruth called out, "This is really nice, but why can't we gallop?"

The Chief Marshal did not reply. It turned out that he was not an expert rider, and he was struggling to control his horse. Suddenly, his horse bucked and kicked at Ruth and her horse, narrowly missing Ruth's leg. This is where David's demeanor as a surgeon, and used to being in charge, kicked in, pardon the pun. He told the marshal, rather firmly, "You almost kicked the justice. I'll give you my horse, but you need to get off your horse right now." The marshal was steaming. But he switched horses with David. The marshal's original horse was tough, but nothing that David couldn't handle. Ruth watched the whole exchange and snickered at the thought that she was a more confident rider than her own security. Which she was. *Notorious RBG* had it right.

FOURTEEN:
FRIENDSHIP IS A CHOICE

No story of friendship is complete without a disappointment, or at least weathering disappointment. Ruth had a very exacting measure for friends. And she had no tolerance for betrayal. But she was also very rational about what constituted betrayal, and she ultimately understood that doing my job was not betrayal, even if it caused her grief and maybe even temporarily pissed her off.

In the middle of July 2016, after the Court's term had concluded, I had a long-scheduled interview with Ruth so that, with her work behind her, she might have some time to reflect. I was not the first to interview her that month. One of her first sit-downs in that cycle was with Mark Sherman, of the Associated Press. In the interview she said that she "didn't want to think about" the possibility of a Donald Trump presidency. Then came an interview with Adam Liptak of *The New York Times,* in which she unloaded on Trump. In a piece filed on July 10, Liptak quoted her as saying, "I can't imagine what this place would be — I can't imagine what the country would be — with Donald Trump as our president. For the country, it could be four years. For the court, it could be — I don't even want to contemplate that." And as if that weren't enough, she added that if Trump were elected, her late husband would have said, "Now it's time for us to move to New Zealand."

The day Adam's story ran, Ruth doubled down in an interview with longtime CNN Court analyst Joan Biskupic, saying, Trump "is a faker. He has no consistency about him. He says whatever comes into his head at the moment. He really has an ego. . . . How has he gotten away with not turning over his tax returns? The press seems to be very gentle with him on that."

The criticism from just about all quarters was instantaneous and intense. Trump himself tweeted, "Justice Ginsburg of the U.S. Supreme Court has embarrassed all by making very dumb political statements about me. Her mind is shot — resign!" Both *The New York Times* and *The Washington Post* editorial pages criticized her comments, and *The Times* headlined its editorial "Donald Trump Is Right About Justice Ruth Bader Ginsburg," opening with the line "Justice Ruth Bader Ginsburg needs to drop the political punditry and the name-calling."

I was absolutely astounded by what she had said. It wasn't that I didn't know her personal political views, just as I knew Justice Scalia's. But I was shocked that she would make such statements publicly. In addition to being astonished at what she had said, I was, let me admit, ticked off. If she was going to make incendiary remarks to reporters, why not to me? Her remarks were news, but they had not been my news.

Of course, Supreme Court justices are not without political views. Indeed, the highly admired Justice Charles Evans Hughes resigned from the court in 1910 to run for president and lost. Twenty years later, though, he would be appointed chief justice. For the most part, though, justices don't think of themselves as political players. And they have on many occasions joined and written opinions that did not please the men who appointed them. What's more, the ethical rules that are supposed to guide the federal courts instruct judges not to engage in partisan politics.

So when Ruth said those things to reporters, she was waaaaay out of line. By Thursday, four days after the original piece in *The Times,* she had walked back her comments, issuing the following statement: "On reflection, my recent remarks in response to press inquiries were ill-advised and I regret making them. Judges should avoid commenting on a candidate for public office. In the future I will be more circumspect." Notably, she did not retract what she had said; she just expressed regret about verbalizing it.

Before our interview, I followed my usual practice; I told Ruth beforehand that I was going to ask her about what she had said. She immediately responded, "Oh, please don't do that." It was the only time she had tested our friendship from our respective professional roles. I told her I simply had to ask the question, explaining, "That's my job. I'm going to ask you about it as I would anybody else. And if you want to get mad at me right there, that's fine." And she did, letting me have it quite directly in the formal interview when I pressed her. I kept my first question neutral: "Why did you just think that it was time to say you were sorry you had made these remarks?"

"Because it was incautious," she replied. "I said something I should not have said, and I made a statement." She then proceeded to repeat her official statement, concluding with, "In the future I will be more circumspect. And that's exactly how I feel about this whole business."

I pressed her, saying that she had been candid in the past about making mistakes, so did she just "goof"? Her voice flinty, she answered, "I stand, Nina, by what I said. I would say yes to your question, and that's why I gave the statement. I did something I should not have done. It's over and done with, and I don't want to discuss it anymore." And she didn't. Her blind spot, and hardly hers alone, was her belief that come November 9, Trump would be old news. Hillary Clinton would be president-elect, and thus the first woman president would be able to appoint Ruth's female successor.

In June 1788, the Constitution of the United States was ratified. Article 3, section 1, covers the appointment of federal judges. It reads, "The judicial Power of the United States, shall be vested in one supreme Court, and in such inferior Courts as the Congress may from time to time ordain and establish. The Judges, both of the supreme and inferior Courts, shall hold their Offices during good Behaviour." That single phrase, "during good Behaviour," establishes the lifetime appointments of federal judges, including Supreme Court justices. Only impeachment in the House and conviction by the Senate can forcibly remove them. Until 2020, during the years that I covered the Court, only two justices had died while in office, Chief Justice Rehnquist in 2005 and Justice Scalia in 2016. Every other vacancy had come through retirement, though Justices Black and Harlan had resigned just before they died.

After Donald Trump's election, all eyes were on Ruth, as the oldest justice and the head of the Court's liberal wing.

She had colon cancer in 1999, pancreatic cancer in 2009. In 2014, she experienced chest pain during a workout and subsequently had a stent placed to open an artery blockage. That was her last major health scare for several years. In July 2013, President Barack Obama had invited her to the White House for lunch to all but suggest that because of the political calendar, she should think about retiring. She didn't take the hint. And she never told me about it. The luncheon stayed private until reported by *The New York Times* shortly after she died.

But in our public interviews, I had started

to ask Ruth about her health because it was on everyone's mind. In January 2018, when we were at the Sundance Film Festival for a conversation before the premiere of the documentary *RBG*, I mentioned her exercise routine. Ruth recounted the story of how she began working out with a trainer after her bout with colorectal cancer nearly twenty years earlier. "I was in pretty bad shape. Marty said I looked like a survivor of Auschwitz, and I had to do something to build myself up." So, she found "this guy" who was working at the federal courthouse not far from the Supreme Court. He had a reputation as a wonderful personal trainer. The "guy" was Bryant Johnson, a federal court clerk and Army reservist who moonlighted as a personal trainer. Until the onset of Covid-19, he and Ruth met at the Supreme Court twice a week to work out. As she explained, "I tend to be compulsive about my work. But when it comes time for me to meet Bryant, whatever I'm doing, I drop it." In October 2017, Bryant released a book, *The RBG Workout,* which is 128 pages of illustrated Ruth routines. It was, even for those who were half her age, a challenge.

My final question at Sundance was simply "How's your health?"

And Ruth replied, "It's very good." Then she launched into a discussion of the other question that she had heard over the years, "Isn't it time for you to go?" She gave a multipart answer that, well, judge for yourself. "My first answer was Justice Brandeis. Louis Brandeis was appointed to the Court at the same age as I was. He was sixty. And he stepped down at age eighty-three. I expect[ed] to stay just as long. I know I'm there almost two years longer than Justice Brandeis. The next excuse was the Museum of American Art has taken away my Josef Albers, a painter I loved. I couldn't think of leaving until I get my Albers back." But now, she admitted, the museum had re-loaned the Albers painting for her to display in her chambers, so her "current answer," she said, would be her forever answer. She would remain on the Court "as long as I can do the job full steam."

By August 2018, Ruth had honed her answer further, saying, "I'm now eighty-five. My senior colleague, Justice John Paul Stevens, he stepped down when he was ninety, so I think I have about at least five more years." She also pointed out that to apply term limits to Supreme Court justices, "you'd have to amend the Constitution." Referencing Article 3 and good behavior, she added slyly, "And most judges are very well behaved."

But in early November 2018, she fell and fractured three ribs. I interviewed her five weeks later, at the Museum of the City of New York. This time, my first question was about her health. "I'm going to start out by asking you the question that — oh, I don't know — probably 70 percent of Americans want to know the answer to. That would be the 70 percent who offered you their body parts and organs in case you needed them. How's your health?" And Ruth replied, "It's fine, thank you."

I followed up. "And those ribs you busted?"

"Almost repaired."

"That's good. And have you gone back to your trainer, Bryant Johnson?"

"Yes. We went back immediately after the fall. We could do legs only, but yesterday we did the whole routine."

"The whole routine?"

"Yes."

But it wasn't fine. In December, we did a series of interviews related to the premiere of the biopic about Ruth's early career, *On the Basis of Sex*. The last of these appearances was on a Sunday night at Lincoln Center, and I cut it short because when I looked into her eyes, I could see Ruth was terribly tired. David had come up for the event, and he knew the truth. After her fall, Ruth had called him.

A CAT scan of her broken ribs had revealed "an abnormality" in one of the lobes of her lungs. That's a nice way of saying that she might have lung cancer. David helped supervise the biopsy that followed, which revealed two cancerous nodules. He worked with her and her children, Jane and James, to navigate the treatment that came next.

I knew nothing of what was transpiring. David treated Ruth as he would any patient, with complete confidentiality. He would rather deflect or lie to me than betray a confidence, so I was kept entirely in the dark. At times my colleagues would ask me, Do you know what's going on with her? And I'd say, "David may, but I don't," which was the truth.

The morning after that last interview, David and I had planned to go to the Tenement Museum, but he gave me some cockamamie excuse, and I believed him. In fact though, David, Ruth, and her two children met at Memorial Sloan Kettering Cancer Center with an array of doctors to make plans for the surgery scheduled for that very Friday to remove part of her lung and to discuss any subsequent treatment. Late the night before her operation, David sat me down to tell me what was going to happen. In that moment, I was not a journalist; I was Ruth's friend, and I wept.

The next day I followed her example and did my job. First, I identified several thoracic surgeons, got their phone numbers, and called them to inquire about the prospects of recovery for a mythical member of Congress who had this condition. Then I waited, and before long, when the announcement of her surgery from the Supreme Court press office hit my email, I reported the information about the procedure and her condition, adding the details that I had gathered from surgeons around the country. That night I met David for a quick dinner before I prepared to do a TV spot, and as we sat in the restaurant, at about 8:00 p.m., my cellphone rang.

It was Ruth. She was calling from the ICU, but her voice sounded strong. "I'm sitting up in a chair eating a consommé soup that is far better than I had any right to expect at a hospital," she said. After a minute or so of meaningless chitchat, she got down to it. She was calling because she wanted me to know why she had "forbidden David to breathe anything about her diagnosis and surgery." The reason, as she put it, was "I just didn't want you to be trapped between your friendship for me and your obligations as a journalist."

As I write these words, tears sting my eyes as they did that night.

At different moments in life, there are choices of lasting consequence. And I had one of those before me. For the next eighteen months, I chose friendship.

It was the best choice I ever made.

Ruth weathered the surgery and went straight back to work, but her doctors told her to cancel all her engagements. No speeches, no travel. Ruth's ever-vigilant judicial assistant, Kimberly McKenzie, listened to the doctors, and then did what the justice wanted. She rebooked most of the events for later in 2019 and into 2020.

Ruth lived up to almost all those obligations, even after a month of enervating radiation in August. In that time I saw her incredible determination, her complete unwillingness to shirk or disappoint. But I also saw something else, how deeply she felt Marty's absence. What she conveyed in private, she eventually shared in public, in a

July 2019 interview she did with me in her chambers and not in front of an audience. It was for a speech I was giving to the American College of Surgeons. As I look back now, so many things about that video look like two old broads just gossiping, and I guess in some ways we were.

She told me that she missed Marty every day, especially now. Her children visited frequently to lift her spirits, but her husband, she said, was always there before, taking care of her, sleeping next to her on some uncomfortable cot or couch in the hospital, despite his bad back. Marty had looked after her so completely that at one point, when she was getting a blood transfusion, he ripped out the IV because he noticed that one of the antigens did not match. "I might not have lived if he hadn't been there," she said, adding, "So, [not] to have his loving care and yet his determination that I do what was necessary to heal faster, it was hard to be alone."

Daily, Marty had buoyed her spirits and goaded her to do the physical therapy that she needed to become stronger. He cooked her tempting meals, and he would entertain her, reading her short stories by Tolstoy and serving as her news clipping service. Without fail he found articles that would interest and amuse her. With a wistful smile, she told me in that practical Ruthian way that betrayed so much emotion underneath, "I miss him every morning. I have no one to go through the papers and pick out what I should read."

This latest brush with mortality had somehow amplified her loss. Intellectually, she remained as fierce and indomitable as ever. Outwardly, she was thoroughly stylish and elegant. But now there was also a tender vulnerability that she had rarely allowed to surface before.

How she handled it was to work. Her response to three cancer diagnoses was to follow the advice of the opera singer Marilyn Horne, who when asked about her pancreatic cancer diagnosis in 2005 had said, " 'I will live,' not that 'I hope I live,' or 'I want to live,' but 'I will live.' " Ruth took Horne's advice to heart.

"The work is really what saved me," Ruth went on to explain, "because I had to concentrate on reading the briefs, doing a draft of an opinion, and I knew I had to get it done. So, I had to get past whatever my aches and pains were just to do the job." At the same time, she waved away any worries about her future. "There was a senator, I think it was after my pancreatic cancer, who announced with great glee that I was going to be dead within six months," she recalled. "That senator, whose name I have forgotten, is now himself dead, and I," she added with a dramatic pause and a wicked semigrin, "am very much alive."

Work and optimism were a strategy that she was about to employ again. On August 5, she began three weeks of radiation at Sloan Kettering for a tumor on her pancreas. The day she completed the daily radiation sessions, the Supreme Court press office disclosed the treatments, describing them as "stereotactic ablative radiation therapy, administered on an outpatient basis to treat a tumor on her pancreas. The abnormality was first detected after a routine blood test in early July, and a biopsy performed on July 31 at Sloan Kettering confirmed a localized malignant tumor.

"As part of her treatment, a bile duct stent was placed. The Justice tolerated treatment well. She cancelled her annual summer visit to Santa Fe but has otherwise maintained an active schedule. The tumor was treated definitively and there is no evidence of disease elsewhere in the body. Justice Ginsburg will continue to have periodic blood tests and scans. No further treatment is needed at this time."

I didn't consider asking David what any of this meant — or what Ruth might have asked or told him — but I did ask another doctor, Timothy Cannon, a gastrointestinal oncology specialist at the Inova Schar Cancer Institute in Virginia, who told me, "That is the cutting-edge new cancer treatment, but it is not a cure for a pancreatic mass. The mystery is what kind of cancer this is. Is it a slow-growing metastasis of her lung cancer? Is it a recurrence of her pancreatic cancer from ten years ago, or is it a new cancer in someone predisposed to getting cancer?"

During her radiation treatments, Ruth maintained a busy schedule in New York, often going out in the evening to the movies, the opera, and the theater. One of the performances she attended was *Fiddler on the Roof* at the off-Broadway theater Stage 42, and when word spread during intermission that she was there, the audience stood for several minutes to applaud. Ironically, in the audience that night was Kate McKinnon, whose frequent portrayals of Ruth on NBC's *Saturday Night Live* had become a marquee event on the show. As the musical's performers watched, the two women, the icon and her imitator, met for the first time, clasping hands in appreciation.

During the day, Ruth worked, window-shopped, and searched for her red shoes at Stuart Weitzman. She had eleven events scheduled for September and still more in October and November; that fall marked her twenty-fifth anniversary on the Court. It would have been a killer schedule for anyone, let alone someone who had endured three weeks of radiation. I was joining her for the first event, a September 3 conversation at the Clinton Center, in Little Rock, where she would be introduced by former President Bill Clinton.

Fifteen:
Losing Friends

After a certain number of years, being a justice on the Supreme Court comes with the added burden of being on either a retirement or a health watch. Once Joe Biden was sworn in as president, a near hysteria built in some liberal quarters for Stephen Breyer to retire in 2021. These campaigns don't always have the desired effect. In Breyer's case, the ferocity of those requests, I think, made him if anything less likely to retire immediately, though it was clear to me that he would pull the trigger, as he did early in the following year.

There was a similar, albeit slightly quieter, campaign launched around Justice Anthony Kennedy back in 2017, immediately after Donald Trump took office. The conservative Federalist Society folks spread rumors that Kennedy was not totally with it, that his health was failing, all whispers that my eyes and ears told me were not true, even though some of his colleagues thought he was slowing down a bit. And in the courtroom, astute observers could see that his hands often were a little shaky, that slight unsteadiness that sometimes comes with age. But what Kennedy said to me, and others, was that he was still very much undecided — until his wife broke her wrist. Suddenly, he had to do everything for her. He had to help her dress and do her hair. He had to put in her earrings and help with her makeup. Doing those things for her, his caregiving, he said, brought them even closer together.

One night, as he sat reading briefs, he looked over at her, sitting in her own chair, patiently reading something else. He thought to himself that since he'd been in his thirties, when President Reagan appointed him to the Ninth Circuit Court of Appeals, he had spent his evenings like this, immersed in work. And it was time to spend more of his time with his wife again. They had grandchildren in New York doing interesting things. He wanted to see them regularly too.

I believed what he told me. Not everyone did. Ruth Marcus of *The Washington Post* reported something else in her book, *Supreme Ambition: Brett Kavanaugh and the*

Conservative Takeover. She says her sources told her that Kennedy retired because he'd been largely assured that the White House would name Kavanaugh, his former law clerk, as his replacement. Kennedy himself denied that to me and other reporters at the time. But while I trust what he told me, the redoubtable Ms. Marcus believes what her sources told her. And maybe in their own way, both stories are true. I really don't know. What everyone knows is that Anthony Kennedy retired in 2018, and Brett Kavanaugh was in fact nominated and had the most contentious confirmation hearing since Clarence Thomas's.

This time, though, the allegation did not involve a boss and his subordinate. It involved two people now in their fifties; Christine Blasey Ford said that Kavanaugh had sexually assaulted her at a party when they were in high school, and he categorically denied the allegation. Like others in the media, as soon as the reports broke, I began hearing additional reports, but none of what I heard was provable. I did one interview with a classmate of Ford's, Christine King Miranda. I tracked her down in Mexico City, with the aid of my reporter-niece, Emily, who was living there. Emily went to King Miranda's house so we could do what is known as a tape-sync. Each of two people are recorded on their ends and then merged — synchronized. King Miranda had become a part of the story after she posted on Facebook that the Kavanaugh incident "DID happen," but when I asked her about it directly, her response was very different. "That it happened or not, I have no idea. I can't say that it did or didn't."

In short, she retreated from her social media words, telling me she had no first-hand knowledge; she only remembered a "buzz." And, unlike Anita Hill's contemporaries, she would not agree to a Senate committee interview.

Having been in the eye of the storm for the Thomas hearings, I saw much about this episode that made me feel queasy. We were not talking about grownups. We were talking about a Supreme Court nominee as a teenager, with alcohol in the mix, and in a different place and time. I've never completely understood why Kavanaugh didn't just say, "I have no idea if I did anything like this, but if I did, I'm horrified." But he didn't. Instead, he blew his stack in front of the Senate Judiciary Committee, accusing the Democrats of a "calculated and orchestrated political hit, fueled with apparent pent-up anger about President Trump and . . . revenge on behalf of the Clintons . . ." The Clinton reference was apparently his belief that this was an effort to get back at him for his role in investigating them when he worked for Special Prosecutor Kenneth Starr in the 1990s on the Whitewater investigation, which was broadened to include Bill Clinton's relationship with White House intern Monica Lewinsky. Ultimately, Kavanaugh was confirmed by the Senate, amid tremendous rancor.

Ruth missed his investiture ceremony at the Court; she was in the hospital for her three broken ribs, the same hospital stay during which doctors would see the concerning and ultimately cancerous spot on her lung. But these contentious confirmation hearings and the swirl of controversy around the Court provided a backdrop for Ruth's approach to her own health challenges in 2019 and beyond.

Aside from her family, Ruth's greatest love was the Court. She was an incredibly fierce defender of the institution and its independence. In July 2019, during the interview when she spoke so endearingly of her love for Marty, she waxed philosophical about her workplace. She opposed expanding the Court, saying, "If anything would make the Court look partisan, it would be that — one side saying, 'When we're in power, we're going to enlarge the number of judges, so we would have more people who would vote the way we want them to.'

"We are blessed in the way no other judiciary in the world is," she continued. "We have life tenure. The only way to get rid of a federal judge is by impeachment. Congress can't retaliate by reducing our salary, so the safeguards for judicial independence in this country, I think, are as great or greater than anyplace else in the world." But she also noted that the whole notion of the country's independent judiciary hinges on public trust.

"The court has no troops at its command. [It] doesn't have the power of the purse, and yet time and again, when the courts say something, people accept it." Ruth spoke specifically of *Bush v. Gore,* in which the Supreme Court stopped the Florida recount after the 2000 presidential election. "I dissented from that decision. I thought it was unwise. A lot of people disagreed with it. And yet the day after the Court rendered its decision, there were no riots in the streets. People adjusted to it. And life went on." Remember, as you read this, that she said those words in 2019, well before the riots at the Capitol on January 6, 2021.

Ruth believed deeply in that mission — to uphold the Court's public trust. That's what she was fighting for in that final year by continuing her work — more even than her own health or survival. She had rolled the dice on retirement in 2013 when President Obama broached the subject with her. Back then, she was healthy, at the top of her game, and she thought that anyone who could possibly win Senate confirmation would not be the force she was on the Court. What's more, she wanted desperately to give the first female president the power to nominate her successor. It was a gamble, and she lost. The Republicans won control of the Senate in 2014, and what she had never imagined, that a candidate like Trump would become president, came to pass. So now, she was stuck.

I do not think that Ruth would have fought so hard to live if Trump were not president and if she were not trying to make it to the 2020 election. There were stretches when something went wrong every week. Her little body took an enormous amount of punishment as she kept going.

It is a natural human instinct to keep your health a private matter. But if you are a Supreme Court justice you should not and realistically, likely cannot do that. Marty's instincts and Ruth's own had ingrained in her the idea that it was stupid not to disclose a serious health issue, because if you tried to keep it hidden and somebody found out, it would look awful. In fact, it would look like a deliberate deception.

As far as I know, she never went to the hospital for anything major without disclosing it, nor did she try to hide major cancer treatments, although she did, as in the case of that August radiation, wait until it was complete. For two decades, she took every cancer in stride. She never missed a day at work. She might be physically hurting, but it never affected either her thought processes or her relationships at the Court.

Other health challenges, she shared, but in a more limited way. Before her new cancer diagnosis in 2018, she had been suffering from shingles, a viral infection caused by the same virus as chicken pox, which produces a very painful rash and blisters on the skin. It was a measure of her grit, her sometimes foolish grit, that she simply suffered through and soldiered on for two weeks, convincing herself that whatever it was, it would go away. It didn't. And by the time she was diagnosed, it was too late. The blisters ultimately subsided, but because she had waited so long, the pain never went away, despite all the creative things that David and Ruth's fabulous internist, Beth Horowitz, came up with.

The best of their solutions was a lidocaine patch at night so Ruth could sleep, but it could be used only for twelve-hour stretches, so when she went to Court, Ruth was always in pain. Yet in the courtroom, no one saw her complain or appear to be suffering. In his remembrance of her, her friend Judge Robert Katzmann, now deceased, candidly recalled how she had traveled to New York in April 2018 to speak to the young lawyers of the Immigrant Justice Corps "about the importance of access to justice for everyone, even though, unbeknownst to the rest of us, she was battling a painful case of shingles."

Shingles was not her only affliction. Ruth read for such long stretches with her head bent over that her neck muscles atrophied, and she needed specialized physical therapy. She had chronic problems with her teeth, partly from all the cancer treatments she had endured. She still struggled with the lingering bowel issues from her colon cancer surgery nearly two decades earlier. But it was the proliferation of these challenges and how she soldiered through each and all of them that made her seem, ironically, more steely and more invincible. She refused to allow herself to be defeated.

One of Ruth's main problems toward the end of her life was concealing how thin she was. She was likely well under a hundred pounds. In addition to well-padded jackets, she often wrapped herself in shawls, sometimes holding them away from her body using one hand to give the appearance that she was more substantial than she was. She was cold too, from being so thin. She still wore her custom crocheted gloves to hide the marks on her hands from all the IV lines stuck into her for chemotherapy. And in public, she always remained elegant, made up with just a dusting of powder and a swipe of lipstick, her hair pulled back in her trademark scrunchie.

But it was impossible to conceal everything. I don't fully understand how she remained as independent as she was while she got sicker. I was never invited into her room when I traveled with her. It was an unspoken veil of privacy that I did not lift. There was only one time when I went to see if she was all right, while we were in Arkansas for the Clinton Center event. I knocked on her door, and she opened it, looking quite frantic, with her hair hanging down. Only one thing was clear: she really wanted me out of there. She was tearing apart her suitcase — she never had anyone pack for her, she did it herself — looking for antidiarrhea pills that she knew she had put in there.

In the film clips of that interview, she looks serene, though she could not have been. And she was, as always, funny and feisty. About her years as the only woman on the Court, she said, "It was a lonely position, and viewing the Court, it was something wrong with the picture. The public would see these eight rather well-fed men coming on the bench and then there was this rather small woman."

She also recalled how as a young woman, fresh out of law school, she used to ride home in a car with Judge Edmund L. Palmieri, for whom she clerked, and the famous Judge Learned Hand, who lived one block away from Palmieri. As Ruth remembered it, when she finished her work on time, "I would ride uptown with them, sitting in the backseat. And this great jurist would say anything that came into his head — words that my mother never taught me. And [one day] I asked him, 'You say you won't consider me as a clerk because you would have to censor your speech and yet in this car you don't seem inhibited at all.' And his response was 'Young Lady, I am not looking at you.' "

By September 21, when we were together at Columbia University for an extended discussion of her twenty-five years on the Supreme Court and a celebratory dinner, more of her old vibrancy was back.

I had come to celebrate Ruth, but I was incredibly sad. Four days earlier, my darling friend Cokie had died. So, after posing for smiling photos with Ruth, I raced back to Washington for Cokie's service, scheduled for a day later. Just as Cokie and Linda had been my faithful ushers/chuppah holders at two different weddings, Linda and I were to be among a small group of ushers — all women and including the Catholic nuns who were also dear to Cokie — at her funeral.

When Cokie's cancer recurred fourteen years after her first diagnosis and treatment, she did what Cokie always did; she researched the hell out of what was happening to her. She found that the outside survival rate for her at that point was three years. As she pragmatically put it, "You just hope they'll find something new, and you just keep lasting as long as you can last."

She tried, but she did have her moments.

371

Once I was at a very boring gala when my phone buzzed. It was Cokie, asking if I had a moment to talk. I told her I would call her right back, walked out of the ballroom, and sat in an empty lobby at the Ritz Carlton in suburban Tyson's Corner, Virginia. Cokie was having "a moment," a bad one, and was in tears. My job, as she once told David, was to say, "Poor baby." There are times when you just offer sympathy — "You poor baby!" — and after that, you try to make the poor baby laugh. That's what I did that night. For at least twenty minutes, I sympathized and then pivoted to funny stories until Cokie finally said, "Okay, I feel much better."

Cokie did last for three years after her diagnosis, managing for most of that time to remain relatively stable, and hiding just how affected she was by the disease. But that started to change early in 2019. I'd known for several months that her health was getting worse, largely because she wasn't eating, and she was losing weight. She simply couldn't hold down much food. We brought her the best-tasting liquid nutrition that we could find, tried to figure out ways that she could keep down supplements, anything to help. But I still couldn't process that she wouldn't pull through. In retrospect, I guess the lucky thing for Linda and me is that we had as much time as we did to prepare for her death. We had more of those special evenings at the movies where it was just the three of us, and our husbands.

Then too, her illness had lasted so long that I talked myself into thinking she might survive. I knew that Cokie was exhausted, a lot, but so many times she picked herself up and did a speech — like the one she gave at the National Archives for the Fourth of July. It was almost impossible to imagine someone who was that ill being able to rally herself. But she did. She was very much like Ruth that way.

Cokie was also still doing her Monday morning live slot on NPR's *Morning Edition.* But in August, Steve Inskeep, one of the hosts, pulled me into his office. He asked point-blank, "What is going on?" I told him that this was not my story to tell. He said that morning they had needed to do a retake of the interview, and it ended up okay, but clearly there was something wrong. My answer was, "Just do what you can."

The first time I fully realized how close to death she was came the last time we met for our standing three-couple movie date, about ten days before she died. As I was riding down the escalator, I saw Cokie, but I didn't recognize her. Her back was to me, and I could only see Linda's face. I thought, "Who is that talking to Linda?" My eyes are not great, and I was only looking at her general outline from behind. But the woman I saw was so thin and not standing the way that Cokie typically stood, and her hair didn't look like Cokie's because for the first time, she was wearing a wig. Only as I drew closer did I realize, "Oh, my God, it's Cokie." At that moment, I knew we really didn't have long. She made it through a short dinner, we laughed a lot, but she hardly touched a thing on her plate.

By Thursday, she was back in the hospital, had been given a blood transfusion, and she sounded great, much more like her old self. I thought, "Maybe we have a stay of execution." But on Monday, I got the call that she had taken a turn for the worse, and I knew I had to see her. By the time I arrived — it took me forever to get inside the Naval Hospital in Bethesda — it was 11:30 p.m., and she was no longer conscious; I didn't know for sure if she could hear me at all. The nurses had placed her wig on her little bald head, but it wasn't really on her head. It was just perched on top of it, and she had tubes all over. Her eyes were half slits. I pulled a chair close, held her hand, and talked to her. She died just hours later, at 5:00 a.m., surrounded by her family.

Soon after, I went into the NPR office and wrote my remembrance. It came out in a flood, a torrent of the details that stood out in that one terrible moment. Cokie, I wrote, "was the embodiment of our better angels — whether it was her work for Save the Children or the millions of kindnesses large and small that she dispensed daily, without ever thinking that what she was doing was unusual or remarkable.

The country knew her as this always polite political reporter, willing to ask the impolitic question if necessary — this funny, wise, smart woman, who could write circles around most reporters. For the past three years, as she battled the return of a cancer vanquished some fourteen years earlier, she carried on, always with that infectious laugh. She gave speeches, appeared on TV and radio, and even called me a few days ago from the hospital to get a "fill" on my reporting about the new NPR president. Indeed, she was planning to go to Houston for the debates . . . until her disease finally trumped her grit.

She didn't want people to know she was

sick. She loved life and she was determined to live it as long as she could. And that meant doing what she always did, including being a super wife, mother, and grandmother. There was not a chance she was going to cancel commitments, no matter how rotten she felt. There was not a chance she would just lie in bed.

To know Cokie was to see the personification of human decency. There is a reason she was asked to speak at so many funerals. People felt such a deep connection to her because she touched their lives. Casual friends would find Cokie visiting them in the hospital. People in terrible financial straits would find her bailing them out, hiring them for work that perhaps she did not need, but work that left them with their dignity . . .

On a larger scale, she was always the voice of people with less power, and the voice of what is right. I remember one day many years ago, when we were in negotiations with NPR management over a labor contract. Management didn't want to extend health care coverage to one group, and we were at an impasse. Then Cokie, who was working on a piece of embroidery, looked up at the management team and said, "You know, the position you are taking isn't immoral, it is simply amoral." The room got very quiet, and soon the impasse was over.

And of course, she was the voice of women. She understood injustices large and small. She understood the hurdles that blue-, pink-, and white-collar women face — in raising and providing for a family, in dealing with husbands and bosses. She understood the whole balance of life.

If she were still with us, I'm confident Cokie could tell a whole bunch of stories for this book that I don't remember. Cokie and Linda and I saw each other through all kinds of things — things which, especially when you are young, you can't see in context, and have no idea how they will turn out. The two of them were always there to catch my fall, and I learned to be there to catch theirs. I think they both taught me how to do that. I am without a doubt a better person because of their friendships.

Even as Cokie was dying, Ruth was determined to make up the appearances she had had to cancel six months earlier. One of the postponed events was at the Berkeley School of Law in California, where she was to give the inaugural Herma Hill Kay Memorial

Lecture. Kay taught at Berkeley for fifty-seven years and had been the law school's first woman dean. She had also been an instrumental part of Ruth's career. The two were coauthors of the first-ever casebook on sex-based discrimination. More than that, they were very good friends until Kay's death in 2017.

Ruth made it clear from the first words of her memorial lecture that she was throwing down the gauntlet to force the completion of Herma Hill Kay's last major effort: a book on the first female tenure-track professors at accredited law schools in the United States. There were fourteen of them, most in the first part of the twentieth century, after women got the vote. Kay would have been the fifteenth, but with her typical modesty, she didn't include herself. So Ruth did, focusing on Kay in the introduction she wrote for the book. And then, in her lecture, she did it again, noting that she had written that introduction in 2015, and the book remained unpublished. She was sure, she said pointedly, that the Berkeley law faculty would now be pushing "to correct that error."

After the lecture, Ruth sat for an hour-long question-and-answer session with Amanda Tyler, one of her former law clerks, who was now teaching at Berkeley. Amanda and the Berkeley dean, Erwin Chemerinsky, thought they could make a book out of her Q & A exchange, intermixed with some of Ruth's favorite opinions. But Ruth would give permission only if Herma Hill Kay's book was published as well. First the carrot and then the stick. That was a lesson she learned early in life from Professor Gerald Gunther, who helped get her a clerkship when no judge wanted to hire her because she was a woman and a mother. Now, frail as she was, she was going to use her leverage to do one more thing on behalf of Herma Hill Kay. No matter how much it cost her physically, and it did cost her.

Behind the scenes, Amanda saw how depleted Ruth was, but when her former boss took the stage, she drew from some hidden reservoir and gave another exceptional performance. During the question-and-answer session, Ruth also talked about how she approached life following Marty's cancer diagnosis. In that moment, everyone likely understood that she was speaking for herself in the here and now as well. "We just took each day as it came," she said. "After those few hard months, I decided that whatever came my way, I could handle it. If you've survived cancer, you have a zest for life you didn't have before. You count each day as a blessing."

In the days and months ahead, I kept thinking, "C'mon, Ruth, you can do it, you can do it." But I was enough of a realist that I would also wake every morning worrying about her.

SIXTEEN: FINDING MY FATHER'S LONG-LOST FRIEND

The summer of 2015 was a very good summer inside a very good year. Ruth and Cokie were healthy. Political strife was, compared to today, contained; the fault lines were manageable. Something else happened that summer, something truly unexpected and extraordinary. My sisters and I had a chance to reconnect with a very important piece of our father and his past. His stolen Stradivarius violin.

Roman Totenberg had been a virtuoso violinist for most of his 101 years when he died in 2012. He made his debut with the Warsaw Philharmonic at the age of eleven and played his last recital when he was ninety-three. After that he continued teaching until just a few weeks before his death. He was a force, onstage and off. When he was ninety, and in the hospital, the medical team urged him to consider signing end-of-life orders. When Amy, Jill, and I arrived that morning, he was in a temper, telling us, "They're trying to kill me. You need to get me out of here." He played a concert four weeks later, and he lived another eleven years.

When he was ninety-something, he made plans with the Boston University School of Music dean to have lunch outside of the school. The dean offered to have a car pick him up. But Mr. T, as he was known, would have none of it, saying, "Don't be silly, I will pick you up." At my father's memorial service the dean did confess that he feared for his life that day: my father was a rather aggressive driver, even at that age, often complaining about "the shrivel" in front of him who was driving too slowly. By "shrivel," he meant an old person, which he did not consider himself to be.

In his final months, he had to have round-the-clock care, but he had no desire to die. We were terrified to even mention the word "hospice" to him. And frail as he was, he continued to teach, and practice. During the last week of his life, as his kidneys began shutting down and he was confined to bed, word got out that the end was near and former students arrived from around the country to visit for one last time. (We had to discourage those from around the world because we feared that by the time they arrived, he might have died.)

He was increasingly weak in his last days, so when his former students walked into his bedroom, he usually had just three words for them: "Play for me." And play they did for their beloved Mr. T, sometimes for hours. My father would listen, with his eyes closed, marking the tempo of the music with one hand. At one point during a movement of the Brahms violin concerto, he commented that the D "was flat." At another point, he showed his former student Daniel Han, by then a member of the Philadelphia Orchestra, how to do some fingering with the violin strings. And when his former student Mira Wang, herself now an accomplished soloist, began to play, Mr. T had just one word at the end of each piece: "More."

The only major unresolved portion of his life was his Stradivarius violin, stolen after a concert in Cambridge, Massachusetts, thirty-two years earlier. In the musical world, Antonio Stradivari was and is considered the greatest violin maker of all time. For decades, my father had played that violin all over the world. And then, one day he turned around, and it was gone.

It was a crushing loss. As he put it at the

time, he had lost his "musical partner of thirty-eight years."

Although he would ultimately buy a Guarneri violin, dating from the same period as the Stradivarius, the new instrument was much smaller and required him to rework the delicate fingering of his entire repertoire. The silver lining, I suppose, was that the more petite Guarneri was easier to play.

My father was a strong man. He moved on from his loss; an object was not the same as a person, as he knew well, having lost so many family members and friends in the Holocaust. But he still longed for that violin. For years, he would dream of opening his violin case and seeing the Strad returned, but he never laid eyes on it again. People used to ask him, "Professor Totenberg, do you think they'll ever find your violin?" His response was always "Not as long as I'm alive. After I kick the bucket, maybe." Indeed, we all believed that the Stradivarius lived on — somewhere.

My father had been dead for three years when I got a call in late June 2015 from FBI Special Agent Christopher McKeogh. Actually, my answering machine got the call, and David called me at work, waiting until after deadline because it was a Court opinion day.

"Oh pooh," I said. "It's just the Bureau doing a security check on some former intern." But David said the call was from the FBI's Art Theft Team. Later that night, we sat on our front porch with some neighbors wondering whether the call could possibly be about the violin. The next morning I called Agent McKeogh and heard him say, "We believe that the FBI has recovered your father's stolen violin."

My father had always suspected who had stolen the violin — a young aspiring violinist named Philip Johnson, who had been seen outside my father's office on the night the violin was stolen. In fact, he had even been questioned by the FBI. Soon afterwards, Johnson's ex-girlfriend told my father that she was quite sure Johnson had taken it. Law enforcement officials believed, however, that there was not enough evidence to request a search warrant. My mother was so frustrated that she famously would ask friends if they knew anyone in the mob willing to break into an apartment and search for a violin. Philip Johnson eventually moved to California, had an undistinguished musical career, and died of cancer at age fifty-eight, a year before my father died.

Fast-forward four years. Johnson's ex-wife and her boyfriend were cleaning the house, and they came across a violin case that her former husband had left to her. It had a combination lock on it. They broke the lock and opened the case to find a violin with a label inside, which said the instrument was made in 1734 by Antonio Stradivari in the city of Cremona, Italy.

A musician friend put her in touch with violin maker and appraiser Phillip Injeian in Pittsburgh. As he would later tell me in an interview, "Of course I hear almost every day from people telling me that they found a Stradivarius in the attic." That's because, while there are only about 550 Stradivarius violins in existence today, there are thousands and thousands of violins that have a "Stradivarius" label stamped inside them — some of them good copies, and most just cheap imitations. So Injeian suggested the ex-wife send him photographs rather than waste a trip to the East.

The photos she sent looked "remarkably good," the appraiser said, after looking up violins made in 1734 in the *Violin Iconography of Antonio Stradivari,* the compilation of all Stradivarius instruments known to exist. There he saw that a famous violin belonging to violinist Roman Totenberg had been stolen and never recovered. It was known as the "Ames Stradivarius," after violinist George Ames, who performed on it in the late 1800s. Soon the appraiser and the ex-wife agreed to meet in New York. And on June 26, Injeian went to her hotel.

Injeian opened the case, looked at the instrument, and examined it. He told her, "Well, I've got good news for you, and I've got bad news for you. The good news is that this is a Stradivarius. The bad news is it was stolen thirty-five, thirty-six years ago from Roman Totenberg." And, he added, as he pulled out his cellphone, "I have to call the FBI right now."

Within two hours Special Agents McKeogh and John Iannuzzi from the FBI's Art Theft Team were at the hotel. En route, they had pulled up old photos of the Ames Stradivarius on their cellphones, along with its measurements to the millimeter. And once at the hotel, as Injeian measured the instrument, he called out the numbers, while the agents checked them against those listed for the Ames Strad.

They matched exactly.

It was an incredible case of "one-stop shopping," as McKeogh put it. The stolen violin, the person who possessed it, and the expert appraiser were all there. The next day McKeogh told me, "I have probably never been so excited to come to work as I was [that] morning, simply because I couldn't wait to see the instrument again." But the FBI's case wasn't closed. The instrument had to be authenticated again, and that was part of the reason he was calling me.

My first response, after all these years, was total skepticism. "Are you sure?" I kept asking. He told me the violin had already been appraised once and was going to be appraised again, but asked, "Is there anything else you can tell me about it?" I told him I knew one thing; the violin had mother-of-pearl-inlaid tuning pegs.

I could almost hear him smiling as he said, "Well, sitting right here on my desk is one of the most beautiful things I've ever had in my hands, and it has mother-of-pearl tuning pegs." My heart started to beat faster. McKeogh told me he didn't think there was any doubt that it was my father's violin, but he asked me not to tell anyone else yet. I began peppering him with questions: Who stole it? How did you get it back? And he answered, "Well, we want to see what we can verify about this, so I can't tell you much yet." He also emphasized that he didn't want anyone to know. But of course,

I told him I had to tell my sisters.

The first person I called was Amy, only to learn from her husband, Ralph, that she was out running. "Tell her to call me back the minute she walks in, right away, and it's not bad news." She called maybe twenty minutes later, and we got my sister Jill on the phone. "I have news, unbelievable news. Sit down. The FBI called me. They found Daddy's violin."

There was this moment of dead silence followed by a gasp, then laughter, and then all three of us were crying and laughing. We didn't want to get off the phone. We just talked and laughed and cried and then I began thinking about how to handle this. What do we do?

My mind was racing with theories. Maybe it had been stolen by the mob, but then they couldn't sell it — not unlike a popular theory of what happened to the fabulous paintings stolen from the Isabella Stewart Gardner Museum in Boston in 1990. At one point, somebody had in fact offered to sell the violin back to my father. The insurance representative came to Boston with $25,000 in cash packed in a suitcase to meet the caller, who never showed.

Agent McKeogh was looking for more information about the actual theft, so I started working to track down the contact information for my father's former assistant, who had been there the night the violin was taken. She knew everything about that period. Remember, this was thirty-five years earlier. She was only in her mid-twenties when she had worked for my father, but he thought she was terrific. And when I found her, all these years later, she remembered everything. She recounted the whole story, I took detailed notes, and then I read those notes back to McKeogh. That's when he told me that the violin had been stolen by Philip Johnson. The final irony was that my father had once risen to Johnson's defense when other members on a musical jury wanted to give him a low grade. The FBI concluded that Johnson had stolen the violin, believing that it would help him play better. Certainly, a good violinist can play better on a very good violin, but that is hardly enough.

My seven-minute radio version of the story (https://www.npr.org/2015/08/06/427718240/ a-rarity-reclaimed-stolen-stradivarius-recovered-after-35-years) was neat and clean, ready for a fast-paced, happy reunification. But it was actually a bit more complicated than that. The ex-wife wanted to make a claim that the violin was hers. I immediately realized that my sisters and I needed a lawyer, and fortunately my friend Jamie Gorelick offered up Sharon Levin, a newly recruited lawyer at the firm of WilmerHale, who for years had been the Justice Department lawyer overseeing art theft cases. After several conversations, including with the U.S. Attorney's Office, it was made clear to Johnson's ex-wife that if she made the claim, she would be subject to a charge of fraud. So she relinquished the violin.

Still, it wasn't automatically returned to us. Because it had been insured, and the insurer had paid out its value at the time of the theft, we had to pay back that amount to the insurance company, which by then was in receivership. The dollar amount was paltry compared to the violin's current value, but I still had to write the largest check of my life, and then lovingly inform my sisters that they each now owed me one third of the amount, and if they left the country without paying, there would be a reckoning worthy of *NCIS*.

This was a major recovery, and the FBI and the U.S. attorney wanted some attention for it. There would be a full press conference and a very public announcement.

Of course, I am a reporter, so I was damned determined to make sure that I had the exclusive on this story. Nobody else was going to get it first. The U.S. Attorney's Office agreed to hold its press release until 10:00 a.m., after the required court filing, to ensure that I could get my piece on NPR's *Morning Edition* first. I spent several days writing the piece. I sat at my desk with all of my father's recordings, weeping, trying to figure out which pieces of music worked best.

My sister Jill, who is a fabulous PR person, also flew into action, devising a strategy in which she could alert select publications that something big was afoot but have them embargo any mention until the event. Everything was embargoed, and miraculously, the embargo held.

Even I, who recognize a big story, never imagined the coverage we would get. To this day, listeners remember this piece more than anything else that I have done, including the Anita Hill story. They have forgotten that I broke that story, but they remember "the violin story." People would come up to Cokie or Linda in the supermarket and say, "Please tell Nina we're so happy about the violin." And Ruth, who really loved my father, was over the moon.

Even as the piece aired, Amy, Jill, and I were in New York for the unveiling at the U.S. Attorney's Office in Lower Manhattan. It was August 6, and about five weeks had passed since that first FBI phone call. No one I've talked to has ever heard of a piece of property being turned over from the Justice Department to a private individual so quickly. Thank you, Jamie Gorelick and Sharon Levin.

The day before we converged on Manhattan to reclaim the violin, we realized that the one thing missing was the instrument's provenance, its record of ownership from the time it was made. We had searched for it everywhere, including in the list of my father's papers at the Library of Congress. Finally, I called Bruno Price, one of the partners at Rare Violins of New York, which had handled the sale of my father's Guarneri after his death. All three of us were on the phone as I said, "Bruno, do you by any chance have the provenance for my father's Strad?" And he replied, "It's sitting in my vault."

"Are you sitting down?" I asked. And then I told him the news, which was followed by the now usual response: silence, laughter, tears. "The provenance has been waiting all this time," he told us. It turned out that

Amy had given it to him for safekeeping when we were packing up my father's house and sending stuff to the Library of Congress. She had just forgotten.

At the U.S. Attorney's Office, the press conference was enormous. I've never seen so many cameras squished into one room, except maybe when Robert F. Kennedy announced that he was running for the presidency. Beforehand, Preet Bharara, the U.S. attorney, took us backstage, so to speak, into the library. And I do have to say that I have never seen so many high-ranking representatives of every law enforcement agency you could imagine, each seeking some credit for the recovery of the violin. The most dashing was an NYPD policeman in by far the most dapper attire, or maybe it was that he was just the most buff.

On the table at center of the room was the violin. It was missing its strings, so it looked a little naked. But it was truly wonderful to see the old girl again. Even after years of neglect, it was such a beautiful instrument. For nearly three hundred years, it had maintained that breathtaking beauty, and its incredible varnish. The three of us also marveled at how much it felt like a living thing. It felt like Daddy was with us again, along with Mommy. (Sorry if this sounds silly. It's still what we call them.)

Then we walked out to meet the press. Jill, Amy, and I each spoke. U.S. Attorney Bharara followed, saying, "It's nice to return something of great value to a family or a country or an institution," adding that these "are moments of celebration that we don't have that often here."

With the media frenzy behind us, we decided to go out for lunch, but as we were preparing to walk out of the building, we realized that Bruno was going to take the instrument back to his shop to begin the restoration. He had come by subway, and he was about to get on the subway with this multimillion-dollar violin. I turned to Agent McKeogh and asked, "Can you take him back to his office?"

"Oh, yes we'll do that," he assured us. And presto, a big SUV appeared to transport Bruno and the magnificent fiddle.

By now it was nearly two o'clock, and it was getting hard to find a place to eat. My cousin Elzunia, who had lived through the Holocaust as a toddler, was with us. She was the young woman spirited out of Poland by my father when she was about nineteen. She had lived with us initially as something between a sister and an aunt. Now the four of us found a mostly empty hole-in-the-wall restaurant and slipped into a booth. Elzunia had brought shot glasses and a bottle of Bison Polish vodka, my father's favorite. He would sip a shot before dinner each night, or on his way out the door before a concert. When we buried him, we toasted him from a similar bottle, and then poured the remains onto the grave site where his ashes are buried with my mother's.

But on this afternoon, as we raised a glass to Roman Totenberg, the restaurant manager thought he was being shortchanged and demanded to know if we were drinking liquor. "Oh, no, no," we all answered, as Elzunia sneaked the bottle back into her tote bag.

The rest of the day, two stories led the news: my father's violin and Donald Trump's first presidential debate. Every station seemed to toggle back and forth between the two. Amy, Jill, and I spent the next day in New York, and after an early dinner, we left Jill in Manhattan and flew back to our homes, I to DC and Amy to Atlanta.

When I got home, David opened the door and said, "You can't imagine what you look like. You look just elated." In a very real sense, the father I knew and loved for so many years was back in my head. Instead of the fading father of his last year, the father who I worried would become a lesser version of himself, my father was fully restored in my memory, the father of his youthful eighties who could still dance the lively *kozatsky.*

When that violin reappeared, it felt like part of the family had been returned to us, that in some way my sisters and I had our father *and* our mother back. I could see the whole arc of Roman Totenberg, an incredible human being who lived for more than a century. And there too was my mother, who supported everything he did in every way, and who presided over all of us, loving us, and teaching by example. It was a wonderful coda to everything that had happened, a second joyful celebration of his life and hers.

Our plan for the Stradivarius was to have it carefully restored. Philip Johnson knew that he could not take the violin to a dealer for needed maintenance because it would have been instantly recognized. So the Strad needed some work, and it would take Rare Violins of New York quite a while to complete the job. Ultimately, it was sold to an anonymous donor who, in a plan worked out with Rare Violins, lent the violin to a wonderful young violinist named Nathan Meltzer. He played it with great success for a little over a year, but Covid-19 intervened, the benefactor decided to liquidate his assets, and the violin was sold again, remaining silent during the pandemic. Rare Violins did not immediately share the name of the new owner. As Ruth would have said, we expect that error to be corrected so we can once again hear the soaring sound of the Ames-Totenberg Strad.

Stradivarius owners, of course, are really only guardians of these great artistic instruments. We hope that in the future, the violin will be in the hands of another virtuoso so that the beautiful, brilliant, and throaty voice of that long-stilled Strad will once again thrill audiences in concert halls around the world.

Seventeen: Farewell to My Friend

We are all going to die. I had watched my mother go, then Floyd, then, after a hiatus, my father, Cokie, and so many others. I have, after all these years, a funeral attire section in my closet. But for the final year of Ruth's life, I want to focus on just that: her life. Because even with a slew of health indignities and a global pandemic, Ruth embraced life until the very end. So, we let the end sit off in the distance, like a fog-shrouded point, out of view from the shore.

Ruth ensured that she had fulfilled her outstanding obligations in the fall of 2019. In January 2020, in an interview with CNN's Joan Biskupic, she declared herself "cancer free. That's good." Joan added that Ruth was "sounding energized and speaking animatedly." And she was. The Court calendar was busy. Across the street, the House and Senate were taking up the first impeachment trial of Donald Trump.

Rooms were packed, people traveled. It was a very different world.

We didn't know it then, but January 2020 was a reprieve — for Ruth, for all of us. As for so many people from all walks of life, what came next would deepen friendships in profound and powerful ways.

As close as Ruth and I were, and as often as we were together in professional and social contexts, there was a distinct limit to our private time together. Much of that stemmed from the demanding nature of our respective jobs. It had taken me years to recognize the type of friendship we could have; it took until Marty's illness for me to fully appreciate that she might need me, really need me, as a friend. And it took a pandemic for me to truly understand what that friendship meant, to both of us.

Once Covid-19 hit and Washington went into lockdown in March 2020, our house became her only refuge outside her apartment. Every Saturday, almost without fail, she came for dinner. If Jane or James and their spouses, George and Patrice, or her granddaughter, Clara, were in town, she brought them too, everyone always pretested. On one occasion relatively early on, I asked if Clara would be joining us for dinner, and Ruth answered that it would be Clara; her husband, Rory; and "the dog, Wallace." After that, we used to tease her and ask if "the dog, Wallace," was coming, a reminder that Wallace, sadly for him, had no rights under the Fourteenth Amendment by virtue of being a canine.

Wallace, a poodle mix of unknown heritage, is the calmest dog I've ever known. He is also a real sweetheart — and was very happy waiting for crumbs under the table with our own Connie Mack, named after both the baseball manager and old Philadelphia stadium, and who is also a very chill dog. Wallace was not initially in Ruth's good graces, especially after he peed on her bed, a crime that Ruth forgave him for only when he became a visitor-fixture during the pandemic.

The truth was that Ruth, having lived in New York for much of her life, was not a dog person. We always told Connie Mack, a twenty-two-pound West Highland terrier, to give her a wide berth because we understood that. But the last time Ruth ate at our house, Ruth and Connie seemed to acknowledge that each had played a role in the other's life. Connie, a service dog, walked very deliberately over to Ruth's chair in the dining room, sat down, and looked up at her. And Ruth looked down and said, "You're a good dog, Connie Mack."

In some ways, Covid-19 extended Ruth's life. Without it, she would have been in much more danger because she would have been exposed to everybody all the time. She also would have tried to do more that she could have done. Instead, the demands on her just stopped. No one was traveling or giving speeches.

Why our house? Two reasons really. Ruth knew lots of people. Even during the pandemic, she would not have lacked for invitations. But she had known me long before she became famous. We had a different bond. She had also seen how protective we tried to be — David, in particular. And of course, for years he was her medical confidant, the person she called in times of need, so much so that she gave permission for her doctor to confer with him. They would, I learned after Ruth died, bounce around ideas and consider treatment options, and at different points console each other.

For David and for me, feeding Ruth was one of the great privileges of our lives together. He was the cook, always. Ruth was still a slow eater, and her various health issues also required a very specific diet. She couldn't have butter or fats or sugar. Meat was also not allowed. Ruth and I were at a prepandemic dinner once during her last year of life, and our hosts served meat. Ruth was hungry, and she ate it. It's not really possible to reach over to a Supreme Court justice and say, "You're not supposed to eat that," not out in public, so I didn't, much to my regret because Ruth was horribly sick afterwards.

Even in the past, when she had come for our anniversary dinner, cooked always by our friend Frederik DePue, a fabulous professional chef, he would prepare an alternative course if there was anything that wouldn't agree with Ruth's dicey stomach.

One pleasure she was still allowed was a glass of wine or champagne. And Ruth was serious about her wine. Once when David poured her a half serving in a large glass, she handed it right back and said, "This is not a full glass. I want my glass of wine," and she looked at him as if to say, "You've gravely disappointed me."

David prepared a medley of fish dishes for her, but Ruth's favorite was the classic bouillabaisse that he made, with some tweaks, following Julia Child's French cookbook recipe for the traditional fish stew. Periodically, I would leave a message on her answering machine, asking what she'd like for dinner — swordfish, shrimp, snapper, bouillabaisse? Hours later I'd check our answering machine, and this quiet but commanding voice would have replied, "Bouillabaisse, of course!"

To protect her, we would scrub every surface in the kitchen, bathroom, and dining room with antiviral liquids, and we put all the leaves in the dining room table so she and Jane or whomever could sit at one end, and we could sit at the other. After drinks in the living room, often with a roaring fire to keep her warm, she would sit at the table eating her beloved bouillabaisse oh so slowly, even on rare occasions asking for seconds.

No matter how weak she might feel, she never came to dinner looking frumpy. Never. Whether it was at our house, or in her apartment, she was consciously elegant. Typically, she would wear long flowing trousers, some sort of jacket or more often an elegant blouse or sweater with a large, warm shawl, and jewelry that ranged in style between Santa Fe and New York. The one thing that never varied was the ever-present scrunchie in her hair. She also always walked up our front stairs, though by summer one of her female security guards had her arm firmly around Ruth's waist. Ruth was hardwired not to be one of those "I don't care what I look like or how I present myself" people.

Until Covid-19, she did like to shop. Many Sunday afternoons before the pandemic, she combined her love of opera and shopping. She would go to a movie theater in DC to watch a matinee Metropolitan Opera performance from Lincoln Center. And during the half-hour intermission, she would go one floor down to Neiman Marcus.

For our dinners at home, in that last year and especially those last six months, I always tried to find some story or anecdote that would make her laugh. David's role was to cook and mine was to entertain. I hunted for good jokes too — because she really did like jokes. I'm not the best joke teller, so David would make me practice so I didn't ruin the punchline. And our friend Bob Taraschi, a talented artist, who came to live with us after his wife's long illness and death, could definitely make her laugh. At one point in his life, he wrote jokes for *Saturday Night Live.* Bob, by the way, is Connie Mack's father. I am her grandmother.

I also looked for gossip. Ruth was interested in Washington gossip — indeed any kind of gossip — and she knew plenty in return. Maybe my best find was some decidedly unlegal gossip about a Supreme Court religion case. A teacher at a Catholic school had been diagnosed with breast cancer. She had asked to take leave for her chemotherapy treatments and instead the school fired her. The case was a test of whether lay teachers at parochial schools were covered by the Americans with Disabilities Act. Unbeknownst to any of the justices, I think, *Esquire* magazine had previously written a story about the school and the nuns who ran it — particularly the two nuns who were in charge and had fired this woman. It turned out that they had embezzled a significant amount of money from the school and had spent weekends in Las Vegas gambling. I quoted a bit of the *Esquire* piece in my report before the case was heard, but I told Ruth the whole long backstory, which had been laid out in the article, including how parents eventually got wind of it and were furious. They demanded answers because it was their money that had been stolen, but they never got any real answers from the Church. The entire episode was a little reminiscent of the movie *Spotlight*. The archdiocese refused to discuss anything substantive with the parents, and then the two nuns abruptly left the parish.

I shared every lurid detail with Ruth, and it was an article with lots of lurid details. At each new turn of the tale, her eyes opened wider and wider, until at one point she actually squealed. She so enjoyed the saga that she made a crack about the embezzlement during the oral argument of the case.

In the beginning, I had conned myself into thinking that there was every reason to believe Ruth would survive this, if it were only lung cancer. But as the months rolled on, it became clear that this illness wasn't just lung cancer. It was a return of the old pancreatic cancer. I thought often about my mother's death. My father had died rather suddenly, but I knew how my mother had suffered when five years after her surgery for lung cancer, we learned the cancer had reappeared, metastasized in her brain.

Being married to a doctor who has seen the worst and can be the voice of doom has pushed me to always hope for the best. But at some point, I had to accept that there was going to be an end, and that I needed to prize every one of these moments. Because Ruth was a very internalized person, I hadn't understood until I was quite a bit older how close we had become; it was so gradual. But now I knew. She had chosen me, us. These choices were largely unspoken. Ruth really never entirely let her guard down. Even when Marty died, she was more stoic than I was, and probably more stoic than her kids were. She was always controlled. One time, as we were listening to a performance at the Kennedy Center by one of my father's former students, I somehow sensed that she was hearing the music and thinking of Marty. I never said a word, I just reached over and took her hand. She did not pull it away. Not all friendships have to be chatty confessionals. There is great power in the unsaid, in the simple knowing that comes after so many years. I knew that she was my friend, and anything I could do for her now I would do to make her life better.

For those final months, Ruth stuck to the routines that she had established throughout her life, modified for a pandemic. She came to see us for dinner, and the other nights, when she was in her apartment, she would watch livestreams of Metropolitan Opera performances on her iPad while she ate dinner. I walked in on her once in her dining room, saw her glued to the tiny screen, and it was clear that she was in another world.

That transport could not have happened for me — I need the live performance — but it certainly did for her.

And she worked. She kept up a furious pace through the June opinion season, even as her health declined. The summer did not provide the Court its usual break; instead, July was riddled with emergency applications, particularly for issues related to Covid-19, and she was feeling the strain. Because she was the senior liberal justice, she often had the responsibility for assigning dissents, and she gave Justice Sotomayor some of the responses that she would have written herself earlier in the year. At one point, she told me, "Poor Sonia. There are some things I can't do, and I'm loading too much stuff on her." This was a woman who was less than two months away from death, and she felt guilty that she could not maintain her expected pace. She was trying to survive, but at that point, she knew she was losing the battle. The question was how fast.

In 2005, I knew Chief Justice Rehnquist was dying. Not that Rehnquist told me anything, but I only had to look at him to know. I think everyone in the press corps knew something was not right. When the Supreme Court put out a statement that he had been diagnosed with thyroid cancer, and had a tracheostomy, it didn't take much to find out that a surgeon doesn't put in a tracheostomy under these circumstances unless it's a very rare and very serious cancer. David told me that Rehnquist couldn't live for more than a year and indeed, he didn't.

But with Ruth, the fade was more gradual, and her spirit remained so steadfast. She still wanted to come to our house. There were a couple of times near the end of July when I don't know how she made it up those six stairs. But she wanted to get out. We left open the option that we would bring dinner to her, and we did do that, but only a few times.

Again, colleagues would ask me, Do you know what's going on with her? And I'd answer, David may, but I don't, which was, of course, true. Even the women who worked at Neiman Marcus wanted to know. Everyone wanted to know, but at a certain point, I had to decide, as I had with Cokie, that it was Ruth's story to tell, not mine. Reporting had always stopped at our front door, and this time was no different, especially since my take was only observational, not factual.

Years before, I had been at a party when

an attorney general made some comments, off the cuff, which were big news, but which had not been meant that way. The AG had spoken before thinking. I didn't want to play gotcha from a night off. The next morning I called the Justice Department press office to follow up on what I'd heard. We found a compromise. I delayed reporting the story, but still got a scoop a short while later. In Ruth's case, reporters were free to ask questions, and the press office did provide technical updates on her treatments. What those press releases did not capture was something less clear, something that only a friend seeing her every week could observe, and at a time that the Supreme Court itself was meeting by telephone.

Underneath, of course, Ruth was still Ruth, and she was still determined to do the things that mattered to her. Among those things were . . . wait for it . . . weddings. As I wrote earlier, she loved performing weddings for friends and the children of friends.

The last wedding that she performed was for the son of Beth Horowitz, the internist who had taken such exquisite care of her. The ceremony was held in a small outdoor terraced area off Ruth's apartment at the Watergate on August 30, 2020. In the days leading up to the wedding, Ruth had been hospitalized at Johns Hopkins for another intestinal problem, and yet she was practically banging on the gate telling doctors, "Let me out of here, I have a wedding to officiate at in two days." They kept her another day, and then they caved. She came home and took a nap. Beth was not sure that Ruth would have the strength to get out of bed and come downstairs, she was so frail. But suddenly, quite a bit later than the appointed hour, there was Ruth, her thin legs carefully picking their way down the staircase. She was wearing proper shoes and her judicial robe, and her hair was pulled back in a scrunchie. With a wan but still radiant smile, she walked out and performed an absolutely beautiful wedding ceremony. I think everyone cried except for Ruth.

It was not just her doctors who kept Ruth alive that last year or years. It was her amazing assistant, Kim McKenzie, who was absolutely devoted to Ruth and worked morning, noon, night, and in between. During the pandemic, she would come to Ruth's apartment to work with her. Kim was the lioness at the gate, the protector, but once she knew that you were a friend, she let you in.

That said, there was no one more devoted to Ruth than her children, especially in that final year. Jane, who lived in New York City, basically decamped to Washington from March on. James came frequently from Chicago for the weekend, which meant he had to be tested for Covid-19 before making the roughly eleven-hour drive to Washington.

The only time I worried was in August, when David and I went to Cape Cod for what had become our annual monthlong vacation. Before I left, I rewrote Ruth's obituary and wrote my remembrance of her. The objective reporter in me said that I had to have everything ready, so that if she died, my written stories could be posted online immediately, and the tape-recorded versions could be on the radio — for the hourly newscasts, *All Things Considered,* and *Morning Edition.* That would give me time to fly back to DC. I had three cycles of stories prepared, one political about her and the politics of her passing. The second was her complete obituary. The third cycle was the remembrance. The whole time, I kept in touch with Ruth and Jane, and David also kept in touch with her doctor. But Ruth survived. The calendar turned to September, and we returned to DC.

After a brief hospitalization, Ruth was released on September 11, and we brought her dinner that weekend. It was the only time that she said to me, "I thought I was going to die. But I came home." And then in her very soft, resolute voice, she added, "And I'm not going to die." The day before, she had even participated by phone in the Court's private conference to discuss the long list of cases that had accumulated over the summer, cases in which the losing side was seeking a review. To anyone who heard her, Ruth's voice sounded the same.

But it was clear from the moment that we arrived that she was even more frail and tired than usual. She was sitting at the table in a beautiful bathrobe, a blue pattern on pale white, which looked like one of her scarves. We brought David's bouillabaisse, and she kept falling asleep, still holding her fork in her hand. Jane would try to take the fork away and she would say, "No, I want to finish my bouillabaisse." And then she'd eat a few more bites and start to nod off again. Finally, I said to her, "Ruth, you're too tired. We'll save your bouillabaisse for you. You can have it for lunch tomorrow. Go upstairs and go to bed." Then David walked her upstairs. That was the last time I saw her. I talked to her once after that, just days later, when it was clear she was dying. By then, she had lost the ability to speak. Jane put the phone to her ear, and I just talked, telling my darling friend goodbye and how much I loved her. When Jane took the phone back, I told her I wasn't sure if her mother had heard me. "Oh yes, she heard you," Jane answered. She had raised her left hand, the hand she wrote with, like a wave.

On Friday, September 18, as the day was closing and the Jewish holiday of Rosh Hashanah was beginning at sundown, Ruth left this earth, surrounded by her family, with James holding her in his arms.

Jane called to let me know and told me the Court would be making the official announcement soon. She asked me to wait for the Court press release, and I did. This was not news that I needed to break. Thinking that none of her family had eaten, David and I packed up a box of food and dropped it off at Ruth's apartment. Beth Horowitz, her doctor, was there too, looking beyond wiped out.

The next morning, I wrote on Twitter, "A Jewish teaching says those who die just before the Jewish new year are the ones God has held back until the last moment bc they were needed most & were the most righteous. And so it was that #RBG died as the sun was setting last night marking the beginning of Rosh Hashanah."

It really is impossible to cry and drink water at the same time. I learned that from the businesswoman and philanthropist Adrienne Arsht after Floyd died. I had been stoic for nearly five years of illness, was back on the air and appearing on TV the week after his death. I spoke at his funeral and practiced every word to hold it together. Then, while I was giving a little talk to maybe a hundred young women at Radcliffe College, I started to talk about Floyd, and I began to cry, and could not stop. I told Adrienne about it later, and she said if that ever happens to you again just grab a glass of water because you physically cannot keep crying and drink water at the same time. It works, but I did not take any water with me to Ruth's burial. And I cried the entire time. Buckets and buckets of silent tears.

I had accumulated so many pieces of Ruth over the years, but Jane wanted David and me to have a few more wonderful reminders of our friend. She gave David Marty's party-size paella pan and possibly the world's largest cleaver, as well as a cast-iron skillet that I'm sure we will pass down to someone else when the time comes. For me, the gift was one of Ruth's favorite necklaces that she wore often as well as some of the collars she wore with her robes, a beautiful scarf, and a pair of her crocheted gloves

I wear the necklace whenever I am feeling stupid, and think I need a dose of brains to help me write.

These bits of Ruth are scattered through the house. Even our basement still has three unopened bottles of Campari that David bought at some point because Campari and soda was Ruth's predinner cocktail of choice in the years when her liquor intake was not curbed for medical reasons. Alas, she was the only one who drank it.

And of course, there are the photos. It is as if the house expects her to come back. As if I do.

EPILOGUE

The Supreme Court's authority is derived, in large part, from the strong voices of its justices. But Ruth's voice, on and off the Court was unique and uniquely powerful, especially for women.

Ruth's mark was so great that she had two services and lay in repose at the Supreme Court and in state at the U.S. Capitol. The first service was for the Court, staff, family, and a few friends. The second was at the Capitol, with much of the pomp normally accorded a president. Presiding at all of these events was Rabbi Lauren Holtzblatt, whose husband, Ari, had been one of Ruth's 159 clerks during her more than forty years on both the Supreme Court and the DC Circuit.

Chief Justice John Roberts eulogized her at the Court ceremony attended by her fellow justices, offering condolences to her children and grandchildren, but reminding everyone that "the Court was her family, too. This building was her home, too."

Outside the Supreme Court Building, a makeshift memorial of thousands of bouquets of flowers, candles, notes, and small items spread like a great carpet flowing down the steps to the sidewalk beyond. It was as if the tributes were laying a beautiful path for a true pathbreaker, one final time.

Despite Covid-19 infections and still no vaccines, for two days the line of people waiting to pay their final respects at the Court building reached back to the National Mall. Many wept. Then on Friday, Ruth's casket was moved into the Capitol, to lie in state. The thirty-three men who had preceded her in receiving this honor included everyone from Abraham Lincoln to Ronald Reagan civil rights icon John Lewis. Three days of viewing had been chosen because it quickly became clear that one day would never be enough to accommodate the large crowds. Yet even this recognition could not be accomplished without partisan drama.

The original request had been for Ruth's casket to be placed in the Rotunda, the soaring space between the House and Senate chambers. But Mitch McConnell, then the Senate majority leader, declined the request. So instead, House Speaker Nancy

Pelosi authorized Ruth's casket to lie in state in Statuary Hall, which is the domain of the House of Representatives. Due to Covid-19, only invited guests were able to pay their respects inside the Capitol. One of those was Ruth's personal trainer, Bryant Johnson, who dropped to the floor to honor her with a final set of push-ups.

The following week, she was buried with full honors at Arlington National Cemetery, beside Marty.

Ruth's last wish, dictated to her granddaughter, Clara Spera, was that no one be appointed to fill her position until after the rapidly approaching November election. That, of course, was not to be. Before she was even laid to rest, President Trump nominated conservative jurist Amy Coney Barrett, who was quickly confirmed by a Republican-controlled Senate.

Despite the various labels attached to RBG's name during her years on the Court, she was, in a very pragmatic sense, quick at assessing what she could get done and what she couldn't. For much of her tenure, there were five conservative or fairly conservative votes on the Court. And yet, the more liberal interpretations of the law and the Constitution prevailed at key moments. Ruth's side kept winning cases that many observers thought were unwinnable. Some were high-profile cases, like upholding the Affordable Care Act for health insurance, in which Chief Justice Roberts made the difference. Others were less high profile, like Ruth's decision upholding an Arizona referendum that established a nonpartisan redistricting commission to draw new legislative district lines after the census every ten years. She told me during an interview in 2015 that one way she was able to be persuasive on the bench was that the conservatives were often divided over their approach. Ruth may have been known for her fierce but restrained dissents, but she never overlooked the need for common ground and consensus if it was possible.

That said, today's Court is very different from the one she sat on. With Republicans having blocked any consideration of President Obama's nominee when Justice Scalia died, and with Trump having named three very conservative justices, the conservative majority is 6 to 3, and the liberals are watching helplessly as decades of precedents are being dismantled.

Even more is at stake than is immediately apparent. I think often of Justice Brennan's philosophy of how to achieve consensus on the Court, particularly his view of the give-

and-take among justices. I have long regarded his approach as the most constructive way to engage in opinion writing. It aims to collaborate, not to clobber. Both the leak of Justice Alito's draft opinion in the 2022 abortion case and the language used in the draft itself represent the antithesis of Justice Brennan's approach. The unprecedented disclosure of the Court's internal deliberations is surely shocking, and Ruth would have been appalled by such a breach, as is the case with other members of the Court who have spoken publicly. But for the future of the Court — and the institution that Ruth and so many others have revered — there is more than the actual leak to worry about.

The leak seemed to pull back the curtain on long-simmering tensions inside the Marble Palace, as the Court is sometimes known. In a May 2022 appearance in Dallas, Justice Clarence Thomas, who for years has made a practice of saying how much he admires and respects his colleagues, implied that he now trusts no one. While he spoke fondly and respectfully of his one-time pro-choice colleagues, Justices Ginsburg and O'Connor, he had no similar praise for his current liberal colleagues. And while he spoke with affection and respect for the late

Chief Justice Rehnquist, he had no words at all for the current chief, John Roberts, with whom he has served for seventeen years.

Even some of the Court's longest-held traditions are being summarily dismantled. In modern times, justices who feel particularly strongly that the Court has erred do, on occasion, dissent orally from the bench to underline, in public, their strong disagreement. The late Justice Scalia felt so strongly about this tradition that he dissented orally in one case because there had been no oral dissent that term, and he thought it important to preserve the practice. But in the wake of the Dobbs case leak in the spring of 2022, none of that sense of tradition seemed to remain when the liberal justices wanted to orally dissent from the bench. There was, of course, an excuse, of sorts. With oral arguments over, and security fences erected in the wake of the leak, the Court was officially closed, and opening it up to the Court's small press corps required a vote. The justices may or may not have held a formal vote, but the result was that no oral dissents from the bench were permitted.

While the human dynamics of the Court are deeply affected by the leak, at risk too is the entire concept of legal precedent, the concept of building established law, one brick at a time, and respecting that law as having been "settled." Among the conservative justices, Alito at his confirmation hearings, as well as Justices Kavanaugh and Gorsuch, professed great respect for precedent. Indeed, respecting precedent has long been seen as a major cornerstone of our legal system. People in all walks of life rely upon precedents to make decisions in business, policy, and their personal lives. The importance of precedent explains why the reaction to the leaked Alito draft opinion has been such a double shock. The opinion's tone is the opposite of Brennan's approach. It is not an attempt to persuade and respectfully pull together a majority under one tent. It is score-settling, angry, and bitter in its language.

If Ruth were still alive, she would be white-faced with fury at Alito's attempt to enlist her nuanced legal writing in a *New York University Law Review* article thirty years ago to support his argument. She did not agree with him at all about *Roe v. Wade.* And he knows that perfectly well. She was fervent in her support of a woman's right to determine when and if she will have children. So too was Justice O'Connor, who was privately troubled by Alito's appointment to the Court, in part because of a position he had taken as an appeals court judge in 1991 in another reproductive rights case, *Planned Parenthood v. Casey*. Among other provisions, the Pennsylvania state law at issue required a woman seeking an abortion to declare, in writing, that she had notified her husband of her planned abortion. Alito, then an appeals court judge, supported this restriction, arguing in his opinion that there was no "proof" of how many women "are victims of battering" and would be "harmed" by having to tell their husbands.

In her portion of the Supreme Court's subsequent decision in the case, O'Connor directly rebutted Alito, citing numerous studies of domestic violence and abuse. Noting that 11,000 women were victims of domestic violence each day (that number has grown in the decades since), she concluded that the "mere notification of pregnancy is frequently a flashpoint for battering and violence within the family." In short, she said, this provision of the law puts women who "most reasonably fear the consequence of notifying their husbands that they are pregnant in the greatest danger."

Further seeking to dismantle Alito's argument, she recalled how previous Courts had ruled that a woman "had no legal existence separate from her husband," and even as late as 1961, she noted that the Court had failed to grant women "full and independent legal status under the Constitution." Were Alito's view to prevail, she said, it would be a step backward for women.

O'Connor's words in *Casey* matched the tone that Justice Brennan tried to take in forging a majority opinion. Firm, pointed, but not needlessly insulting. Abrasive language, when it occurs at the Supreme Court, has almost always been reserved for dissenting opinions — until the 2022 Alito draft majority opinion. Its visceral tone, plus the needless legal landmines planted for exploitation later, undermine not just the image of the Court, but the reality.

As I write this epilogue, the abortion opinion has just been released. While I and others speculated that some of the most combative language in the draft might not appear in the final opinion, that did not happen. In form and tone, the final product is almost unchanged, and it even includes the contentious RBG citations.

Polls show public approval for the Court is plummeting, and some conservative justices' homes resemble armed camps. No longer is it just Supreme Court Police in an SUV outside their houses, but armed U.S. Marshals in their driveways, even dressed in full tactical gear, plus other elite police agencies at the ready. Yes, there are at times when more than a handful of angry demonstrators gather outside their homes, sometimes yelling. But after a long life in Washington, I can tell you it is not this smattering of demonstrators that has provoked this armed reaction. Even before a potential shooter was arrested outside Justice Kavanaugh's home, it was clear that there were a very unsettling and large number of death threats against these justices. How far we have come from the days less than a decade ago when the entire Court celebrated the posthumous publication of Marty Ginsburg's favorite recipes in a cookbook, with Martha-Ann Alito a moving force in getting it done.

In this climate of division, even some staunch conservatives may come to miss the more centrist Court of the past. A Court that, as Ruth observed in our interviews, rocked the boat from time to time, but seemed to know it couldn't go too far beyond public opinion. Proof of that wisdom is now on public display.

■ ■ ■ ■

The woman who sat at our dinner table and never, ever raised her voice, turned out to have one of the strongest voices in the room. As our table had to go quiet to hear her, so did her colleagues and everyone else around her. What she said was invariably written with what the Chief Justice called "the unaffected grace of precision." Her words were careful, brilliant, and expressed sparely, in language that was legally elegant but understandable to the nonlawyer, too. Perhaps most important, she spoke only when she had something to say. The silencing of that voice has made her irreplaceable.

In Jewish tradition, we wait for a year to have passed before unveiling the gravestone of the deceased. And so, right before Rosh Hashanah in 2021, David and I traveled back to Arlington National Cemetery for the unveiling of Ruth's headstone. Above her name is the engraved seal of the U.S. Supreme Court.

I expected to cry that day, and I did. What I did not expect was to learn that her gravesite has become a pilgrimage place for people from all over the world. And they do not simply come and reflect. They come and leave pieces of themselves behind. They leave small notes or objects, such as smooth stones (a Jewish tradition at gravesites) and coins, as well as many bouquets of flowers and tiny American flags, visible signs that they have been there. It is a testament to this woman that thousands of people who she never met are moved to attest to the transformative influence she had on their lives.

I had wanted to quote from some of the notes left at Ruth's headstone, but sadly, they have not been preserved. The U.S. Army's public affairs division responded with a terse, one-sentence reply: "We don't collect at Justice Ginsburg's gravesite." In fact, I learned that Arlington National Cemetery has a policy of gathering the objects once a week and tossing them. As if any of us needed further proof of how ephemeral life — and even death — is in our world today.

And yet, I hope that the objects, the notes, the coins, the flowers, and the stones, keep appearing in remembrance of this remarkable woman. I hope that many generations continue to seek out Ruth and her wisdom. She is one of those rare people who truly changed the world and had something important to say to every generation.

I still wake up many mornings, thinking of Ruth, and also Cokie — and sometimes Nino, and Lewis Powell, and Bill Brennan, too. I have been so fortunate to have them all, and many more, as friends. For the ones who are gone, I often wonder what they would have to say about the current state of the world. Yet, I am struck by the fact that no matter their origins or paths in life, all of them shared a common trait: optimism. Today's events, at home and abroad, would surely test that optimism, but while I think each of them would be realistic about the challenges we face, they would all be determined to persevere. As Ruth often said, "My story is hopeful."

So, I will be, too. I am not hanging up my spurs anytime soon. As my mother used to tell me, "I'll see you on the radio."

NOTES

One. The First Stirrings of Friendship

Invariably, the people gave us . . . Nina Totenberg, "Roman Totenberg: A Musical Life Remembered," NPR, May 12, 2012.

devastating to both of my parents . . . Full exchange in Ruth Bader Ginsburg in Conversation, Museum of the City of New York, December 8, 2018, https://www.mcny.org/rbg.

A Tree Grows in Brooklyn, *and "that kind of risqué nasty boy's" . . .* Ibid.

For women of my generation, getting the first job . . . Ibid.

had the guts to stand up . . . Author's private papers.

malicious lie . . . walked a respectful one step, faceless informers . . . Nina Totenberg, "Hoover: Life and Times of a 76-Year-Old Cop," *National Observer,* April 12, 1971, and "Hoover vs. National Observer," *Na-*

tional Observer, July 5, 1971.

exclusive on the horrid six . . . Author's private papers.

Two. Making Friends and A Few Enemies

nice to see two roses . . . Nancy Boxley Tepper, "The Education of a Harvard Lawyer: An Alumna Looks Back," *Harvard Magazine,* January/February 2021, https://www.harvardmagazine.com/2021/ 01/ feature-education-harvard-lawyer.

The attitude to sexual harassment . . . Full exchange from Cinema Café with Ruth Bader Ginsburg and Nina Totenberg, conversation, 2018 Sundance Film Festival, January 21, 2018, https://www.youtube .com/watch?v=pDXxsRB4s7Y.

when necessary to the point of exhaustion . . . Author's private papers.

Three. Unexpected Friends

Mr. Powell, would you come . . . Author's personal notes.

After that I thought to myself . . . Ibid.

like nine different law firms . . . Nina Totenberg, "Behind the Marble," *New York Times,* March 16, 1975, sec. SM, p. 14.

This child was what . . . Full exchange from

Cinema Café with Ruth Bader Ginsburg and Nina Totenberg.

Four. Friends and Love

I learned very early on . . . Full Exchange in NPR, "At the High Court a Tribute to a Chef Supreme," December 12, 2011. https://www.npr.org/transcripts/143352 409.

I have great affection for your daughter . . . Letter from Ruth Bader Ginsburg to Roman and Melanie Totenberg, author's private papers.

Six. Friends of the Court

had no idea that the Justice knew . . . Twitter, @palmore_joe, 6x thread, September 18, 2020.

You're late . . . Story told in Sandra Day O'Connor and H. Alan Day, *Lazy B* (Random House, 2002).

"Back to your kitchen" and "This is a job" . . . Evan Thomas, "Behind the Scenes of Sandra Day O'Connor's First Days on the Supreme Court," *Smithsonian,* March 2019.

O'Connor in particular . . . Stuart Taylor, "Rehnquist's Court: Tuning Out the White House," *New York Times,* September 11,

1988, sec. 6 p. 38.

He would come and sit . . . Richard Harris, Forbes.com,/Next Avenue, March 19, 2019, https://www.forbes.com/sites/next avenue/2019/03/19/sandra-day-oconnor-and-alzheimers-a-personal-story/?sh= 24137b 616091.

"could barely recognize" his wife . . . Full quote in NPR, "From Triumph to Tragedy, 'First' Tells Story of Justice Sandra Day O'Connor," March 15, 2019, https://www.npr.org/2019/03/15/693542112/from-triumph-to-tragedy-first-tells-story-of-justice-sandra-day-oconnor.

it would be an intellectual feast . . . Nina Totenberg, "Robert Bork's Supreme Court Nomination 'Changed Everything, Maybe Forever,' " NPR, December 19, 2012. https://www.npr.org/sections/itsallpolitics/2012/12/19/167645600/robert-borks-supreme-court-nomination-changed-everything-maybe-forever.

The nomination changed everything . . . Ibid.

Seven. Friends and Confidences

I believe there are certain things . . . Nina Totenberg, "A Timeline of the Clarence Thomas–Anita Hill Controversy as Kavanaugh to Face Accuser," NPR, September 23, 2018, https://www.npr108.org/2018/09/23/650138049/a-timeline-of-clarence-thomas-anita-hill-controversy-as-kavanaugh-to-face-accuse.

By the time Clarence Thomas was testifying . . . Transcript of Nina Totenberg's NPR report on Anita Hill's charges of sexual harassment by Clarence Thomas, *NPR Weekend Edition,* October 6, 1991, published in Jewish Women's Archive: https://jwa.org/media/transcript-of-nina-totenbergs-npr-report-on-anita-hills-charges-of-sexual-harassment-by-0.

Purposeful plagiarism . . . Thomas Rosenthiel, "Media Squabble over Coverage of Thomas Hearings: Conduct," *Los Angeles Times,* October 18, 1991.

That is how serious leaking an FBI file is . . . "Senate Launches Probe into News Leaks," in *CQ Almanac 1991,* 47th ed. (Washington, DC: Congressional Quarterly, 1992), pp. 46–47.

dangerous assaults on the First Amendment . . . Neil A. Lewis, "Senate Counsel Seeks Phone Records of Reporters," *New York Times,* March 17, 1992, sec. A, p. 14.

It's not as if any crime was committed . . . Quoted in Douglas Turner, "Laurels for Moynihan for Quashing Subpoena of News People in Anita Hill Leak," *Buffalo*

News, March 30, 1992.

"rolling Southern accent" — *"I've known her [Nina] since I was sworn in"* . . . Ann Louise Bardach, "Nina Totenberg: Queen of the Leaks," *Vanity Fair,* January 1992.

Justice Ginsburg and I often disagreed . . . Clarence Thomas, "Remembering Ruth Bader Ginsburg," Supreme Court Historical Society, https://supremecourthistory .org/clarence-thomas-remembering-ruth-bader-ginsburg/.

Concise advice: Stay strong . . . Quoted in https://www.publichealth .columbia.edu/ public-health-now/news/student-poster-honors-justice-ruth-bader-ginsburg.

Eight. Supreme Friends

The women are against her . . . Jill Lepore, "Ruth Bader Ginsburg's Unlikely Path to the Supreme Court: Before She Became a Hero to Feminists, She Had to Overcome Their Distrust," *New Yorker,* October 8, 2018.

It was one of the happiest moments . . . All quotations from Totenberg/Ginsburg Interview, "Justice Ruth Bader Ginsburg in Conversation at the Clinton Presidential Center," September 10, 2019, https://www .youtube.com/watch?v=a2rz5tuSm2U.

I pray that I may be all . . . https://www.c-span.org/video/?42908-1/ginsburg-supreme-court-nomination, 21:55.

What's not to like . . . Nina Totenberg, NPR, February 13, 2015, https://www.npr.org/sections/thetwo-way/2015/02/13/38608 5342/justice-ginsberg-admits-to-being-tipsy-during-state-of-the-union-nap.

The right to determine one's own . . . Nina Totenberg, "The Ginsburg Rule: False Advertising by the GOP," NPR, July 13, 2018, https://www.npr.org/2018/07/13/628626965/the-ginsburg-rule-false-advertising-by-the-gop.

the answer comes out . . . Lori A. Ringhand and Paul Collins, "What Two Legal Scholars Learned from Studying 70 Years of Supreme Court Confirmation Hearings" *Popular Media,* 2016, p. 259, and Nina Totenberg, "The Ginsburg Rule: False Advertising By The GOP."

the most helpful big sister . . . All quotations from "Ruth Bader Ginsburg in Conversation at the Clinton Presidential Center."

Just do it . . . Quotations from Remarks at the National Museum of Women and the Arts, Washington, DC, April 15, 2015. Justice O'Connor accepted an award from the Seneca Women Global Leadership Forum, Ruth Bader Ginsburg with Mary

Hartnett and Wendy W. Williams, *My Own Words* (Simon & Schuster, 2016), pp. 90–91.

When I was a new justice . . . Katherine Baicker, "Supreme Court Justice Ruth Bader Ginsburg on Polarization, Discrimination and Her Favorite Dissent," *Big Brains — University of Chicago,* episode 30, https://news.uchicago.edu/podcasts/big-brains/supreme-court-justice-ruth-badergins burg-polarization-discrimination.

cited a 1982 precedent, written by O'Connor . . . the Case is *Mississippi University for Women v. Hogan, 458 U.S. 718 (1982).*

As often as Justice O'Connor and I have disagreed . . . Joan Biskupic, "Ginsburg: Court Needs Another Woman," *USA Today,* May 5, 2009.

In addition to not following up . . . All quotations from Supreme Court *Redding* proceedings taken from www.supremecourt.gov/oral_arguments/argument_transcripts/2008/ 08-479.pdf.

They have never been a thirteen-year-old girl . . . Biskupic, "Ginsburg: Court Needs Another Woman."

It was almost as if . . . Dahlia Lithwick, "Fire and Ice," in *The Legacy of Ruth Bader Gin-*

sburg, ed. Scott Dodson (Cambridge University Press, 2015), p. 230.

Her style has always been very ameliorative . . . Quoted in Linda Greenhouse, "Oral Dissents Give Ginsburg a New Voice on the Court," *New York Times,* May 31, 2007.

Just a minute, I'm not finished . . . Quoted in an interview with Emily Bazelon, "The Place of Women on the Court," *New York Times,* July 7, 2009.

Nine. Male Friends

charmed by the way he said it . . . Baicker, "Ruth Bader Ginsburg on Polarization."

said it in an absolutely captivating way . . . The Kalb Report, National Press Club, April 17, 2014, https://www.youtube.com/watch?v=z0utJAu_iG4.

mutual improvement society . . . Antonin Scalia, *Scalia Speaks* (Crown Forum, 2017), p. 378.

We also cared about not only . . . Baicker, "Supreme Ruth Bader Ginsburg on Polarization."

Our styles were not at all alike . . . Ibid.

ruined my weekend . . . Irin Carmon and Shana Knizhnik, *Notorious RBG: The Life and Times of Ruth Bader Ginsburg* (Dey

441

St., 2015), p. 120.

The Justice loved few things more . . . Roy McLeese III, "Justice Scalia the Teacher," in *Harvard Journal of Law and Public Policy,* Vol. 39, p. 581, and author's notes.

That's all I have to say . . . Scalia, *Scalia Speaks,* p. 378.

the two of us riding on a very elegant elephant . . . Baicker, "Ruth Bader Ginsburg on Polarization."

inaccessible voting place proves nothing . . . *Tennessee v. Lane,* Supreme Court of the United States, January 13, 2004.

What good have all these roses done . . . Antonin Scalia, *The Essential Scalia: On the Constitution, the Courts, and the Rule of Law,* ed. Jeffrey S. Sutton and Edward Whelan (Crown Forum, 2020), and Tweet by @cjscalia, Christopher J. Scalia, September 18, 2020.

Because seniority really matters . . . Baicker, "Ruth Bader Ginsburg on Polarization."

Ten. Friends in Joy

the price of admission . . . Author's notes.

Eleven. Nourishing Friendships

it can be pointed at a burglar . . . Opinion of the Court, *District of Columbia v. Heller,*

Supreme Court of the United States, June 26, 2008.

Twelve. Friendship and Hardships

was caught early . . . Lloyd Grove, "The Reliable Source," *Washington Post,* August 6, 2002.

When a book was written . . . Lisa Napoli, *Susan, Linda, Nina, and Cokie: The Extraordinary Story of the Founding Mothers of NPR* (Abrams Press, 2021).

Thirteen. Fame and Friendship

Ruth and I are truly delighted . . . 2010 Tenth Circuit Bench and Bar Conference, C-SPAN, August 27, 2010, https://www .c-span.org/video/?295217-1/life-federal-judiciary.

"silly" and all quotations in this paragraph . . . Ibid.

The court does not comprehend . . . Opinion Announcement, *Ledbetter v. Goodyear Tire and Rubber Co.,* May 29, 2007.

throwing out preclearance . . . Dissenting Opinion, *Shelby County v. Holder,* June 25, 2013.

also explained to me what Notorious R.B.G. *was* . . . Ruth Bader Ginsburg and Dorit

Beinisch with Nina Totenberg, 92nd Street Y, October 19, 2014, https://www.92y.org/archives/ruth-bader-ginsburg-dorit-beinisch-nina-totenberg.

Supreme Court justices are generally robed . . . Nina Totenberg, "Notorious RBG: The Supreme Court Turned Cultural Icon," NPR, October 26, 2015.

"I think the Internet has given . . . Ibid.

He wrote to me that this pin . . . Justice Ginsburg Speaks at Virginia Military Institute, February 1, 2017, https://www.youtube.com/watch?v=6ZXRk6TlSvg.

Fourteen. Friendship Is a Choice

didn't want to think about . . . Mark Sherman, "Ginsburg: If Trump wins, 'everything is up for grabs,' " Associated Press, July 8, 2016.

I can't imagine what this place . . . Adam Liptak, "Ruth Bader Ginsburg, No Fan of Donald Trump, Critiques Latest Term," *New York Times,* July 10, 2016.

is a faker . . . Joan Biskupic, "Justice Ruth Bader Ginsburg Calls Trump a 'faker,' He Says She Should Resign," CNN, July 13, 2016.

Justice Ginsburg of the U.S. Supreme Court has embarrassed . . . Tweet, Donald J.

Trump, July 13, 2016.

Donald Trump Is Right . . . Editorial, "Donald Trump Is Right About Justice Ruth Bader Ginsburg," *New York Times,* July 13, 2016.

Why did you just think . . . Full exchange in Meg Anderson, "Listen: Justice Ginsburg Expands on Decision to Apologize for Trump Remarks," NPR, July 14, 2016, https://www.npr.org/2016/07/14/4860 80234/listen-justice-ginsburg-expands-on-decision-to-apologize-for-trump-remarks.

I was in pretty bad shape . . . Cinema Café with Ruth Bader Ginsburg and Nina Totenberg.

I'm now eighty-five . . . A talk at the 59E59 Theater in July 2018; quotations are mentioned in CNN article https://www .cnn.com/2018/07/29/politics/ruth-bader-ginsburg-scalia-new-york/index.html.

I'm going to start out by asking . . . Ruth Bader Ginsburg in Conversation, Museum of the City of New York.

I might not have lived . . . Full exchange in Nina Totenberg, "Justice Ginsburg Talks About Her Health with Nina Totenberg," NPR, August 2, 2019, https://www.npr .org/2019/08/02/747757921/video-justice-ginsburg-talks-about-her-health-with-nina-totenberg.

calculated and orchestrated political hit . . . Confirmation Hearing on the Nomination of Hon. Brett M. Kavanaugh to Be an Associate Justice of the Supreme Court of the United States, Committee on the Judiciary — U.S. Senate, September 27, 2018.

If anything would make the Court . . . Nina Totenberg, "Justice Ginsburg: 'I Am Very Much Alive,' " NPR, July 24, 2019, https://www.npr.org/2019/07/24/744633 713/justice-ginsburg-i-am-very-much-alive.

It was a lonely position . . . "Ruth Bader Ginsburg in Conversation at the Clinton Presidential Center."

I would ride uptown with them . . . Ibid. Book referred to is Kenneth M. Davidson, Ruth Bader Ginsburg and Herma Hill Kay, *Sex-Based Discrimination: Texts, Cases, and Materials* (West, 1974).

We just took each day . . . "Iconic Justice Ruth Bader Ginsburg Gives Inaugural Herma Hill Kay Memorial Lecture," October 22, 2019, https://www.law .berkeley.edu/article/iconic-justice-ruth-bader-ginsburg-gives-inaugural-herma-hill-kay-memorial-lecture/.

Seventeen. Farewell to My Friend

cancer free. That's good . . . Joan Biskupic, "How Ruth Bader Ginsburg Is Trying to Check the Conservative Majority," CNN, January 9, 2020.

Epilogue

We don't collect at . . . Upon hearing of this policy, Ruth's daughter, Jane, asked a family friend to go by once a week to gather notes and objects left on her parents' gravesite.

The court was her family . . . John Roberts, September 23, 2020, https://www.youtube.com/watch?v=joTTbdcCqj0.

ACKNOWLEDGMENTS

There are many people I have to thank. I could not have tackled this book, and kept my day job, without Lyric Winik, whose help was simply invaluable in helping me braid together the friendships that have blessed my life. I could not have finished on time without the incredible help of my niece, Link Nicoll, a digital marketing and design executive, who helped me select the photos for the book; organized the scanning, production, and permitting process; and advised me on layout as well.

I leaned on a select group of friends and relatives to read my drafts and make suggestions, because, in the end, those "readers," who are themselves good writers, are also meticulous editors. Those include, in alphabetical order: Adrienne Arsht, Linda Douglass, Jamie Gorelick, my niece Emily Green, and my sisters, Amy and Jill Totenberg.

At Simon & Schuster, Jonathan Karp had the idea for this book and talked me into it, aided by Dana Canedy and the lovely Mindy Marques, my editor, who kept my spirits and confidence up, as did my attorney, the indefatigable Bob Barnett, the perfect guide to help me through all the decisions an author has to make, ably assisted by Emily Alden. I'd also like to thank the entire Simon & Schuster team of Hana Park, Phil Metcalf, Susan M. S. Brown, Alison Forner, Clay Smith, Ruth Lee-Mui, and Brianna Scharfenberg.

Then too there is my NPR family, the foundation of my professional life for more than four decades, including my current boss, Krishnadev Calamur, who has made work a real joy, even as I tried to cram in extra hours on the book.

And there are my interns, who continue to keep me young, especially Ryan Ellingson, who helped me crash land the final draft of the book.

There would be no book without my family, all of whom have made me feel lucky. My darling husband, David; our daughters, Beth Wheeler and Alissa Leeman; our sons-in-law, Tim Gunter and Zack Leeman; and our grandchildren, Grace, Carson, Addie, and Althea. Also, Floyd's family, especially his daughter Evie Maxwell and my grand-daughter Cody. And of course, the previously mentioned Totenberg sisters, my sweet cousin Elzunia Wilk and her family, and my parents, Roman and Melanie Totenberg, who taught us all the meaning, and responsibility, of love.

My last thanks, of course, are for Ruth.

PHOTO CREDITS

Insert 1

1. No Credit
2. No Credit
3. No Credit
4. No Credit
5. No Credit
6. No Credit
7. Link Nicoll
8. No Credit
9. No Credit
10. No Credit
11. No Credit
12. No Credit
13. No Credit
14. No Credit
15. Sora DeVore
16. No Credit
17. Sora DeVore
18. Sora DeVore
19. No Credit

ABOUT THE AUTHOR

Nina Totenberg is NPR's award-winning legal affairs correspondent. She appears on NPR's critically acclaimed news magazines *All Things Considered, Morning Edition,* and *Weekend Edition,* and on NPR podcasts, including the *Politics Podcast* and *The Docket.* She is a frequent guest on TV news programs, and has written articles for publications ranging from *The New York Times Magazine* and the *Harvard Law Review* to *Parade* magazine. Totenberg's Supreme Court and legal coverage has won her every major journalistic award in broadcasting. She has been honored seven times by the American Bar Association for continued excellence in legal reporting. On a lighter note, *Esquire* magazine twice named her one of the "Women We Love." She lives in Washington, DC, with her husband, Dr. David Reines, a trauma surgeon.

Jill and me in the embrace of my mother's love.

My mother, Melanie.

An early photo with my father.

4

Carnegie Hall flyer.

5

Aspen Festival Orchestra rehearsal of the Tchaikovsky Violin Concerto.

Some people
never change.

Sisters carrying
out the family
tradition of
musical birthday
roasts, this
one for me.

The whole
family at an
anniversary party
the sisters threw
for our parents.

Floyd and me
at a picnic.

Floyd doing his favorite
thing—sailing.

Floyd affectionately
called me "Doc."

My father playing the
Bach Chaconne at Floyd's
memorial service.

At RBG's family birthday party.

David does same-day return for an award ceremony.

The newly married David and Nina.

A stolen moment at our rehearsal dinner in 2000.

17

RBG signing our marriage certificate just before the wedding.

18

RBG, Cokie, David, and me under the infamous chuppa.

19

I married into a very tall family. David and me with daughters Beth *(left)* and Alissa.

At the press conference unveiling the recovered Stradivarius.

Nina, Linda, Cokie—at NPR, forty years apart.

1

Early days
at NPR.

At the Bork
hearings. Me,
Mara Liasson,
and engineer
Michael Cullen.

A typical press
conference, post
arguments, on
the Supreme
Court steps.

Left: Nightline, the night after my Anita Hill–
Clarence Thomas sexual harassment story broke.

Right: Senator Alan Simpson and I sing "I Get a
Kick Out of You" at an Arena Stage benefit.

RBG swears in Deputy Attorney General Jamie Gorelick.

Turnaround is fair play. Senator
Patrick Leahy took this photo of me
at a Judiciary Committee hearing.

Justice Antonin Scalia and I share a joke
while Chief Justice William Rehnquist
gives us the eye.

This is "the real RBG"—at an opera gala, with me and Judge Sri Srinivasan.

Anniversary dinner 2014. *Left to right:* Linda Wertheimer, Steve Roberts, Debra Kraft Liberatore, Richard Waldhorn, David and me, Rob Liberatore, Jamie Gorelick, Fred Wertheimer, Cokie Roberts.

At a birthday party, Justice Stephen Breyer enlisted Scalia and Ginsburg for karaoke of "My Funny Valentine," subbing lyrics about "Nee-nah-TOE-ten-berg."

Nina, RBG, "Totenterns," surgical residents, and attendings.

13

Brady Gun Control Act challenger Sheriff Richard Mack gives me a shooting lesson.

14

Niece Emily, in Mexico, interviews children trained to shoot if their village is invaded by cartels.

15

At a Not July Fourth Party, former interns Ari Shapiro, Tom Goldstein, me, Amy Howe, and Justice Breyer.

After an interview
with Scalia.

Interviewing
Ruth at the book
fair in DC.

Me, Justice
Anthony Kennedy,
and Steve Roberts
at a Shakespeare
Theater benefit.

The tale of the dogs: Ruth; her granddaughter Clara; Connie Mack; Clara's husband, Rory; and Wallace.

Pandemic dinners with Ruth and her daughter, Jane.